THE AUGUSTINIAN THEOLOGY
OF W. H. AUDEN

THE AUGUSTINIAN THEOLOGY

OF W. H. AUDEN

Stephen J. Schuler

The University of South Carolina Press

© 2013 University of South Carolina

Published by the University of South Carolina Press
Columbia, South Carolina 29208

www.sc.edu/uscpress

Manufactured in the United States of America

22 21 20 19 18 17 16 15 14 13   10 9 8 7 6 5 4 3 2 1

CIP data can be found in the back of this book on p. 217

This book was printed on a recycled paper with 30 percent postconsumer waste content.

For Grace by grace

CONTENTS

ACKNOWLEDGMENTS

In writing and rewriting this book, I have benefited from the generous support, encouragement, and criticism of many colleagues and mentors. I especially wish to acknowledge David Lyle Jeffrey, Michael Foley, Luke Ferretter, and Kevin Gardner at Baylor University, who saw this project in its original form and gave me valuable advice.

Richard Rankin Russell not only read my manuscript closely and challenged weaknesses in the argument, but also exemplified professional mentorship and academic decorum. I am also grateful to my colleagues at the University of Mobile, especially Doug Mitchell, Katherine Abernathy, and Ted Mashburn, who offered friendship and support along the way, and Dwight Steedley, who supported and encouraged my research in many ways, including sending me to present papers at several conferences, including the Southeast Conference on Christianity and Literature, the Southwest Conference on Christianity and Literature, and the Conference on Faith and the Academy.

Permission to quote from Auden's *Collected Poems* and *The Dyer's Hand* was granted by Random House, Inc. My thanks go to the two anonymous readers for University of South Carolina Press, who both affirmed my general conclusions and made excellent suggestions for improvement. Jim Denton and Linda Fogle at USC Press kindly guided me through the publishing process, and, at a providentially propitious moment, my friend Marisa Humphrey offered her expert assistance in editing and proofreading the typescript. My three daughters patiently allowed me to work and provided much-needed diversion, and my wife, Grace, listened to me talk through my ideas at great length, read and critiqued each one of my drafts, and removed innumerable distractions as I wrote—"Many women have done excellently, but you surpass them all."

ABBREVIATIONS

CP	*Collected Poems of W. H. Auden*, ed. Edward Mendelson
DH	*The Dyer's Hand*
FA	*Forewords and Afterwords*
Prose I	*The Complete Works of W. H. Auden: Prose*, vol. 1
Prose II	*The Complete Works of W. H. Auden: Prose*, vol. 2
Prose III	*The Complete Works of W. H. Auden: Prose*, vol. 3
Prose IV	*The Complete Works of W. H. Auden: Prose*, vol. 4

or theological ideas informed Auden's ethics and aesthetics. I hoped that the process of answering these two questions would elucidate the intellectual underpinnings of Auden's poems, and help me clear up some of the obscurities therein.

When Auden first became interested in theology in the late 1930s and early 1940s, he almost immediately identified himself with the Augustinian theological tradition. In a 1941 letter to Ursula Niebuhr, Auden wrote, "Re my theological position, it is I think the same as your husband's, i.e. Augustinian not Thomist, (I would allow a little more place, perhaps, for the via negativa)" (qtd. in Spender 106). For Auden, the terms "Augustinian" and "Thomist" connote not just strictly theological positions, but methodological approaches to exploring human nature in its relation to the divine. Auden explains the difference at some length in an introduction to Kierkegaard:

> As a Christian, Kierkegaard belongs to the tradition of religious thinking—theology is too systematic a term—represented by Augustine, Pascal, Newman and Karl Barth, as distinct both from the Thomist tradition of official Catholicism and from the liberal Protestantism of men like Schleiermacher. As a secular dialectician, he is one of the great exponents of an approach . . . to which the Germans have given the name Existential . . . [and] the same approach is typical of what is most valuable in Marx and Freud.
>
> In contrast to those philosophers who begin by considering the *objects* of human knowledge, essences and relations, the existential philosopher begins with man's immediate experience as a *subject*, i.e. as a being in *need*, as an *interested* being whose existence is at stake. He does not assert, as he is usually accused of asserting, the primacy of Will over Reason, but their inseparability. As Augustine says, 'I am and know and will; I am knowing and willing; I know myself to be and to will; I will to be and to know.' There is, therefore, no timeless, disinterested I who stands outside my finite temporal self and serenely knows whatever there is to know; cognition is always a specific historic act accompanied by hope and fear. (*Prose II* 213–14)

As a poet and as a Christian, Auden placed himself within this "existential" tradition, which Augustine helped him define as a mode of thinking that not only allows for human subjectivity, but emphasizes the hopes, fears, needs, desires, and anxieties of the individual human person. Augustine thus became for Auden a model of a thinker who seamlessly merged psychological investigation with philosophical speculation and theological insight, and it is this combination of the psychological and the philosophical that shapes much of Auden's later poetry, and not incidentally, makes it so difficult to read.

It is hardly surprising, then, that Auden occasionally references Augustine in his poetry and prose, and that he frequently articulates ideas that are clearly drawn from Augustinian thought. The earliest of Auden's many references to Augustine appears in the 1927 juvenile poem "Narcissus," which begins with a quotation from the *Confessions* in Latin (*Juvenilia* 185). At about the same time, he quoted another line from the *Confessions*, also in Latin, in a letter to his friend William McElwee (187). It was only in the late 1930s, when Auden was gradually making his way back to the Christian faith he had abandoned in adolescence, that his work begins to reflect the presence of Augustine. Auden mentions that he was reading Augustine around the same time he was reading Pascal and Kierkegaard (*Prose II* 248). He was clearly reading Pascal in the late 1930s—his abortive prose work "The Prolific and the Devourer" is modeled partly on the *Penseés*—and he began reading Kierkegaard in about 1940. Apparently, Auden was reading the *Confessions* in the early 1940s, during which time he had indirect contact with other works of Augustine. Exact or partial quotations from Augustine's *Confessions* appear in *New Year Letter* and "For the Time Being," as well as in many of Auden's essays and in his 1970 commonplace book *A Certain World*. He also took notes on the *Confessions* in the back of the notebook in which he drafted much of "For the Time Being" in 1941–42 (see Kirsch, Introduction 77), and in a 1942 letter to Stephen Spender he mentioned that he was "reading St Augustine a lot lately, who is quite wonderful" (qtd. in Kirsch, *Auden* 59). The last of his direct references to Augustine is in his poem "Aubade," written in 1972, only a year before he died.

Auden's debt to Augustinian theology has already been noted in several important critical works. Throughout his biography of Auden, Humphrey Carpenter identifies many important figures whose work left notable marks on Auden's writing, specifically Freud, Homer Lane, Charles Williams, Reinhold Niebuhr, and Charles Cochrane, many of whom Auden identified as "Augustinian" in their outlook. Arthur Kirsch adds Blaise Pascal, Søren Kierkegaard, Martin Buber, Paul Tillich, as well as Augustine to the list of important theological figures in Auden's library (*Auden* xiv). Auden himself, in his 1945 foreword to Emile Cammaerts's autobiography *The Flower of Grass*, lists Augustine, Pascal, and Kierkegaard, in that order, as his initial theological influences (*Prose II* 248). John Fuller's *W. H. Auden: A Commentary* offers insightful explanations of a vast array of literary, philosophical, and theological references in Auden's poetry, including many references to Augustine, and Brian Conniff has more recently published enlightening articles on Auden's use of Paul Tillich and Reinhold Niebuhr.[1] Edward Mendelson also remarks briefly but insightfully on Auden's debts to Freud, Kierkegaard, Williams, Cochrane, and Augustine throughout his two landmark studies, *Early Auden* and *Later Auden*. Auden's interest in Kierkegaard has been thoroughly explored, but the influence of other theologians on Auden's later thought and work has not yet been adequately traced. The closest to date is Kirsch's *Auden and Christianity*, which sketches the convergence of several theologians' ideas in Auden's work. Kirsch's study is important as an overview of Auden's distinctly Christian beliefs, and it provides a necessary background for any discussion of Auden's theological influences, though Kirsch is more focused on Auden's general religious tendencies than he is on tracing any given theological position back to particular sources, such as Augustine. Thus, Auden's appropriation of Augustinian theology has been often noted, but seldom investigated.

Augustine's influence on Auden is notable partly because Auden was hard to influence. He had a strong, outspoken personality and was given to dogmatic pronouncements on any subject offered for conversation. Thus, his close associates, such as Christopher Isherwood, Stephen Spender, and Chester Kallman, seem to have exerted little influence on the young Auden, while his opinions and even his poetic style deeply influenced his friends. However, Auden was strongly influenced by books, and although there are only a few lengthy studies of Auden's library, it is generally acknowledged that the themes and concerns that characterize Auden's work, and especially his later work, owe much to his wide reading in psychology, philosophy, and theology. As James Bertram points out, Auden's works were influenced by "a good many patristic as well as modern theologians: as with Coleridge, it is dangerous to assume there is any relevant text Auden had not read" (Bertram 224).

BIOGRAPHY

While Auden had not always been interested in theology, religious practice was an important element of his childhood, and throughout his life he was especially fond of liturgy and ritual. In *The Prolific and the Devourer* (1939), he recalls his family's Anglo-Catholic preferences for high liturgy, including candles, incense, and ancient hymns (*Prose II* 414), and in a 1956 essay in *Modern Canterbury Pilgrims* he fondly recollects, "my first religious memories are of exciting magical rites (at six I was a boat-boy) rather than listening to sermons" (*Prose III* 573–74). A "boat-boy" is a junior acolyte, or altar server, who is responsible for carrying an incense bowl during special services, and Auden implies that the experience contributed to his appreciation of the physicality of liturgical worship. Even after he lost interest in Christianity in the late 1920s, his close friend Christopher Isherwood, with whom he collaborated on several verse plays, stated in 1937, "Auden is a musician and a ritualist. As a child, he enjoyed a high Anglican upbringing, coupled with a sound musical education. The Anglicanism has evaporated, leaving only the height: he is still much preoccupied with ritual, in all its forms. When we collaborate, I have to keep a sharp eye on him—or down flop the characters on their knees . . . : another constant danger is that of choral interruptions by angel voices. If Auden had his way, he would turn every play into a cross between grand opera and high mass" (qtd. in Spender 74). Despite his lifelong attraction to religious ritual, Auden was an atheist throughout his early career. In 1939, he wrote that he did not believe in "a creator who is distinct from and independent of the creation, an omnipotent free-willing immaterial agent," but he added later, "If anyone chooses to call our knowledge of existence knowledge of God . . . I don't mind: Nomenclature is purely a matter of convenience" (*Prose II* 448). Soon after he wrote this statement, a long and complicated series of events brought Auden back to creedal Christianity soon after he immigrated to the United States at age thirty-two, in January of 1939.

A reader of any biography of Auden might well be struck by the biographical parallels between Auden and Augustine as he presents himself in the *Confessions*. Auden and Augustine were both intellectually gifted and possessed great facility with their native languages. Both became schoolteachers, and both had frequent, guilty indulgences in illicit sex during youth. Augustine eventually became a celibate priest and later a bishop, and Auden was also fond of saying that, if he had not become a poet, he might have been an Anglican bishop instead, though he was never willingly celibate. While Auden's sexual preferences were always homosexual, Augustine's were largely heterosexual, though he implies in the *Confessions* that he experimented with homosexuality while at Carthage (3.1), and Auden did have a couple of female lovers. Both Auden and Augustine departed from the Christian faith of their mothers in their adolescence—Auden's mother was almost as strong an influence on him as was Augustine's mother Monica. Both Auden's mother and Augustine's died within a year of their sons' respective conversions.

Both Auden and Augustine experimented with the popular philosophies of their respective historical moments, Auden with Freud and Marx, and Augustine with Manichacism and Neoplatonism. After various forays into the details of these philosophies, certain personal crises led both to convert to Christianity in their early thirties. Both were troubled and fascinated by the ontology of evil, and the Christian explanation of the nature of evil as a privation was a major factor in their respective conversions. In their post-conversion works, both exhibit a taste for finely tuned rhetoric as well as for epigrammatical pronouncements and fierce attacks on what they consider to be heretical ideas, especially false dualisms. Both men were very interested in human psychology and the nature of time, which are themes that run through both the *Confessions* and Auden's entire poetic corpus. Both also had a penchant for revision and retraction. Near the end of his life, Augustine wrote his *Retractions*, in which he corrected mistakes and clarified statements he had made in his earlier works, and Auden became infamous for revising his early poetry in subsequent editions, going so far as to scrawl corrections in his friends' copies of his books. In reading the *Confessions* in 1942, soon after he had returned to the Anglican communion, Auden could hardly have helped noticing the strong parallels between Augustine's life and his own.

Despite Auden's return to the Anglican communion in the early 1940s, his enthusiasm for Christian theology and ethics, and his habitual church attendance, there has always been a strain of Auden criticism that claims that Auden never, in fact, became a real Christian at all. Charles Osborne for example states, "Indeed, whether [Auden] ever returned to the unquestioning faith of his childhood years is highly doubtful. He was essentially a questioning, skeptical temperament" ("Auden"

pray to become, aware always both of one's infinite capacity for rebellion and self-deception and of the infinite patience and love of God" (*Prose II* 250).

For convenience, I will continue to refer to Auden's return to the Anglican communion in 1940 as his "conversion," with the understanding that the formation of his Christian beliefs began earlier and continued for some years afterward, and that his subsequent articulations of his Christian faith seldom conform to conventional religious language. As a talented intellectual and a practicing homosexual, Auden never found the Christian faith easy, but there can be no serious dispute that after about 1940 he accepted the existence of the Trinity and the Incarnation of God in the historical Jesus Christ, and that he firmly believed that it was his Christian duty to love God and to love his neighbor as himself, though he did acknowledge his frequent failures to do so. He was outspoken about many of his opinions, but he tended to keep his faith quiet. He took very seriously Jesus' injunction, "do not let your left hand know what your right hand is doing" (Matt. 6:3), and he was fond of quoting an anonymous Anglican bishop's statement that "orthodoxy is reticence" (*FA* 71).

THE POET'S LIBRARY

Philip Larkin once famously complained that, with the appearance of *New Year Letter* in 1940, Auden had "become a reader rather than a writer" (125). Whereas Auden's early poems had only infrequently named other writers, Auden's later poetry was awash in literary, philosophical, and theological texts, which strongly contributed to the loss of what Larkin calls "poetic pressure" (127). On the surface, Larkin's observation is true enough, but it also plays down the fact that Auden had always written from books. For example, Larkin admired "Spain 1937," perhaps without quite noticing that it is every bit as much a "bookish" poem as is *New Year Letter,* though the books are not the same ones. In *The Dyer's Hand,* Auden lists the wide variety of books and authors that shaped his early imagination—George MacDonald, Jules Verne, and a large number of books on geology and mining. Eventually Freud and Marx emerged as strong influences, as well as William Blake, Thomas Hardy, and D. H. Lawrence (see *Prose III* 577). In the 1940s, Auden became more forthright about his sources than he had been in the 1930s, and his library grew a great deal during his middle period, but his early poetry always contained a mixture of books and personal experience. As Auden remarked in a 1952 essay, "works of art are closer to each other than they are to their creators; a poet's library will enlighten us about his poems infinitely more than his childhood or his love affairs" (*Prose III,* 325). While Auden criticism now includes a number of substantial studies of Auden's sources, the relationship between his poems and his library has yet to be fully explored.

Near the beginning of *The Dyer's Hand,* Auden asks, "What is the function of a critic?" (*DH* 8). He answers,

So far as I am concerned, he can do me one or more of the following services:

1. Introduce me to authors or works of which I was hitherto unaware.

2. Convince me that I have undervalued an author or a work because I had not read them carefully enough.

3. Show me relations between works of different ages and cultures which I could never have seen for myself because I do not know enough and never shall.

4. Give a "reading" of a work which increases my understanding of it.

5. Throw light upon the process of artistic "Making."

6. Throw light upon the relation of art to life, to science, economics, ethics, religion, etc. (DH 8–9)

According to Auden's schema, I am concerned primarily with the third function, to elucidate the relationship between Auden's writings and those of the Augustinian theological tradition, though also touching on the fourth and sixth functions. I hope to fulfill incidentally the first and second functions for some readers.

Augustine's thought was a real and significant influence on Auden's works, and that influence was largely conscious on Auden's part, though it was often indirect as well. Part literary criticism and part intellectual biography, my approach to Auden is one that Mendelson's *Early Auden* and *Later Auden* have legitimated. Not only does Auden's poetry have theological implications—indeed, Augustinian features of Auden's theology appear frequently in his poems—he makes more explicit explanations in his prose.

Despite Harold Bloom's problematization of the idea of literary "influence," I use the term here. By "influence" I do not mean mere slavish imitation, nor do I mean only the borrowing of terms and phrases. I certainly do not mean an agonistic attempt to supplant a predecessor. Rather, by "influence" I mean that Auden was a sympathetic and enthusiastic reader of Augustine, and that he derived several key philosophical and theological ideas both from Augustine's own works and from contemporary works that rely on Augustine. Auden's intellectual debt to Augustinian theology does not consist only in his occasional borrowing of Augustine's language, significant though that is. Such borrowings signal the presence of broader, sometimes latent ideas whose definitive forms were articulated by Augustine. In contrast to Bloom's portrayal of literary influence, Auden's largely sympathetic adaptation of Augustine provides an example, however rare, of a case in which "influence" is more amiable than anxious and more cooperative than competitive.

Any study that employs Augustine must come to terms with two features of Augustinian theology: unoriginality and diffusion. First, what are now recognized as distinctly Augustinian ideas are often not original to Augustine, but are drawn from a wide variety of sources, from Plato and Paul to Cicero and Jerome. It is often the case that, rather than advancing a truly original idea, Augustine instead provided a compelling and memorable articulation of ideas that were already circulating in philosophy or theology. Second, Augustine is rightly called a "church father" because his theology has been adopted in large measure by widely divergent Christian traditions throughout the centuries, from the Roman Catholic Church to Lutheran, Calvinist, and even nonconformist traditions, and so the distinction between ideas that are peculiar to Augustine and ideas that he shares with a large body of orthodox Christian theology is often difficult or impossible to make. Furthermore, Auden certainly came to share with Augustine such central doctrines as the Trinity, the Incarnation, the necessity of faith for salvation, and the possibility of redemptive suffering, but these are ideas that characterize Christianity itself and are not original or particular to Augustine at all. Therefore I focus on ideas whose articulation can be attributed specifically to Augustine rather than on ideas that are general to a much broader community of Christian thought.

Augustine's influence is not limited to only a few of Auden's works but appears throughout his works from the late 1930s to the early 1970s. Therefore any thematic division is artificial, and would be false if followed too closely. The poems themselves often address a whole cluster of Augustinian ideas at once. Thus, certain ideas (for example, the *acte gratuit* and *fantastica fornicatio*) appear in several of the following chapters. Since Auden began reading Augustine seriously in mid-career, after he had already written many of his most famous early poems, my focus is on Auden's later poems, which have received far less critical attention than have his early works. While critics rightly assume that Auden's later poetry varies greatly in quality, his status as a major poet is now beyond dispute, and I hope to further confirm him as one of the premier poets of the twentieth century, not only for his poetic virtuosity, but also for his depth and breadth of theological insight.

1. EVIL AS PRIVATION

Auden's 1938 poem "Musée des Beaux Arts" remarks on the usual human response to exceptional suffering in others, describing how disaster appears in the midst of everyday events such as an afternoon stroll (*CP* 179). The poem alludes to two events, the crucifixion of Christ and the fall of Icarus, identifying both as extraordinary examples of suffering that occur "in a corner, some untidy spot," from which all observers turn away "Quite leisurely from the disaster" (179). Human suffering, the poem suggests, is frequently ignored by most ordinary people. Artists, it seems, are in a better position to notice it, at least in retrospect. The poem does not ask the "big questions" about the nature of evil and suffering: Why do people suffer? Can suffering be meaningful? How should ordinary people respond to exceptional suffering in others? The poem is more concerned with revealing the personal guilt that an individual feels after turning away from another suffering person, and it is typical of Auden's existential approach to such questions. He did not approach what theistic philosophy refers to as the "problem of evil" in the conventional, twentieth-century manner. More typical, modern attempts at theodicy begin with the riddle of Epicurus: God is either unwilling or unable to prevent human suffering, for if he were both supremely good and supremely powerful, he would alleviate human suffering. Auden's approach to evil and suffering also began with a moral question, but the rise of European fascism in the 1930s forced him to begin in a very different way: "If, as I am convinced, the Nazis are wrong and we are right, what is it that validates our values and invalidates theirs?" (*Prose III* 578). The question was certainly of great public importance, but Auden asked it from an existential perspective, "as a being in *need*, as an *interested* being whose existence is at stake" (*Prose II*, 213–14). In order to answer that question, even before his official return to Christianity, Auden began to resort to the theological language of Augustine, another existential thinker, to talk about evil.

Augustine, too, approached the nature of evil as "an interested being." According to the *Confessions*, he began his own attempt to understand the nature of evil, not as a philosopher engaged in systematic, theoretical inquiry, but as a young man in search of a religion that would allow him to live the libertine lifestyle that he had already chosen to live. Augustine observes in retrospect that it was not initially a search for truth but for a rationalization of his behavior, even though his search included a strong philosophical component. In the *Confessions*, Augustine details his own intellectual struggle with the ontological nature of evil, which prevented him from embracing Christianity for many years. In books 4 and 5 he describes his involvement with the Manichees, devotees of the teachings of Mani, who believed that all existence was ruled by two eternally opposed gods, an evil god of darkness who ruled the physical realm and a good god of light who created and ruled the spiritual realm. As Augustine explains succinctly in his *City of God*, the Manichees believed "that there is some evil in nature, which is derived and produced from a supposed 'adverse first cause' of its own" and that since the good god cannot redeem the evil, physical realm, "the part which cannot be purified from that defilement is to serve as the prison to enclose the Enemy after his overthrow" (11.22). The Manichees believed that the evil domain of the physical world, especially the human body, oppressed the good, spiritual domain of the intellect, pending an apocalypse in which the souls of the devout would become permanently free of their bodies. Unlike Augustine, Auden was never consciously a dualist in theory, though he came to reject some of his earlier philosophical interests as forms of false dualism, and their respective spiritual journeys are parallel at least in that sense.

The Manichees developed a detailed mythological cosmology along these lines, but Augustine's main attraction to Manichaeism seems to have been its explanation of the origin of evil. The Manichees taught that bodily existence was inherently evil, and thus all morally evil actions arose from the body in which the soul was trapped. Therefore, the spiritual essence of a person was not responsible for evil actions; rather, an outside, malignant agency working through the body was responsible. Augustine says it flattered his pride to think that he was not really responsible for anything bad that he did (5.10). However, the young Augustine was troubled by the fact that Manichean teachings flatly contradicted the mathematics and astronomy he had learned in school as part of his liberal arts curriculum, and he found his intellectual desires at odds with his desire to rationalize his behavior.[1] Disillusioned, Augustine abandoned the Manichees in favor of Neoplatonic philosophy, which he later came to see as a significant step toward his eventual acceptance of Christianity.

Neoplatonism posited the absolute goodness and independence of God, which Augustine thought superior to the Manichean model that limited the power of the good divinity. Better yet, Neoplatonism also refuted the Manichees by explaining that evil was not a positive substance, but an absence of goodness. Nevertheless, Neoplatonism did not offer a satisfactory explanation for the origin of evil, and after studying various Neoplatonic works—Plotinus and Porphyry specifically—Augustine complained, "yet understood I not, clearly and without difficulty, the cause of evil" (*Confessions* 7.3). He had been told, perhaps by Ambrose of Milan, that evil was a result of the free choice of human beings, yet Augustine could not accept the idea that evil could exist contrary to the will of God's all-powerful goodness, whether "God" was the Platonic *primum mobile* or the Christian *Yahweh* (7.5). Eventually Augustine came to recognize that he had been making a categorical error all along. He had continued to assume, contrary to Neoplatonism, that evil was a thing with its own positive, independent existence. This, he realized, was not necessarily true. Evil might "exist" in some other way. He reasoned that if it is possible to corrupt good things, then when good things become corrupted, they must lose some good quality that they previously possessed. "Therefore," he concluded, "if they shall be deprived of all good, they shall no longer be. So long therefore as they are, they are good: therefore whatsoever is, is good. That evil then which I sought, whence it is, is not any substance: for were it a substance, it should be good" (*Confessions* 7.10). He concluded that evil is not a thing at all, but a negative attribute of otherwise good things, and the problem of the existence of evil disappeared at a theoretical level.

Despite his subsequent insistence on the intrinsic goodness of the physical world and the human body, Augustine has earned a reputation for denigrating bodily existence generally and sexuality specifically. In light of the whole of the *Confessions*, that reputation is not entirely justified. It is not the physical objects themselves to which Augustine objects, but the human failure to refer existence and pleasure to their divine source.[2] Augustine objects not to physical things themselves, but to the usual human tendency to misuse physical things, which is ultimately a spiritual problem located in the human will, not a physical problem located in the body. Nevertheless, Augustine's frequent condemnation of sexual lust in the *Confessions*, as well as in other works, implies an ongoing suspicion of physicality that his theology formally rejects. His underlying anxiety about the human body may be due partly to his earlier Neoplatonism, which exhibits a similar ambivalence about embodiment. Augustine never attempted to distance himself from Neoplatonic philosophy as he did from Manichaeism, partly because he believed that the ideas of evil as a privation, as well as the eternal existence of the *Logos* (the divine word that is the origin of the cosmos), were common to both Neoplatonism and Christianity. So while this shift in Augustine's thinking about the nature of evil did not immediately impel him toward Christianity, it did remove a significant philosophical barrier between him and the church. Like Auden's, Augustine's conversion was motivated by a series of personal crises that brought him reluctantly to enter the church.

THE PROLIFIC AND THE DEVOURER

Auden first began to show clear signs of an Augustinian influence in 1939, but several statements he made in earlier writings anticipate his eventual use of Augustinian theology to address the problem of moral evil. He had always tended to speak of evil as some sort of privation, as Edward Mendelson explains in *Early Auden*. Even in Auden's earliest mature poems from the late 1920s, Mendelson argues that "Auden's intractable problem in these poems is finally neither erotic nor social nor linguistic, but the irreducible fact of division itself," so "The question he asked in his first poems was not What should I do now? but Of what whole can I be part?" (*Early* 7). Whatever ailed the poet himself and his culture as a whole, Auden sensed that the real, underlying problem was a privation of some kind of wholeness, and while the early poems suggest that the missing wholeness is psychological in nature, they are never decisive on that question. Mendelson's thorough analysis of the early poems shows that they are largely about "their own failure to be part of any larger interpretive frame," so critics who attempt to read Auden's early poems as strictly Marxist or Freudian allegories are missing the point entirely (10). Rather, Auden was seeking a compelling account for the divided consciousness that he so acutely felt throughout the 1920s and 1930s but did not yet possess an adequate language to describe.

Well before his conversion, Auden had resorted to explicitly theological language to describe the nature of evil. In a 1935 essay, "The Good Life," he asserts that "Psychology is principally an investigation into the nature of evil. Its essential problem is to discern what it is that prevents people having the good will" (*Prose I* 113). Even Freudian psychoanalysis is based, Auden suggests, on the Christian assumption that "a change of heart can, and must, bring about a change in the environment . . . 'Except ye be born again, ye cannot enter into the Kingdom of Heaven'" (113). Auden explains that psychoanalysis is opposed both to Rousseau's attribution of evil to social circumstance and to Augustine's attribution of evil to conscious moral choice (114), a statement that indicates Auden already thought himself familiar enough with Augustinian theology to critique it. The critique is a gross oversimplification of Augustine's psychological theory of moral evil, which Auden eventually accepted. Without knowing it, Auden remained very close to Augustine's belief that evil is a privation, or a kind of "crookedness," a word that appears regularly in Auden's poetry of the late 1930s.

Cicero Bruce notes that "crooked" is "synonymous with the adjective *depraved*, defined in the Christian sense of the word as 'corrupt,' 'wicked,' or that which deviates from what is considered 'right' or 'natural.' In fact, *depravity* itself derives from the Latin infinitive *depravare*: 'to make crooked'" (28–29). However, Bruce's otherwise thorough explanation neglects the sexual connotation of the word, which Richard Bozorth explains is an important element of Auden's post-conversion poetry. Bozorth recognizes "Auden's ongoing proclivity for poetic figures of crookedness, with all the sexual overtones they have in his earlier work. At the same time, crook-edness—or *angularity*—also signifies his sense of the relationship between the fallen human and the divine" (223). Bozorth notes that Auden always regarded his own homosexuality as an abnormality, probably because he believed in Freud's thesis that homosexuality was a form of sexual immaturity (73). Bozorth identifies Augustine as a source for Auden's ideas about the nature of such "crookedness," though he suggests that Auden absorbed such an assumption through Freud, who is the "secular heir to the belief in reproduction as the divinely ordained end of sexual desire, with perversion as a turning away from that end; for St. Augustine, perversion is the definition of evil" (73). To call Augustine's definition of evil "perversion" is right in a sense, but "privation" is the more exact term. The word "perversion" carries so many sexual overtones that it might wrongly imply that the essence of evil is sexuality that deviates from social norms. For Augustine, as for Auden, uncontrollable sexual desire is but one symptom of a much more serious and pervasive deformation in the human soul.

In the spring of 1939, Auden gave lectures at several American schools, including Dartmouth, Bryn Mawr, and the University of North Carolina, in which he explicitly rejected philosophies that he grouped under the heading of "dualism," which included fascism, Platonism, and the romanticism of Rousseau. In opposition, Auden espoused what he called "monism," by which he seems to have meant a conscious reconciliation of opposites, and which he identified with Jesus, Blake, Voltaire, and Goethe. The lectures do not survive in print, but school newspapers reported Auden's saying that "monism" did not, like dualism, reject any aspect of existence as inherently evil (*Prose II* 481–83). While Augustine is not mentioned, the reported critique of "dualist" philosophies suggests that Auden was already leaning toward an Augustinian understanding of the nature of evil, and he would quickly drop the term "monist" in favor of more explicitly theological language. That same summer, he and his newfound lover Chester Kallman took a road trip to New Mexico and California, during which Auden began writing a series of pensées setting out his political, social, and philosophical positions on a number of questions.

This prose work, which he titled *The Prolific and the Devourer*, is the first of Auden's works that displays a strong Augustinian influence. Mendelson identifies Augustine's *Confessions* as a significant model and source for the work, explaining that "Auden set to work renouncing his political errors in the same way Augustine renounced his philosophical and erotic ones" (*Later* 62). *The Prolific and the Devourer* also coincides with the *Confessions* in some specific philosophical positions, especially in its statements on the nature of evil and in its resounding rejection of Manichean dualism. For example, in a characteristically sweeping statement, Auden argues that "the false philosophy in all its forms starts out from a dualistic division between either The Whole and its parts, or one part of the whole and another. One part is good with absolute right to exist unchanged; the other is evil with no right to exist" (*Prose II* 425). His description of dualism as a divided cosmos, one part perfectly good and worthy and the other part completely evil and worthless, comes remarkably close to Augustine's descriptions of the Manichees. In the *Confessions*, Augustine describes Manichean dualism as a belief in "two opposed masses, both infinite, but the evil rather smaller, the good larger; and of this pestilential beginning other blasphemous notions were the corollary" (5.10). While Auden does not use the word "Manichean" in *The Prolific and the Devourer*, he would soon pick up the term as a handy descriptor for false dualisms of any sort.

Auden, like Augustine, found that he had to reject dualism in favor of the belief that all existence is inherently good and that evil has no positive existence whatsoever. Auden follows his statement on dualism with a list of theses denouncing dualism:

1. There are not "good" and "evil" existences. All existences are good, i.e. they are equally free and have an equal right to their existence. Everything that is is holy.

2. No existence is without relation to and influence upon all other existences.

3. Evil is not an existence but a state of disharmony between existences. (Prose II 426)

These first three theses are very similar to many of Augustine's statements on the subject, such as one statement early in the *Confessions* in which Augustine laments his youthful ignorance of God: "I did not know that evil has no existence except as a privation of good, down to that level which is altogether without being" (3.7). Such a definition of evil as disharmony or privation—as the disruption of good relationships between entities—is a clearly Augustinian position, and while it has roots in Platonic philosophy which precedes Augustine, it was Augustine who articulated it in a comprehensive form. No one as well read as Auden could have come to this conclusion without recognizing the idea's source in Augustine, most particularly in the *Confessions*.

While his rejection of the positive existence of evil led Augustine to reject all Manichean assumptions about the physical world, Auden's own denunciations of dualism in *The Prolific and the Devourer* implicate a wide range of philosophies and worldviews that he had come to see as false. His identification of "God and Satan" as a false and dangerous dualism suggests a critique of the institutional Christianity of Europe and perhaps also the low-church fundamentalism of his day (*Prose II* 425). Other dualisms are easier to identify with specific philosophies, such as "the philosopher king and the ignoble masses," which is a direct reference to the idealistic totalitarianism advanced in Plato's *Republic*, and "the State and the individual," a reference to fascist ideology (425). He also identifies "the proletariat and the masses" as yet another false dualism, the basis of Marxist ideology (425), even though Auden ends this section by saying, "Blake and the Marxists are probably correct in their diagnosis: Dualism is thinking about the creation in terms of man's experience of human politics" (425). While Augustine suggests in the *Confessions* that his own early dualistic thinking was an attempt to rationalize his adolescent behavior, Auden argues that modern dualisms derive from human experiences in which the world appears to be clearly divided between good and evil, whatever specific entities might be linked with these opposites.

Auden's thought further resembles Augustine's in the way both articulate the relationship between evil and the nature of the human being. Augustine asserts that humans were created to be naturally attracted to God, and natural or innate attraction becomes one of the dominant themes of the *Confessions*. As Augustine famously states at the outset, "You stir man to take pleasure in praising you, because you have made us for yourself, and our heart is restless until it rests in you" (1.1). Thus, by following his or her truly natural tendencies, a person will seek to resolve his or her anxiety by returning to a right love of God, but it takes a conscious choice to reject the love of God in favor of evil. However, according to Augustine, that initial choice of evil introduces a new, unnatural inclination towards evil, which is no less compelling for its being unnatural, and Augustine was, so far as anyone knows, the first to call this unnatural desire "original sin" (*Confessions,* trans. Chadwick 59n).

Like Augustine, Auden also recognizes that the choice to do evil is unnatural. At the end of his list of theses against dualism in *The Prolific and the Devourer* he claims that evil is foreign to natural inclination: "To do evil is to act contrary to self-interest. It is possible for all living creatures to do this because their knowledge of their self-interest is false or inadequate. Thus the animals whose evolution is finished, i.e. whose knowledge of their relations to the rest of creation is fixed, can do evil, but they cannot sin. But we, being divided beings composed of a number of selves each with its false conception of its self-interest, sin in most that we do, for we rarely act in such a way that even the false self-interests of all our different selves are satisfied. The majority of our actions are in the interest of one of these selves, not always the same one, at the expense of the rest" (*Prose II* 426–27). Auden argues that one can make an evil choice only when one is mistaken about the nature of that choice, for all choices that a person (or an animal, for that matter) makes are made in the interest of securing some perceived good, whether survival or happiness or freedom from pain. The crucial question, then, is the nature of the good to be secured. For Augustine, the good that humans naturally desire is to love God. For Auden in 1939, the answer is less clear, but it seems to have something to do with achieving personal and social unity through the recovery of psychological wholeness, with the reunification of the many contradictory desires that seek fulfillment at the expense of the whole person.

It is this disharmony, this privation of unity within the self, that Auden identifies as evil. In describing moral evil, or sin, as a primarily psychological phenomenon, Auden was closer to Augustine than he probably knew, since he had yet to encounter Charles Norris Cochrane and Reinhold Niebuhr, who explicated Augustine's psychology of sin (see chapter 4) in terms that Auden found easy to accept. It seems likely that in his use of the *Confessions*, Auden was working from memory, rather than from a contemporaneous reading. Furthermore, while Auden implicitly draws on Augustine's definition of evil as privation, he does not hesitate to criticize Augustine's institutional heirs in the Roman Catholic Church.[3] He indicates that Christianity in general and Catholicism in particular had long abandoned Augustine's position on the nature of evil, and he states, "Romanticism is right in asserting against [Catholicism and Protestantism] the goodness of the material world, but wrong in denying against them both the goodness of reason" (*Prose II* 446). Auden detected in both Catholic and Protestant churches of his day the tendency toward dualistic thinking, both in their moralism and in their denunciations of nearly all aspects of modernity, and such religious dualism may have been a significant obstacle to his acceptance of Christianity. Auden's recognition of the nature of evil as privation was certainly a step toward Christianity, but it was not, in itself, a mark of his return to the faith.

CONVERSION

Auden's appropriation of Augustine's definition of evil prepared him to respond to a formative experience he had in 1939 in a New York movie theater. Humphrey Carpenter recounts Auden's shock when, during a newsreel showing Polish prisoners taken during the Nazi Blitzkrieg, German audience members began shouting "Kill them!" Carpenter quotes Auden's later comment on this event: "I wondered then, why I reacted as I did against this denial of every humanistic value. The answer brought me back to the church" (282). As Carpenter proceeds to explain, Auden was now being forced to account theologically for blind, irrational hatred, and every system of thought he had "tried on" since his youth failed to account sufficiently for the virulent rejection of human rights that he had always imagined to be self-evident (Carpenter 282–83, *Prose III* 578). Marxism and even psychoanalysis tended to place the origin of evil outside the individual, conscious person, such that evil was imposed on a person, either by a powerful ruling class or by subconscious drives. But Auden concluded that neither political oppression nor psychological repression was sufficient to explain one person's irrational hatred of a perfect stranger.

This was not the first time that Auden had been profoundly disturbed by the human capacity for evil. Reflecting on his visit to Spain in 1937 during the Spanish Civil War, Auden says, "On arriving in Barcelona, I found as I walked through the city that all the churches were closed and there was not a priest to be seen. To my astonishment, this discovery left me profoundly shocked and disturbed" (qtd. in Carpenter 209). His shock was not due only to his "liberal dislike of intolerance," but to his sudden realization that "however I had consciously ignored and rejected the Church for sixteen years, the existence of churches and what went on in them had all the time been very important to me. If that was the case, what then?" (qtd. in Carpenter 210). These two events, in Spain and in New York, though separated by about two years, appear to have been pivotal in Auden's subsequent turn to Christianity. Citing passages from Auden's *The Prolific and the Devourer*, Carpenter explains, "He had been through many changes of heart since reaching adulthood, all the dogmas he had adopted or played with—post-Freudian psychology, Marxism, and the liberal-socialist-democratic outlook that had been his final political stance before leaving England—had one thing in common: they were all based on a belief in the natural goodness of man. They all claimed that if one specific evil were removed, be it sexual repression, the domination of the proletariat by the bourgeoisie, or fascism, then humanity would be happy and unrest would cease" (282).

While Carpenter is correct that Auden saw fatal flaws in these three earlier philosophies, his assessment of the fault itself could be more nuanced. At issue is the definition of the word "natural." In the sense in which Rousseau, for example, might use the term, humans are "naturally" good in that all their most basic impulses are toward truth, beauty, harmony, and peace, and any impulses to the contrary are artificial, social impositions on the individual. For Rousseau, as for Freud and Marx to a lesser extent, the removal of societal constraints on basically good, "natural" impulses is necessary for the full flourishing of humanity. Thus, all other things being equal, humans tend toward the good, however variously defined. Auden rejected this definition of the "natural" goodness of humans in the late 1930s.[4] He had come to an Augustinian turning point at which he had to admit that his previous philosophies had all been forms of false dualism and that evil did not have its origin in political or economic ills, but rather that evil was a matter of what his 1937 poem, "As I Walked Out One Evening," called a "crooked heart" (*CP* 135).

In November of 1939, after he had abandoned "The Prolific and the Devourer," Auden wrote one of his most celebrated poems of that period, "In Memory of Sigmund Freud," which commemorates Freud's death earlier that year. The poem pays tribute to the famed psychoanalyst who, the poet says, was doing what little he could to improve the lives of his fellow humans (*CP* 273). The poem indicates that Freud's most important contribution was that he "showed us what evil is, not, as we thought, / deeds that must be punished, but our lack of faith, / our dishonest mood of denial, / the concupiscence of the oppressor" (274). In explaining Freud's contribution to his understanding of human psychology, Auden replaces the psychoanalytic language of "neurosis" and "repression" with theological terms like "lack of faith," describing the human problem almost entirely in negative terms: "lack," "dishonest," "denial" (274). "Concupiscence" is an oddly archaic, theological term that suggests the sort of self-centered attempts at gratification that Auden's early love poetry often describes. Auden had never used much psychoanalytic jargon in his poetry, though his earlier poems often do rely on Freud's idea that opposing impulses constantly compete for dominance within one person. Before 1939,

Auden had largely relied on allegory to suggest the divided consciousness, but from 1939 on, he would increasingly resort to such theological language that suggests he was rediscovering the Augustinian theological tradition for the first time in the late 1930s.

NEW YEAR LETTER

After the abortive *The Prolific and the Devourer*, Auden's next major exploration of his own spiritual development came in his long poem *New Year Letter*, written in the early months of 1940 and addressed to his friend Elizabeth Mayer, a fellow expatriate. The verse epistle is written in octosyllabic couplets, which lend a certain formal rigidity to a poem that Edward Mendelson explains "is sinuous, various, and far more elusive than its formal style suggests" (*Early* 103). Few critics besides Mendelson have even attempted a thorough reading of the poem, much less probed its philosophical inquiries. In general, critics have had difficulty detecting coherence in the poem. For example, Randall Jarrell once remarked, "This, *New Year Letter*, consists of a couple of thousand tetrameter couplets about—well, it's always hard to say what long didactic expository poems are about, but one feels quite safe in saying the *New Year Letter* is about the Modern World and how it got to be Modern, about Auden—the poet—and his relations to Things in General" (126). Jarrell's exaggeration signifies a certain frustration that this long, discursive poem appears to lack a coherent thematic structure. However, if the poem is loosely structured, it is thematically coherent. Its grand theme is Auden's rejection of various forms of dualistic thinking, and like so many of his earlier poems that Jarrell and others admired, the poem is about the poet's own spiritual quest for psychological wholeness and social belonging, achieving a balance between opposing tensions, a theme that the very form of the rhyming couplet suggests. More recently, Rachel Wetzsteon has argued that *New Year Letter* "is Auden's dense and ambitious attempt to find a reason for the horrible war just getting started, and, more broadly, to provide satisfying answers to eternal questions of good, evil, and the nature of the self" (91). Indeed, one of the poem's primary concerns is the nature of evil, which Auden consistently describes as a product of fallaciously dualistic thinking and contrasts with a healthy ability to hold opposites in tension. As a long, discursive poem struggling with the nature of good and evil, the poem has many models, including Pope's *Essay on Man*, Blake's *Marriage of Heaven and Hell*, and Goethe's *Faust*. It also bears a strong thematic resemblance to Augustine's *Confessions*, which, although not strictly a poem, also details the author's spiritual journey through a series of false dualisms to a cohesive philosophy.

The close parallels between the *Confessions* and *New Year Letter* are not widely recognized, even though both works speak in the mode of an "overheard" confession in which the authors publicly recount their spiritual journeys, renounce their own faults, and pray for guidance as they seek to reorder their souls according to the truth that they have perceived. Perhaps the link between *New Year Letter* and the *Confessions* goes largely unnoticed because Auden was writing in a confessional genre several decades before "confessional" poetry became popular. And there are, of course, major differences between the two works. The *Confessions* are arranged as one long prayer, addressed to God but overheard, as it were, by the readers, who are only the indirect audience for the work.[5] But unlike Augustine, Auden addresses *New Year Letter* to an individual human, Elizabeth Mayer, in whose Long Island home Auden was a sometime lodger and frequent guest. Mayer, an accomplished musician and the wife of an expatriate German-Jewish physician in New York, became a kind of mother-figure to Auden, who had recently left his own mother behind in England. His addressing of the poem to a mother figure links the poem with Augustine, whose own mother, Monica, played a pivotal role in his eventual conversion to Christianity. So in *New Year Letter,* Elizabeth Mayer plays the role of Monica to Auden's role as the confessing Augustine.

Like the *Confessions, New Year Letter* examines the nature of evil and concludes that evil exists ontologically only as a privation, and the poem proceeds to explore the ways in which this Augustinian view can account for both political and psychological evils of which Auden is constantly aware. The poem says far more about the nature of evil than it does about any likely remedy for it—Hitler is a stronger presence in the poem than is God. But Hitler is not himself the Devil, with whom the speaker of the poem has a long exchange. Rather, the Devil is a personification of evil, whom Auden calls "the great schismatic who / First split creation into two" (*CP* 213). The Devil in the poem is not a literal entity, but represents the contradictory impulses within the human to control everything that exists and yet to renounce certain existences as illegitimate (213). The human attempt at self-divinization is self-defeating because it necessitates the destruction of something upon which the individual depends for his or her own existence.

Auden's Devil figure is most directly indebted to Goethe's *Faust*, in which Mephistopheles tempts the restless Faust to content himself with some worldly good.[6] Auden calls him the "Prince of Lies," and the "Spirit-that-denies" (*CP* 209), the latter epithet being a virtual quotation of Mephistopheles's introduction of himself to Faust in scene 3 of Goethe's *Faust*. Theo Hobson suggests that Auden's use of the Devil "could be seen as a 'mere' personification, a convenient symbol for that which impedes human freedom and moral responsibility, yet even to employ Christian imagery so extensively is suggestive of an essentially religious position" (25). But as *The Prolific and the Devourer* indicates, Auden was probably not even a theist when he began the poem, and while the poem does work its way tentatively toward Christian theology, Auden's earlier use of religious imagery does not necessarily indicate religious belief, since only a year earlier he had stated explicitly that, in the realm of religious language, "Nomenclature is merely a matter of convenience" (*Prose II* 448). But his theological language does indicate a philosophical shift away from the dualism that he personifies as the Devil. Mendelson is closer in suggesting that "The Devil is a convenient name for the cause and agent of this inner division" (*Later* 108). Yet the Devil is not so much the *cause* of the division, but a name for the division itself, the privation that Auden identified in *The Prolific and the Devourer* and that he calls in "New Year Letter" "the great Denier" (*CP* 211).

Given the time of Auden's writing the *New Year Letter,* the nature of evil could never be very far from the poet's mind. The poem was begun in January of 1940, and the first part pictures what it calls "The Thing," the "dreadful figure" of Nazi fascism, advancing steadily across Europe (*CP* 199). The escalation of World War II was calling into serious question Auden's earlier notions that Marxism, post-Freudian psychoanalysis, or liberal humanism could effectively maintain a just society in the face of expanding totalitarian regimes. At the root of all this Auden finds a demonic dualism. In an ambivalent address to this Devil, the speaker says,

> Lame fallen shadow, *retro me,*
> *Retro,* but do not go away:
>
> Although, for all your fond insistence,
> You have no positive existence,
> Are only a recurrent state
> Of fear and faithlessness and hate,
> That takes on from becoming me
> A legal personality,
> Assuming your existence is
> A rule-of-thumb hypostasis. . . . (*CP* 209)

Auden's point in this passage is that evil "exists" only in the wrong actions—fear, faithlessness, hate—which provide evil with a provisional identity that can seem like an essence, or as Auden calls it, an assumed "hypostasis." The syntax in the passage is vague, but the lines imply that that the assumption is wrong. "Hypostasis" is used in the philosophical sense of "substance" or "essence," which the poem clearly says the Devil lacks in actuality, but takes on in a provisional way. Auden's phrase "no positive existence" is very close to Augustine's statement in *The City of God* in which he says, "evil is *not a positive substance*: the loss of good has been given the name of 'evil'" (11.9, emphasis added), though the poem's description of the Devil has confused not a few critics. For example, Randall Jarrell says that in *New Year Letter,* "the status of the Devil (who has 'no positive existence' . . .) is still exactly that of A. A. Milne's bears which eat you if you step on the cracks in the pavement— lovable hypostatized fictions of the pragmatic moralist" (101).[7] But Jarrell misunderstands Auden's developing, Augustinian view of evil as a privation, which distinguishes between Milne's childish picture of evil as an imaginary monster and the philosophical conception of evil as a real, moral absence. Auden's phrase does not suggest that evil is only an illusion, nor even that evil is not real, but merely that evil is not a real existence. It is a real absence.

One temptation of this Devil is the romantic myth of the Fall. Auden's Devil suggests that the prelapsarian Adam and Eve "were totally illogical" and that the Fall consists of a "syllogistic sin" that uses discursive reason to suppress otherwise good instincts (*CP* 211–12), and the Devil encourages the poet to reject the "*ordre logique*" of Enlightenment rationalism and to seek salvation "an *ordre du cœur*," which offers a liberation of instinct and emotion but actually entails the arbitrary tyranny of the passions. The Devil's proposal is fallacious, Auden implies, because it is founded on a dualism that holds one aspect of the inner life—feeling and intuition—to be intrinsically good, while rejecting another necessary aspect—logic and reason—as absolutely evil. A similar temptation is the "False Association," and the poem identifies Wordsworth as an example of the disillusioned revolutionary who rejects the good principles of liberalism because of their abuse in the French Revolution. However, the unmasking of a philosophy as dualist does not in itself constitute a defeat of dualism. When the Devil, as the personification of the human tendency toward dualistic thinking, has led a person to reject a given dualism, he merely offers another, opposite dualism to take its place. Auden pictures the Devil as a patronizing parent addressing a hungover undergraduate: "Well, how's our Socialist this morning? / I could say 'Let this be a warning,' But no, why should I? . . . / . . . / Such things have happened in the lives / Of all the best Conservatives" (219). The disillusioned socialist is tempted to react against socialism by becoming that which he first reacted against, a conservative. Although Auden typically supported leftist causes, he acknowledged that certain brands of extreme socialism could be dualistic because they presuppose the absolute goodness of the working class and the absolute evil of the ruling class. Extreme conservatism is merely the reverse in that it believes the workers to be evil and the ruling class to be good. Auden's choice of socialism in this passage indicates a measure of self-critique, as well as an insistence that his doubts about Marxism will not lead him to embrace conservative ideology. The unnamed idealist in the poem might just as easily have been disillusioned by conservatism or liberalism, for which the Devil would offer him communism or fascism as a remedy. The disillusioned idealist may thus vacillate between political extremes without ever correcting the underlying, dualistic error.

The poem traces several popular ideologies of the late nineteenth and early twentieth centuries, arguing that they are all based on fallacious negations, that is, on false dualism. For instance, Marxism, by its own admission, is a "negation of a negation," a phrase from *Das Kapital*, which Auden uses in *New Year Letter* (*CP* 216). Or, as Michael Murphy argues, Auden observes that ideologies must always identify a scapegoat, such that Freudian ideology privileges the subjective/artistic/inner knowledge over the objective/scientific/outer knowledge privileged by Marxist ideology (118).[8] Auden insists, against modern philosophies, that "guilt is everywhere" and that the evil political regimes of the twentieth century are irrefutable evidence of "vast spiritual disorders" (205). Evil, whatever its origin, is not to be identified with any particular class or element of society, nor with any particular element of the human psyche, because it is a *dis*order, a failure to maintain healthy relations between parts, whether social or psychological.

The answer to false dualism, Auden argues, is not to trade it for yet another false dualism, whose totalizing ideology continues to reject certain existences, but instead to develop what he calls "double-focus" (*CP* 220). The Devil offers "The either-ors," and "he may never tell us lies, / Just half-truths we can synthesize" (220). The poem holds out hope that "hidden in his hocus-pocus, / There lies the gift of double-focus" (220). The Devil's half-truths become clues to the whole truth, so long as one can hold opposing desires and ideas in suspension in order to see them both at once. In his note to these lines, Auden writes, "the Devil, indeed, is the father of Poetry, for poetry might be defined as the clear expression of mixed feelings. The Poetic mood is never indicative," and Auden follows the remark with a brief verse: "Whether determined by God or their neural structure, still / All men have one common creed, account for it as you will: / The Truth is one and incapable of self-contradiction; / All knowledge that conflicts with itself is Poetic Fiction" (*New Year Letter* 119n). Of all Auden's statements questioning the value of his own art, this is one of the most extreme. But it must be remembered that when Auden speaks of the Devil, he does not have in mind a literal, malignant intelligence as Christian tradition might define him. Rather, the Devil is Auden's personification of disorder or conflict, and the associated tendency toward dualistic thinking; and because a good poem must deal with conflicted desires, or as Auden puts it, "mixed feelings," the Devil is a name for the very lack of unity between parts of the psyche that makes possible the expression of that conflict. As Auden would assert many years later, "in poetry, all facts and all beliefs cease to be true or false and become interesting possibilities. . . . [A] poet is constantly tempted to make use of an idea or a belief, not because he believes it to be true, but because he sees it has interesting poetic possibilities" (*DH* 19). A poet finds it easy to entertain false dualism when writing a poem, even if he or she is at some level aware of its falsehood. But even when poetry succumbs to devilish dualism, the poet may be reassured that the "gift of double-focus" is available in the Devil's poetic lies, that a poem may point to a truth that it is itself incapable of expressing. (9)

Mendelson calls "double-focus" "more than a dialectical ability to see both sides of a question," but "a realm of free action in an eternally changing condition to which the poem gives two names: Purgatory, a name Auden had not used before, and the simpler word 'time'" (*Later* 114). Part 3 of *New Year Letter* is driven by this attempt to consistently inhabit the realm of double-focus. Auden's description of his own spiritual journey maintains its Faustian overtones, describing an intellectual climb up Mount Purgatory "Where if we do not move we fall, / Yet

movement is heretical / Since over its ironic rocks / No route is truly orthodox"
(*CP* 223). Auden likely has his own past in mind here, though he might just as easily be referring to the biography of any philosophical pilgrim, from Augustine to
the Buddha, many of whom tried out a variety of false philosophies before happening on the truth. The struggle to achieve the double-focus always entails a
flirtation with dualistic thinking, and so all spiritual journeys involve a series of
failures to escape dualistic thinking, which is at once a source of implicit truth and
a temptation to sin. In a review written at the same time as *New Year Letter,* Auden
describes "double-focus" as the knowledge "that all absolutes are heretical but that
one can only act in a given circumstance by assuming one" (*Prose II* 56). Perhaps
the word "absolute" should not be taken too absolutely, as Auden seems to mean
by it the assertion that one has perfect and total knowledge, the idea that a human
can achieve a transcendent, God-like perspective on history, which would give that
person unquestionable moral authority.[10] Although one must occasionally take up
a position that appears to be dualist, one must do so only tentatively and provision-
ally, never absolutely.

Another appropriate term for the idea of double-focus, which Auden was about
to discover in Charles Williams's book *The Descent of the Dove,* is the word "co-
inherence," a little-used theological term that Williams adopted to describe any
union of distinct or diverse things in which both unity and diversity are harmoniously maintained, in the orthodox conception of the Trinity for example, in
which God is regarded as a single substance existing in the three persons of the
Father, the Son, and the Holy Spirit, such that the three persons maintain difference without violence; the single divine substance is never divided while the three
distinct persons are never conflated. The term may also refer to the hypostasis of the
human and divine natures of Jesus Christ, who is regarded in creedal Christianity
as both fully God and fully man. Williams's book argues that, throughout history,
Christianity has always struggled to maintain a balance between pairs of seemingly
opposed ideas which have threatened to pull the church apart, successfully at times.
Williams gives Augustine as one of the first examples of successful co-inherence in
church history, since it was Augustine who led the fourth-century church to reject
the dualist philosophies of his day—Manichaeism and Neoplatonism—while arguing that both spirit and body could co-inhere and were redeemable. In other words,
Augustine succeeded in demonstrating to the church that the human body was not
intrinsically evil, that sin was ultimately a defect in the soul rather than the fact of
embodiment, and that through faith in God, spirit and body could co-inhere. Williams acknowledges that, for all his philosophical insistence on the basic goodness
of the body, Augustine maintained a certain, culturally conditioned suspicion of the
body. Williams states, "Formally Augustine did not err; but informally? For all his
culture . . . [h]e has always been a danger to the devout, for without his genius they
lose his scope. Move some of his sayings but a little from the centre of his passion

and they point to damnation" (64). Even for Augustine, the spiritual journey up Mount Purgatory was not entirely orthodox.

While the term "co-inherence" does not appear in Auden's poem,[11] Mendelson notes that Auden did read Williams's book shortly after its publication in February of 1940 and that other phrases from the book begin to appear in the last hundred or so lines of *New Year Letter* (125). The American title of the book in which *New Year Letter* was originally published, *The Double Man*, came from *The Descent of the Dove*, in which Williams cites Montaigne's reflection on what Williams calls "co-inherence": "We are, I know not how, double in ourselves, so that what we believe we disbelieve, and cannot rid ourselves of what we condemn" (qtd. in Williams 192). This intellectual doubleness, in which one continues to be attracted to ideas that one has already acknowledged to be false, always threatens to become mere duplicity, but in Auden's estimation, it also makes double-focus possible. But the title *The Double Man* is a double-reference, since Williams also quotes an unnamed Egyptian monk who said, "It is right for a man to take up the burden for them who are near to him, whatever it may be, and, so to speak, to put his own soul in the place of that of his neighbor, and to become, if it were possible, a double man. . . . For thus it is written *We are all one body . . .*" (qtd. in Williams 55).

Some years later, Auden wrote an introduction to a reprint of *The Descent of the Dove* in which he explains Williams's concept of "bearing one another's burdens": "the first law of the spiritual universe is that nobody can carry his own burden; he only can, and therefore must, carry someone else's. Whose burden in particular he should carry is up to him to decide: usually, this choice is dictated by his character and his social circumstances." Auden adds, "Choosing to bear another's burden involves at the same time permitting another to carry one's own, and this may well be the harder choice, just as it is usually easier to forgive than be forgiven" (*Prose IV* 25–26). That is, the Christian is required to both give and receive aid from those closest to him or herself without reducing the exchange to economic manipulation, and without allowing the relationship to become one-sided with one person only giving and the other only receiving. Probably Auden had already drafted the lines concerned with "double-focus" when he read *The Descent of the Dove*, although, as Mendelson puts it, there are many ideas that "had been in the poem before Auden found them in Williams, but they looked different in the light that Williams reflected on them" (*Later* 127). Once Auden happened upon the concept of co-inherence in Williams, he was able to develop a language in which he could more clearly explain his antipathy toward any kind of philosophical dualism.

New Year Letter returns repeatedly to one particular philosophical rejection that Auden sees as fallacious: the denial of time. Following Goethe's *Faust*, in which the protagonist is in danger of damnation only if he rejects the future in favor of prolonging some present moment,[12] Auden recognizes that evil in the modern world often consists of the rejection of some element of time, whether past, present, or future. Sin occurs not in the mythic act of eating from the Tree of Knowledge of Good and Evil, but rather in lingering at the tree instead of "depart[ing] / At once with gay and grateful heart, / Obedient, reborn, re-aware" (*CP* 222). To "stop an instant there" is to find that "Horror . . . / . . . has sprung the trap of Hell" (222). Potential human destiny will not be realized by merely mulling it over. Once an enlightenment is achieved, it must be acted upon, not rested in. But the problem remains as to what exactly a human being must do with newfound knowledge, a problem that had plagued Auden for his entire poetic career. Whatever the action is, to attempt to stop moving through time is to condemn oneself. But in the middle of his movement through time—the mythic climb up Mount Purgatory—the poet must pause to listen to the "calls of conscience" that surround him in the contemporary world, in case one of these just causes demands his personal devotion (224).

In Auden's estimation, there is far more injustice than any one person can redress, and the present evil of fascism threatens to destroy civilization. While the current enemies of civilization are often imagined as the barbarians at the gates of civilized Rome, Auden insists that such a historical analogy is false: the immediate future looming over the modern West does not resemble the Dark Ages when Rome's superficial cultural coherence was destroyed by "artless and barbaric foes . . ." (*CP* 225). Rather, "The cities we abandon fall / To nothing primitive at all" (225). The modern destroyer of civilization, the disembodied "Voice" that comes out of Europe, is not a backward barbarian but an industrial populist who contrives a mechanical social order (225). It is also "A theologian who denies / . . . / The basis of civility" (225). Like other forms of evil in the poem, Hitler is characterized not by any affirmation, but by his dualistic denial of something good. Auden later explained that, even before his conversion, he recognized that Nazism was an "utter denial of everything liberalism had ever stood for" (*Prose III* 578). As the war was escalating in 1940, it was clear to Auden that the evil present in his historic moment demanded a prompt response, in part because it fit in so well with modern industrial society. So it is not the Dark Ages to which Auden turns in *New Year Letter* for a historical analogy with his own time, but to the Renaissance which saw the birth of the modern "Economic Man" (*CP* 230). Auden suggests that the Renaissance introduced the idea of settling theological disputes on the battlefield with "the / Opinions of artillery" (230). The combination "Of LUTHER's faith and MONTAIGNE's doubt, / The epidemic of translations" with "The scholars' scurrilous disputes / Over the freedom of the Will" produced the modern capitalist whose sole aim is economic profit and who is "urban, prudent, and inventive" (230), but who also makes Nazi fascism possible.

New Year Letter proceeds to identify two opposing philosophical traditions, the romantic and the Platonic, that Auden denounces as dualistic mirror-images of each other. The error of Platonism is evident in its eventual support of totalitarianism, though like Augustine, he identifies dualistic thinking as the source of the

Platonic error. Elitism is only a symptom of "PLATO's lie of intellect" that produced the philosopher-kings who are really tyrants: "knowing Good, they will no Wrong / United in the abstract Word / Above the low anarchic herd" (*CP* 234). The poem refers particularly to the *Republic*, which rejects the physical world in favor of the abstract, ideal world of the Good. Thus Platonic Idealism proposes that only those elite philosophers who know the Good are fit to rule. The problem, as Auden sees it, is the equation of knowledge with virtue. Plato does not recognize that the moral corruption that leads to injustice and oppression comes not from ignorance but from the many contradictory desires that compete within each individual. If the material world is good, then a philosopher's knowledge of the abstract world of ideas does not necessarily make him morally superior to the ignorant. The poem equally denounces "ROUSSEAU's falsehood of the flesh" that attempts to find the basis of social equality in "the Irrational" (234).

Both the Platonic rejection of the body and the romantic rejection of the intellect have the same psychological result in their respective followers. Whatever dualistic philosophy it embraces, the human ego ends in narcissistic self-loathing. Auden pictures the self-conscious ego as a mad woman in the attic, but unlike the conventional woman in the attic, the ego is imprisoned by her own choice. She asserts "the right to lead alone / An attic life all on her own, / Unhindered, unrebuked, unwatched, / Self-known, self-praising, self-attached" (235). Left to itself, the ego naturally turns inward to narcissistic introspection. Whether the ego is obsessed with the intellect or with the irrational, the self-centeredness is pleasurable enough at first, but once the introspection becomes self-absorption, it leads to panic and despair, and at that point self-loathing is inescapable (235). Then the ego undergoes yet another transformation, from a committed lunatic to "A witch self-tortured . . . / . . . . / She worships in obscene delight / The Not, the Never, and the Night" (235). The ego has regressed from atmospheric self-consciousness to the madness of self-absorption, and finally to the witchcraft of self-worship, and what the ego finds to worship in the self is expressed in almost totally negative terms: "Not," "Never," "Night," as well as "The formless Mass without a Me." The self is now stripped down to the Eros and Thanatos drives that Freud identified as the root of human desires, and which Auden reminds us are really "Synonymous with one another" (236). The ego wishes to be not-itself by relinquishing self-consciousness and returning to the pre-conscious fetal state in the mother's womb, either in sex or in death, but the recognition of this fact by the ego does not solve the problem of self-consciousness. In fact, Auden is implying that psychoanalysis might make the problem of self-consciousness worse if it encourages morbid, narcissistic introspection.

Auden's description of the psychological results of philosophical dualism is an attempt to cast an Augustinian denunciation of false philosophy in the language of post-Freudian psychoanalysis. Although the practice of confession is important to both Augustine and Freud—the sinner confessing to God or the patient confessing to the analyst—the confessional nature of *New Year Letter* almost disappears in its ruminations on history and philosophy. Auden returns formally to the theme of confession at the end of the poem, in which he points out the distinct limitations of human perspective, and thus of humans' inability to achieve anything like a just society because "good intentions cannot cure / The actual evils they endure" (*CP* 240). It is a bleak outlook, but a few lines later, Auden suggests a tentative starting point for social justice:

> . . . all that we can always say
> Is: true democracy begins
> With free confession of our sins.
> In this alone are all the same,
> All are so weak that none dare claim
> "I have the right to govern," or
> "Behold in me the Moral Law" . . . (241)

The lines weave together a number of thematic threads in the poem—the quest for psychological and social unity, the rejection of absolutist political agendas, and the necessity of personal humility. A few lines later, Auden offers a prayer to an absconded deity, and Augustine's presence in the poem finally comes to the surface.

The prayer asks for conviction, as well as for a disturbing of the speaker's complacency. Acknowledging the moral demands for "locality" and "peace" that his attempt at double-focus makes on him, he quotes a line from the *Confessions*: "*O da quod jubes, Domine,*" or "O, give what you command, Lord" (*CP* 242). Auden found the Latin clause in *The Descent of the Dove* (Williams 65–66), which he began reading as he was finishing the poem. The line is taken, slightly altered, from the *Confessions*, where the command refers specifically to chastity, but the line also implies Augustine's broader recognition that he is incapable of obeying any of God's commands unless God also gives him the grace to believe and obey (10.29). Auden quoted the line again a few months later in a book review, in which he claimed, "Augustine . . . was not denying free will, but only saying that in order to will you must first believe that you can" (*Prose II* 88). At this point, Auden interpreted the passage as an affirmation of free will, not necessarily in reference to Christian faith.

In orthodox Christianity, faith is a gift of God, to which the human will contributes obedience, but despite the explicitly theological language at the end of *New Year Letter*, Auden was apparently not altogether convinced of the existence of the Christian God in early 1940. It is not clear from the poem's language whether his understanding of God falls within creedal Christian Trinitarianism (which he would soon accept explicitly), or whether he is addressing a protean deity of his own imagining. The prayer addresses the hidden deity with many names, most of which are drawn from Christian tradition: Unicorn, Dove, Ichthus, Wind, Voice, and finally in the words of Augustine, *Domine*, or Lord (*CP* 241–42). The poem also quotes Athanasius' definitive statement against the Arians on the eternity of Christ: "*Non est quando not fuerit*," or "There is not when he was not," which Auden also took from Williams. But Auden also uses names like Clock and Keeper of the years, which are not necessarily Christian references (*CP* 242). Nor is the epithet, "It without image," a name that suggests Auden does not yet have the Incarnation or the *imago dei* in view. As Mendelson points out, Auden found most of these names in Williams's *Descent of the Dove*, and regardless of the deity's exact identity, the poem is clearly a significant step toward Christianity and toward a specifically Augustinian theological position.

Monroe Spears argues that the Christian language in *New Year Letter* is mythic and is entertained as a theoretical possibility and even a cultural necessity, but that the poem nevertheless "hesitates on the edge of belief" (*Poetry* 172). The poem is tentatively theistic, but as a statement of belief, it is the "clear expression of mixed feelings" that Auden claimed was the definition of poetry (*New Year Letter* 119). As Mendelson points out, "Auden hoped to receive instruction and strength from the divinity he had prayed to earlier. But it was Elizabeth Mayer to whom he looked for forgiveness" (*Later* 126). The poem's second, final prayer is a direct address to Mayer, to whom the entire poem is dedicated. Perhaps it seemed impolite at the end of the epistle to neglect the first addressee, even for God, but it is certainly an appropriate ending given the poem's concern with rebuilding a just society through confession and forgiveness. In any event, he expresses his gratitude for Mayer's forbearance and forgiveness, which leads Auden to remind himself that "Our life and death are with our neighbor" (*CP* 243). Extra-textual evidence suggests that Auden did not yet consider himself a Christian when he wrote the lines. Mendelson reports that in March 1940 Williams wrote to his wife and mentioned that Auden had written him a letter saying "he just wanted to tell me how moved he was by the Dove (and he no Christian)" (qtd. in *Later* 125); presumably Auden told Williams explicitly that he was not a Christian. Auden would not begin attending church until the autumn of 1940, and then only "in a tentative and experimental way," as he put it, when he had already finished the *New Year Letter* (qtd. in *Later* 148). The poem does not reflect a conversion as such, but it does show that he was seriously considering Christian theism as a possible remedy for the social and psychological privations that lay at the root of all human ills.

CHARLES NORRIS COCHRANE

The year between the summer of 1940 and the summer of 1941 saw Auden undergo a series of personal crises that led him back to the Christian faith, but during that time he also read several theological books that helped him make sense of his own personal history and of the modern world he inhabited, and these books became crucial to his intellectual and spiritual development during the 1940s. In his 1955 essay for *Modern Canterbury Pilgrims*, Auden recollects that his reading of "some theological works," including Kierkegaard, were important factors in his return to Christianity (*Prose III* 579). He does not say what works other than Kierkegaard he read at that time, though he favorably compares Kierkegaard's existentialism with Augustine's exploration of the interaction of free will with faith and grace in the human consciousness (*Prose III* 579), and the notes to *New Year Letter* contain quotations from Pascal and Paul Tillich, as well as references to Charles Williams. In a 1945 essay Auden claimed that Augustine, along with Pascal and Kierkegaard, were some of his initial theological influences (*Prose II* 248), so it is likely that Augustine's *Confessions* was one of the theological works that Auden was reading between 1940 and 1941. In addition to Augustine himself, Auden was reading contemporary works that retraced the contours of Augustine's thought. One was Williams's *Descent of the Dove*, but another was Charles Norris Cochrane's *Christianity and Classical Culture*, whose analysis of the importance of Augustinian theology to the cultural development of the West became a centerpiece of Auden's early theology. It is not clear exactly when Auden first read Cochrane, but in a 1944 review of the revised edition, he claimed to have read it "many times" since its original publication in 1940 (*FA* 33). Soon after the book's initial publication, Auden began drawing heavily from Cochrane's account of Augustine's confrontation with classical philosophy.

Christianity and Classical Culture is part history, part political philosophy, and part theology; in some ways it is an early and admirable example of what would come to be called "cultural studies" later in the twentieth century. Part 1 of the book traces the decline in late Roman political philosophy, focusing on the failure of both Neoplatonism and classical materialism to provide a stable rationale for the maintenance of the Roman state. Part 2 describes the ill-fated attempt to shore up the Roman *imperium* by replacing the state religion with Christianity. Part 3 concludes the book with a detailed analysis of Augustine's theology of the Trinity and of divine providence, and Cochrane details the ways in which Augustine's theology solved many of the theoretical problems that had plagued the irreconcilable classical philosophies of idealism and materialism, offering in their place a coherent metaphysics that affirmed both body and spirit, the finite and the eternal, the particular and the universal.

Cochrane explains that one of the many significant philosophical problems that classical philosophy was unable to solve concerned the nature of evil, and Cochrane helped Auden see that Augustine's theory of evil as privation was a direct response to the failure of classical, dualistic philosophies to account for moral evils. Cochrane points out that, while Augustine opposed the Manichees, who presupposed that evil choices were imposed on the individual from without and denied that individuals were morally responsible for their evil choices, "Augustine was no less concerned to expose the error of the Platonists which, as he insisted, rested upon a false antithesis between body and soul" (447), which held the body primarily responsible for moral evil. Cochrane explains that Augustine's definition of moral evil as a privation in the will, far from dismissing the seriousness of evil, actually reinforces the fact that evil has great power because of its pervasiveness: "Augustine concludes that sin is due originally to a corruption, not of body but of soul. As such, it begins with a wrong determination of the will and develops as the result of physical satisfactions derived therefrom, until it is finally confirmed by the bond of habit. Its consequences are thus insidious, far-reaching, and cumulative; the ultimate nemesis being frustration or self-defeat through the loss of genuine freedom and power" (449). Evil cannot therefore be defeated by social or political pressure because it infects every human being, including those who make and enforce the law. Nor can evil be corrected by the individual, because every person's will is always already corrupted by past choices and experience. The corruption of each human will produces a willful ignorance of the principles of love and justice, and it cripples the mind's ability to resist additional seductions, plunging it ever deeper into hatred, selfishness, and despair. Every corrupted person, Cochrane states, "may thus be described as a slave to sin, that is, to his own aberrations of mind and heart" (449).

Auden may have read these words either while he was finishing *New Year Letter* or shortly after he completed it, and Cochrane's summary of Augustine's definition of evil resonated strongly with him. *New Year Letter* had advanced a very similar argument: that all evil could be traced to an insidious corruption of the human mind. *New Year Letter* hesitates to explain specifically how evil might be addressed and corrected in the day-to-day world, though the poem does suggest that the mode of thought it calls "double-focus" is the way to resist the corruption of one's own mind (*CP* 220). The prayers that end the poem suggest that the author had begun to suspect that the corruptions in his own will could be corrected only by outside intervention. And yet, the poem conveys the hope that double-focus may be found in the morass of dualistic philosophies that the poem confronts. Each false philosophy deprives itself of some important truth, but each diabolical lie also paradoxically reveals an element of truth that must be recognized and synthesized with other truths found in other false dualisms. Auden's sentiments in *New Year Letter* are very similar to Cochrane's distillation of passages from Augustine's *City of God*, among other works: "the nature even of the devil, in so far as it is a nature, is good; *even his lies, in order to serve their purpose as lies, must have verisimilitude, i.e. they must be interspersed with elements of truth.* The goodness and truth which are thus original in nature are, moreover, final to it. In the secular conflict with sin and error they are substance confronting shadow, unity division, the whole a distorted and partial image, a mere parody of itself" (513, emphasis added). Cochrane then remarks, "In such a conflict who can doubt to which side final victory must belong? Accordingly, the apparently irreconcilable antitheses which present themselves everywhere in nature are not to be accepted as ultimate" (513). The similarities of Cochrane's words and Auden's description of the Devil in *New Year Letter* could hardly have escaped Auden's notice. He had denounced dualism, but he had no ready philo-sophical point of view to adopt in their place until Cochrane provided a theological standpoint for a critique of the various dualisms.

"FOR THE TIME BEING"

Williams and Cochrane had provided Auden with a theological vocabulary with which he could continue to make reference to evil in terms of the privations exacer-bated by dualism, although after *New Year Letter* Auden would never again explore the nature of evil at such length. However, "For the Time Being," a Christmas ora-torio that Auden wrote in 1941–42, regularly describes evil as a privation that the Incarnation subsequently repairs. The poem is unconventional in both theology and form, for while it follows the form of a traditional oratorio in the sense that the verse is written for singers and not stage actors, it also borrows from the medieval mystery play in which the biblical story is represented by melodramatic actors in contemporary modes of dress and speech. Thus, Simeon becomes a modern philos-opher, the shepherds represent the working classes, and Herod is a liberal humanist dictator. In this way, Auden is able to draw some ingenious parallels between the story's original setting in the early first century and his own time in the mid-twenti-eth century by recasting the political conflicts of the past as social and psychological conflicts in the present. The comparisons are largely indebted to Cochrane's analy-sis of social and political disintegration of late classical culture, which he implic-itly compares to the twentieth century throughout the book. "For the Time Being" makes Cochrane's comparisons more explicit, especially in its dramatization of the psychological fragmentation in each individual, in which all social and political ills are rooted. Mendelson has identified much of the material that Auden appropriated from Cochrane and integrated into the poem, and Mendelson's reading focuses on the poem's double view of history, specifically the historical parallels Auden draws between the first century and the twentieth. But extending that analysis into fully theological territory shows that the poem is strongly concerned with perennial metaphysical and moral questions.

The second part of the poem, entitled "The Annunciation," begins not with Gabriel and Mary, but with the Four Faculties as distinguished by Jung: Intuition, Feeling, Sensation, and Thought. Together they identify themselves as dissociated parts of the human psyche, saying that they were "one" before the primal, human rebellion (*CP* 355). Deprived of their co-inherence with the self in the unfallen psyche, Adam's "error became our / Chance to be" (355). The divided nature of the human person goes all the way down to the cellular level, as a later "Boys' Semi-Chorus" says in a prayer to Saints Joseph and Mary:

> Joseph, Mary, pray for us,
> Independent embryos who,

Unconscious in another, do
Evil as each creature does
In every definite decision
To improve; for even in
The germ-cell's primary division
Innocence is lost and sin,
Already given as a fact,
Once more issues as an act. (366)

The semi-chorus speaks in the voice of pre-conscious, pre-sexual embryos who, nevertheless, are subject to the division that constitutes evil. Even individual cells reproduce asexually by fission, which Auden uses to foreshadow the divided consciousness that will inevitably emerge later in the speakers' lives. The pre-conscious embryos imply that their development is inherently selfish and violent, that it takes place at the expense of another and is therefore evil, though not yet sinful because not conscious. In *The Prolific and the Devourer* Auden had distinguished between "evil" committed unconsciously by animals and "sin" committed consciously by adult humans (*Prose II* 426–27), but this passage in "For the Time Being" suggests a disturbing continuity between animal evil and human sin.

The stanza recalls one of the most controversial passages in Augustine's *Confessions*, in which Augustine traces his own rebellious selfishness as far back as his own infancy. Augustine says that, even though he does not remember his own infancy, "Myself have seen and known even a baby envious; it could not speak, yet it turned pale and looked bitterly on its foster-brother. Who knows not this? . . . Is that too innocence . . . ?" (1.7). Augustine observes, "We bear gently with all this, not as being no or slight evils, but because they will disappear as years increase . . . ," and if children do carry such overt greed and jealousy into adulthood, they are sternly rebuked (1.7). Like Augustine, Auden suggests that the path toward the conscious choice to sin has already been established at conception. Some years later Auden would say in *The Dyer's Hand* that "No human being is innocent, but small children are not yet personally guilty" (415), so he would not hold a baby judicially guilty of willful sin. However, he also notes in a later essay, "From the moment consciousness first wakes in a baby (and this may possibly be before birth) it finds itself in the company of sinners, and its consciousness is affected by a contagion against which there is no prophylaxis" (*FA* 54).

Auden indicates that no human being, however young, is able to escape the sinful destiny established by its circumstances, and while no one is actually *forced* to sin initially, it is inevitable that sin will eventually occur at some point.[13] According to Gabriel, who speaks directly after the Four Faculties in "For the Time Being," that trajectory of all humans toward sin was set by Eve, who, enamored with her own willfulness, "denied the will of Love and fell" (*CP* 359). Mary, then, becomes an antitype of Eve, whose mythic fall fragmented the human consciousness. As Gabriel tells Mary, "What her negation wounded, may / Your affirmation heal today; / Love's will requires your own . . ." (359). This is not to say that Auden believed in a literal, historical Eve; rather, Eve stands for conflicted desires, the emergence of which are more or less synonymous with the prehistorical advent of self-conscious human beings. Though Eve is mythical and Mary is historical, Mary can begin to repair the Fall through her own willful acceptance of Christ's presence in her body. For Auden, evil is a negation, even of the will, so restoration must initially involve a willful affirmation. Throughout "For the Time Being" Auden continues to think of evil largely in terms of privation, and especially as a psychological privation of single-mindedness—hence the Narrator's statement to Joseph and Mary: "Sin fractures the Vision, not the Fact" (365). Evil is primarily a corruption of the human person, not of the non-human world at large.

The portrayal of evil as privation is more subtle in the most obvious manifestation of evil in the poem, "The Massacre of the Innocents," which is spoken in prose by a modernized Herod the Great. He does not speak in terms of privation as explicitly as do Gabriel and the Four Faculties, but his speech is immediately recognizable as the product of dualistic thinking, which Auden often associates with Manichaeism as described by Augustine. At the outset, Herod admits that he has to make a decision about what to do with the newborn Christ, but he virtually renounces his own responsibility, saying "my decision must be in conformity with Nature and Necessity" (*CP* 390). He then expresses his gratitude to his parents and teachers who have formed his nature and have, as far as he is concerned, turned every choice he makes into a foregone conclusion. Although the monologue is modeled on the *Meditations* of the stoic Marcus Aurelius, Auden turns Herod into a Platonic dualist who believes that knowledge is equivalent to virtue, so he fears the loss of "objective truths" available to anyone willing to undertake the requisite educational program (393). When he begins his monologue, Herod has already executed a twenty-year campaign to banish all forms of irrationality and superstition from his realm. He has outlawed crystals, Ouija boards, and alchemy, and the apparently happy result is that crime rates are down, food supplies are steady, and the economy is growing (391–92). Still, Herod laments the fact that magic and many other forms of the irrational are still prevalent, complaining that the captain of his guard "wears an amulet against the Evil Eye" and the most successful businessman in Jerusalem "consults a medium over every important transaction" (392). Not the least among Herod's accomplishments is that he manages to make his dystopia attractive, a rare accomplishment in twentieth-century dystopian literature.[14] A society that values allotment gardening and fair prices for soft drinks and sandwiches looks vastly superior to a barbaric society in which "Mongolian idiots are regarded as sacred and mothers who give birth to twins are instantly put to death" (391). But Herod's state is a dystopia. His subjects have not willingly chosen to live in his perfectly rational society, so he must impose rationality by force.

The problem is that the covert barbarians within Herod's realm are just as dualistic as he is. The opposing dualisms of Herod's dystopic Judea are largely drawn from Cochrane's account of the philosophical antitheses that plagued classical civic theory: "To Classicism morality is a matter *either* of emotion *or* of reason. The former it regards as subjective, particularist, barbarian; the other as objective, universal, the morality of civilized man" (Cochrane 507). Herod exemplifies the Platonic dualism that Cochrane describes; his chief political concern is to suppress the subjectivist materialism that he regards as irrational barbarism. In a 1941 essay, Auden explains that "an intellectual evil, i.e. a heresy, is always either a reaction to a previous heresy which it attempts to correct by thinking the exact opposite on every point, or a revolt against hypocrisy. . . . Every heretic, like every neurotic and every tyrant, has a real grievance; the Evil One seduces us by an appeal to our sense of justice" (*Prose II* 148–49). Herod's rational tyranny is an attempt to correct the barbaric worship of the irrational. His dualistic philosophy displays a reactionary desire for justice, but its actual result is injustice.

Thus Herod's Platonic dualism leads him to believe that, if the Christ child is allowed to live, "Idealism will be replaced by Materialism" (*CP* 393). Herod's language here is drawn directly from Cochrane, who explains that classical philosophy "falls into two general divisions, (1) that of classical materialism, and (2) that of classical idealism; the former of which envisages the cosmos as one big machine, the later as one big soul" (508). Cochrane's subsequent analysis of Augustine's response to these divisions helps explain why Auden chose to characterize Herod as a Platonic idealist: "To Augustine the machine-cosmology is so grotesque that it hardly merits the attention of a serious thinker. . . . The other, the one-big-soul cosmology, was . . . much more seductive and dangerous, inasmuch as it appealed to the spirit of devotion and self-sacrifice which is one of the fundamental and most deep-seated instincts of the race. Yet it evoked this spirit only to degrade, pervert, and destroy it. . . . What it demanded was, in effect, that the individual should abnegate his God-given status, in order to prostrate himself before, not a reality but a figment of his own imagination, the so-called 'group spirit' as exemplified in family, class, or state" (508–9). For Auden no less than Augustine, the "liberal" idealism represented by Herod is highly attractive, first because of its strong emphasis on knowledge and reason, and then because of its ability to inspire social and political loyalty. While Platonism as Cochrane presents it is a form of false dualism, it can nevertheless be the source of significant political power, as Herod's republic demonstrates. Because it seeks to suppress all forms of irrationality, it is very difficult to refute on the grounds of experience or reason.

The flaw in Herod's idealism is not a strictly logical flaw but a moral one. The logic of his political idealism necessitates the murder of innocent children. Herod assumes that his resistance to the Christ child is just another step in his campaign against the barbarian materialists who argue, "'I like committing crimes, God likes forgiving them. Really the world is admirably arranged'" (*CP* 395). Were it not for the epigraph to the poem from Romans 6:1 ("What shall we say then? Shall we continue in sin, that grace may abound? God forbid."), Herod's assessment of the moral flaws of romanticism would seem compelling (347). It is in the best interests of civilization to maintain law and order, and if this child is about to disrupt the entire social order that Herod has spent his life building, then the subversive element must be eliminated. But of course, Herod is wrong. Even though he cannot imagine a world in which reason co-inheres with magical rites and law co-inheres with mercy, that is exactly the world that Christ has come to build in place of both Herod's Neoplatonic Republic and the barbarians' anarchic wilderness. To his credit, Herod attempts to imagine what would happen, hypothetically, if "this child is in some inexplicable manner both God and Man," but he concludes that, if it were so, "God would expect every man, whatever his fortune, to lead a sinless life in the flesh and on earth" (394). "Then indeed," he continues, "would the human race be plunged into madness and despair," even though he obviously thinks that his romantic, barbarian opponents are already subject to madness (394). He momentarily tries and fails to imagine something that transcends his own Platonic dualism, and he therefore plunges himself into despair. He ends his speech saying, "I wish I had never been born" (394).

The coming of Christianity does not, as Herod imagines, entail a plunge into romantic irrationalism, but it will reveal the futility of his attempt to establish a utopian society force. To those whose philosophical opinions are merely one of a set of competing dualisms, Christianity promises not a return to a static, pre-conscious univocality, but the difficult task of inhabiting the tensions that dualisms insist on collapsing. To those who accept the Incarnation in which opposites co-inhere, the final Chorus of "For the Time Being" offers not security and serenity but increased tension. "He is the Way," the Chorus says, "Follow Him through the Land of Unlikeness" (*CP* 400). The phrase "Land of Unlikeness" comes from the *Confessions* in a passage in which Augustine looks back at his youth and remarks, "I perceived myself to be far off from Thee, in the region of unlikeness [*in regione dissimilitudinis*]" (7.10).[15] Auden's appropriation of this phrase suggests that, paradoxically, the Incarnation has both brought God near to humanity and revealed the great remaining distance between humans and God, and as *New Year Letter* had observed, the way to salvation is through a series of spiritual failures.

After "For the Time Being," Auden's poetic works do not explain so much as assume the theological position of evil he had staked out in the 1940s. Spears notes that "For the Time Being" "is the fullest and most balanced expression of Auden's religious attitudes; the ideas and dominant images that have been seen partially and transitionally in other poems here may be seen in their final place as part of an ordered whole" (*Poetry* 206). It is reasonable, then, that some of Auden's theological assumptions would recede into the background of his subsequent poetry instead of being foregrounded as they are in *New Year Letter* and "For the Time Being," both of which feature Augustinian ideas, especially at their respective conclusions.16 Although Auden's later poetry often has religious overtones and deep theological implications, "For the Time Being" remains the most explicitly religious and theological work that Auden would ever attempt.

"THE SEA AND THE MIRROR"

"For the Time Being" was first published alongside another long poem of Auden's, "The Sea and the Mirror," and while "The Sea and the Mirror" came first in the volume, it was written after "For the Time Being."17 The publication sequence reflects a logical progression in theme, since "The Sea and the Mirror" ends by describing the world's need for God, and "For the Time Being" examines God's entry into the world. The poems are quite different from each other, but they do share similar concerns about human nature and social order, as well as a philosophical underpinning that includes the Augustinian view of evil as privation that Auden had articulated more explicitly in *New Year Letter.* While "The Sea and the Mirror" is not as openly theological as "For the Time Being," dealing as it does with the difficult relationship between art and life,18 Arthur Kirsch briefly points out that "*The Confessions* is reflected not only in a number of important details in 'The Sea and the Mirror,' particularly in Prospero's speech, but also in Auden's broader identification in the poem with Augustine's rejection of the temptations of Manichaeism . . ." (Introduction xiii). The poem contains several passages that express doubt about the false dualisms that Auden rejected in *New Year Letter,* and it also includes some relatively overt statements that reveal a consistently Augustinian position on the nature of evil.

In the first section, "Prospero to Ariel," Prospero remarks that, when he looks into Ariel's eyes, the "mirror" of art that reflects life, "All we are not stares back at what we are" (*CP* 405). Ariel, who represents the idealistic, artistic impulse, shows up all human shortcomings, making clear the areas in which the viewers are deprived of good. Once art has revealed his deficiencies, Prospero finds that Ariel has no power to restore what is lacking, so Prospero must leave his contrived artistic world and once again inhabit the real one where he will not be able to manipulate characters and events at will. His initial renunciation of his art will have to continue in the real world as he follows his own *via negativa*, or his Way of Rejection of images, in Charles Williams's words (*Descent* 57–58). Prospero anticipates this Negative

Way with some hesitancy, asking himself, "can I learn to suffer / Without saying something ironic or funny / On suffering? I never suspected the way of truth / Was a way of silence . . ." (*CP* 409). In this "way of silence," Prospero will have to reject the magic of artistic impulses, even the innocent arts of conversation and music, lest he be tempted to remake a new magical world in Italy. His excessive interest in art must be corrected by an asceticism through which he will practice relinquishing control of his circumstances.

Williams had introduced Auden to what he calls the "Negative Way" and the "Affirmative Way" (Williams *Descent*, 57). The "Negative Way" characterized the desert fathers, early Christian ascetics who retreated to hermitages or small communes in the wilderness, renouncing physical pleasures and comforts in their efforts to maintain holiness, so the Negative Way is generally identified with contemplative mysticism.[19] The "Affirmative Way," on the other hand, describes those Christians who, often maintaining an urban presence, affirmed the innocence of physical pleasures and developed iconographic art as a means of perceiving the glories of the divine through the medium of the material world. As Williams presents them, these two contrary tendencies appeared to be polar opposites, and so they had to either co-inhere or split Christendom into two separate religions adhering, respectively, to the Affirmative and Negative ways. Either tendency, if isolated from the other, would reject some crucial aspect of existence and generate a false dualism. Williams identifies both Kierkegaard and Augustine as followers of the Negative Way, and while Auden insisted that he was not himself a mystic in his own religious practices, he had a high regard for certain followers of the Negative Way.[20] Auden had used the Latin form of the phrase "Negative Way" (*via negativa*) in his 1941 letter to Ursula Niebuhr, in which he called himself an Augustinian in the vein of Reinhold Niebuhr, adding that "I would allow a little more place, perhaps, for the via negativa" (qtd. in Spender 106). Auden's statement was likely made in response to Ursula and her husband Reinhold's general skepticism about the value of Christian mysticism (see Spender 109). And yet, Auden also associated Augustine with the tendency toward co-inherence that attempted to maintain a healthy tension between the Negative and Affirmative ways.[21] There is, then, a certain willing privation of pleasures that is not evil but spiritually healthy for those who are tempted to make too much of them. Paradoxically, Prospero has lived according to the Affirmative Way while on the island, but on his return he finds he must renounce his magic and become a follower of the Negative Way.

While Prospero has come to acknowledge the limits of his art and prepares himself for the silence that will attend the restoration of his dukedom, other characters from *The Tempest* have yet to come to terms with their own psychological fragmentation, which Auden had come to see as the source of personal and social problems. Stephano, the drunken butler, finds himself pulled in conflicting directions by his many contradictory desires, and he wonders which of his opposing selves is supposed to be dominant: "Exhausted glasses wonder who / Is self and sovereign, I or You? / We cannot both be what we claim, / The real Stephano—Which is true? / A lost thing looks for a lost name" (*CP* 413). Prospero's magic arts may have brought a temporary halt to political hostilities, but his art could not repair the characters' inner psychological damage that lies at the root of the political conflicts. His arts have no power to reunify Stephano's divided and conflicted self. Neither can they generate genuine love between the other characters, and while Gonzalo suggests that "All our loves were altered" on the enchanted island, Gonzalo himself finally "stood convicted of / Doubt and insufficient love" (414). Like Stephano, Gonzalo's faults lie strictly in what he lacks, faith and love, which Prospero's art has the power to reveal but not restore.

Alonso addresses his speech to his son Ferdinand,[22] and it is, according to Mendelson, "the poem's structural center" as it recasts in concrete political terms the dilemmas that Caliban will raise in abstractly aesthetic terms at the end of the poem (*Later* 237). Returning to the questions of politics and justice that Prospero had raised in his monologue, Alonso explains "The Way of Justice is a tightrope" stretched between the sea and the desert, for "How narrow the space, how slight the chance / For civil pattern and importance / Between the watery vagueness and / The triviality of sand" (*CP* 416, 417). Though he does not use the term, Alonso indicates that the good ruler must maintain a sense of double-focus, the gift that can be found within the errors surrounding him and that will help the sea and the desert to co-inhere. He hopes Ferdinand will "find / The spring in the desert, the fruitful / Island in the sea, where flesh and mind / Are delivered from mistrust" (418). Isolated from each other, the sea and the desert are false dualisms, but it is not clear in the poem exactly what the sea and the desert symbolize. As Spears's perceptive analysis suggests, "the sea is associated with the flesh, the senses, potentiality, and subjectivity; the desert with mind, abstraction, the temptation to ignore the limitations of the human creature" (*Poetry* 223). Or, in the terms set up by *New Year Letter*, the desert seems roughly equivalent to Platonic idealism, which denies the good of bodily existence, while the sea is similar to Rousseau's romanticism,[23] which in Alonso's speech suggests a subjectivism that rejects all claims of universality in favor of a crude pragmatism. Either dualism will lead Ferdinand to become a tyrant if he does not achieve the double-focus necessary to perceive the co-inherence of body and mind.

Fuller further argues that "the sea represents the life of the senses, the realized; the desert represents the life of the spirit, the potential. One is reached by the *via activa*, the other by the *via contempliva*" (*Reader's Guide* 362). Alonso's speech evokes the tradition of Christian mysticism beginning with the desert fathers. In the West, the mystical tradition comes largely through Augustine, who distinguished between what came to be called the active life, the contemplative life, and the mixed life in a famous passage in *The City of God*: "As for the three kinds of life, the life of leisure, the life of action, and the combination of the two . . . no one ought to be so leisured as to take no thought in that leisure for the interest of his neighbor, nor so active as to feel no need for the contemplation of God" (19.19). Augustine's brief instructions would become the basis for the long-standing distinction in Western Christian practice between the contemplative life of the hermit or monk and the active life of the pastor or layperson. However the two were variously defined, it was generally maintained that, while both were good and necessary to the general life of the church, it was also possible to lead a "Mixed Life" in which an individual maintained a balance between contemplation and business activities. Alonso's speech in "The Sea and the Mirror," then, draws on the mystical tradition's insistence that the mixed life is desirable for the just ruler.

Nevertheless, even if the fledgling ruler were to achieve the mental coherence necessary to maintain that double-focus as an individual, it is no guarantee that he will build the just city. His subjects may not share his breadth of vision. Antonio's ironic reply to Alonso's speech reveals his own total rejection of the just state, or indeed, any state at all: "One crown is lacking, Prospero, / My empire is my own; / Dying Alonso does not know / The diadem Antonio / Wears in his world alone" (*CP* 418). Even under a just ruler, willing participation in the just state cannot be coerced without the state becoming unjust. Antonio remains the demonic voice that insists on total self-rule, subverting all noble aspirations of even the just rulers, but the demonic voice does point to the truth at which Auden arrived in *New Year Letter*: "Aloneness is Man's real condition" (*CP* 238). Antonio has gone far beyond the mere isolation inherent in fallen human nature. He has isolated himself from all human society and has begun to resemble the privation-worshiping witch who represents the self-conscious self's fixation on its own fragmentation in *New Year Letter* (*CP* 235–36).

In a 1942 series of notes published in *Commonweal*, Auden remarks that evil in one's own will is neither self-evident nor undeniable, and the admission of an evil will "is a subjective religious event" (*Prose II* 169). Furthermore, the mere confession of one's own corrupted will does not correct it. Rather, Auden argues, "The conversion of an evil will into a good will cannot be its own act, for it is impossible to will the opposite of what one wills; that is, it is an act of God's" (169). So in *The Tempest*, Prospero's arts can bring Antonio face-to-face with his own evil will, but they cannot make Antonio wish to repent. Earlier in the poem, Antonio had spoken a defiant monologue in *terza rima*, perhaps suggestive of Dante's *Inferno*, but Mendelson argues that Antonio is really "unconvincing as the speaker of a monologue, because he embodies the motiveless malignity that, after it is revealed, withdraws into total silence" (*Later* 228). Indeed, a perfect representation of evil as privation would be total silence. But as a cast member, Antonio must speak, and in each of Antonio's subversive lyrics, he distances himself from the other characters, and his final lines are particularly emphatic: "I am I, Antonio, / By choice myself alone" (*CP* 412).

Antonio has achieved what Caliban later calls "the ultimately liberal condition" in which "your existence is indeed free at last to choose its own meaning, that is, to plunge headlong into despair and fall through silence fathomless and dry, all fact your single drop, all value your pure alas" (*CP* 438). Caliban reveals that Antonio's complete self-absorption has cut him off from all other existences, and he is approaching a state of total evil, an almost complete privation of existence. As Spears points out, the passage is cast in "terms that parody those of atheistic existentialism" (*Poetry* 227); the passage also recalls Auden's anticipation and critique of existentialism in *New Year Letter,* in which he suggests that, if being and becoming were the same, then we would actually be trapped in the hell of unchanging singularity for the rest of our lives [24] (*CP* 222). As Auden had asserted in the notes to *New Year Letter,* "Evil is not an existence. . . . Pure evil would be pure passivity, a denial by an existence of any relation with any other existence; this is impossible because it would also mean a denial of its own existence" (*New Year Letter* 109). Antonio comes very close to such a state of "pure evil," in that he asserts his absolute independence from all others. He does not, of course, achieve absolute solitude; his ironic answers are parasitic, all depending for their existence on the other characters' lyric monologues. It is impossible for Antonio to achieve a state of "pure evil," though he clearly wishes to do so.

Antonio's defiant silence is a mirror image of the ascetic silence to which Prospero looks forward in his monologue, and although the two silences cannot be easily distinguished from the outside, they are diametrically opposed in both the motives for silence and the social results of silence. Antonio's silence is absolutely self-centered and results in total isolation and despair. Prospero's silence entails the restoration of his political responsibilities but also his submission to the infirmities of old age, when he will "Not . . . be interesting anymore," and Prospero asks himself whether he will be able to maintain his silence "When the servants settle me into a chair / . . . / And arrange my muffler and rugs" (*CP* 409). Prospero must now live a quiet life of faith and self-denial, but he must not talk about it, for "if I speak, I shall sink without a sound / Into unmeaning abysses" (409). To explain his silence would not only break the silence, but it would also turn his faith into an object to be admired, thus negating the sincerity of his faith. Prospero implies that his future position will always be precarious, and that he will escape Antonio's fate narrowly if he escapes it at all.

Other attempts to avoid Antonio's fate of wallowing in absolute denial are widely varied, but according to Caliban, they operate on similar principles: "Religion and culture seem to be represented by a catholic belief that something is lacking which must be found, but as to what the something is, the keys of heaven, the missing heir, genius, the smells of childhood, or a sense of humor, why it is lacking, whether it has been deliberately stolen, or accidentally lost or just hidden for a lark, and who is responsible, our ancestors, ourselves, the social structure, or mysterious wicked powers, there are as many faiths as there are searchers, and clues can be found behind every clock, under every stone, and in every hollow tree to support all of them" (*CP* 440–41). Caliban's statement accords with accounts that Auden gave elsewhere of his frustrations with modern philosophies. In his essay for *Modern Canterbury Pilgrims* he points out, "The various 'kerygmas,' of Blake, of Lawrence, of Freud, of Marx" were all searching for some suppressed or overlooked element of existence, whose discovery would make the establishment of the just society possible (*Prose III* 577). Auden remarks that "each of them brought to some particular aspect of life that intensity of attention which is characteristic of one-sided geniuses (needless to say, they all contradicted each other), and such comprehension of Christian wisdom as I have, little though it be, would be very much less without them" (577). For Lawrence, the thing that is "lacking which must be found," as Caliban puts it, is sexual freedom; for Freud the knowledge of repression; for Marx the liberation of the working class. Or, as Caliban argues, every modern philosophy believes in something like Augustine's theory of evil as privation in that they all begin with the supposition that the source of disorder in the world is the privation of some crucial element that, once restored, will bring order and wholeness to existence.

In an ironically self-referential turn, Caliban reminds his audience that, while he represents life in the body, he must nevertheless speak as the work of art he is, for he speaks from the stage within a poem, though his own words are prose. As the voice of art—and he has never really spoken apart from that role, since it was an artist who taught him to speak[25]—Caliban announces the inability of art to offer solutions to the audience's problems as he has described them: "I begin to feel something of the serio-comic embarrassment of the dedicated dramatist, who, in representing to you your condition of estrangement from the truth, is doomed to fail the more he succeeds, for the more truthfully he paints the condition, the less clearly can he indicate the truth from which it is estranged, the brighter his revelation of the truth from which it is estranged, the brighter his revelation of the truth in its order, its justice, its joy, the fainter shows his picture of your actual condition in all its drabness and sham . . ." (*CP* 442). That is, the artist may choose to depict the reality of the human condition, but in that case it is impossible to depict the ideal world from which the real world has fallen. Or the artist may choose to depict the ideal, but then it will be impossible to depict the real. The artist can never make realism and idealism co-inhere within a single, coherent work. In his speech, Caliban has chosen to reveal the problem, which bars him from clearly articulating the solution, but that also promotes "your delusion that an awareness of the gap is in itself a bridge, your interest in your imprisonment a release" (442). There is a difference between recognizing that a gap between the ideal and the real exists and actually restoring the condition of innocence.

Caliban must think his attempt to portray humanity's estrangement from truth very successful, since he is only barely able to hint at the truth from which it is estranged. But just as the poet in *New Year Letter* had found the gift of double-focus hidden in a tangle of half-truths, Caliban uses the utterly disastrous human attempt to order life to point to the human need for divine grace. As it turns out, the world really *is* a stage on which every human being, no doubt ad-libbing his or her part, has attempted to bring artistic order to life in the form of a grand opera[26] that turns out to have been "indescribably inexcusably awful" (*CP* 443). In the dead silence following the final, dissonant chord, the players can finally hear "the real Word which is our only *raison d'être*," so it is not in spite of human failures "but with them that we are blessed by that Wholly Other Life from which we are separated by an essential emphatic gulf," of which the gaps between art and life "are feebly figurative signs" (444). This "Word" or "Life," for which Caliban gives several other names like "Mercy" and "perfected Work," appears in the disasters of the real, physical world itself. Auden rejects a modern Manichaeism that would deny embodied existence in order to escape into the ideal world of art. As he explains in *The Dyer's Hand*, "it is difficult for a modern artist, unless he can flee to the depths of the country and never open a newspaper, to prevent his imagination from acquiring a Manichaean cast, from *feeling*, whatever his religious convictions to the contrary, that the physical world is utterly profane or the abode of demons" (460). And yet, as Caliban indicates, it is only through that untidy, physical world, through "the massacres, the whippings, the lies, the twaddle, and all their carbon copies, . . . our shame, our fear, our incorrigible staginess, all wish and no resolve" (*CP* 444), that redemption can come. As "For the Time Being" would assert, humans are redeemed through the appearance of the Word in the physical world.

The hesitance of the poem to fully describe redemption points up the double role of silence in the poem, and the poem's conclusion emphasizes the frequent ambiguity of gaps, renunciations, and privations. All evils may be rooted in a privation, but not all privations are evil, and while the silence of the mystic is not immediately distinguishable from the silence of the reprobate, the difference between the two is profound. Both silences are forms of rejection, and as such might both be described as privations of speech and even of art. The difference is not the fact of rejection itself, but the motive and inevitable results of reticence. As Auden explains in a 1957 review of *Mysticism Sacred and Profane* by R. C. Zaehner, "The main purpose of even the most austere, enclosed and contemplative Christian orders is a corporate one, to worship God and to pray for the world, and the Church has always been a bit suspicious, often most unjustly, of her mystics, because she has always rejected the notion that there can be a class of Superior Persons in the Kingdom of God" (*Prose IV* 94). The holy silence required of Prospero is fundamentally a renunciation of pride and of personal control over circumstances, which will result in a humble acceptance of communal life among ordinary people. Although he will remain exceptional in his abilities, he will never again be allowed to become a "Superior Person," manipulating his surroundings to serve even noble purposes. Antonio's silence, on the other hand, is an absolute renunciation that not only prevents him from accepting forgiveness and reconciliation, but also cuts him off from all human community, isolating him in a kingdom of irony in which he is a king without subjects, a high priest without a god. What Prospero and Antonio have in common is their mutual inability to speak once they have entered fully into their respective renunciations. Like the poem itself, they can only hint indirectly at the full realities they signify.

LATER POEMS

In a 1950 lecture, Auden relates his approach to his art, both concretely in terms of the composition and revision of single poems, and abstractly in terms of the philosophical and theological presuppositions for his aesthetics. He identifies the doctrine of the Fall as a key element in his aesthetics, arguing that, while "Adam was created in the image of God," the advent of sin "effaced and obscured" the image of God in which humans were created (*Prose III* 652).[27] Auden explains the psychological results: "Fallen man retains a unity-in-tension of existence and essence; but, whereas, in prelapsarian man this unity-in-tension was one of perfect balance and harmony, in him it is one of unbalance and discord, for which he feels guilty, knowing that he ought not so to be, and feels a nostalgia for his former state, even if he cannot imagine accurately what it could have been, knowing only that it must have been balanced and harmonious" (652). Therefore, Auden concludes, "Evil does not exist positively, but is the deprivation of good. That is to say, evil has no essence of its own. Essence is what evil destroys, but it cannot create or destroy existence, even its own" (652). The Augustinian doctrine of evil-as-privation had become for Auden a necessary presupposition, and an article of faith. Since a poet's raw materials are his own feelings, he must both acknowledge the fact of his own fallenness and affirm that, whatever his feelings are, they are neither wholly evil nor unredeemable. Auden goes on to state that "every beautiful poem" is "an analogy of forgiveness of sins," but that in a poem, there is no repentance of evil intentions, but the reconciliation of contradictory feelings (652–53). Here Auden qualifies his statement in the notes to *New Year Letter*—"poetry might be defined as the clear expression of mixed feelings" (*New Year Letter* 119). A good poem achieves a reconciliation of mixed feelings—not an erasure of one feeling or the other—which resembles the resolution of guilt when a fault is forgiven.

In the 1964 poem "The Cave of Making," part of the "Thanksgiving for a Habitat" sequence, Auden describes his personal study where he writes his poetry. He meditates on the solitary nature of his art and welcomes the ghostly presence of his recently deceased friend and fellow poet Louis MacNeice, but the poem ends with a postscript partly made up of a series of epigraphs on the nature of poetry and language, one of which states, "Speechless Evil / Borrowed the language of Good / And reduced it to noise" (*CP* 695). As he characterizes it here, evil has no language of its own; all it can do is corrupt good speech that does not properly belong to it, making evil essentially parasitical and silent in itself. The poem's final address to MacNeice acknowledges the extent to which vice inspired his friend's poetry (695). Indeed, Auden admits, acquiescence to temptation makes for "many a fine / expressive line," for an immoral life is often an interesting one (695). But still, the poet concludes, if evil is only a corrupt derivative of good, he tells his friend, "God may reduce you / on Judgment Day / to tears of shame, / reciting by heart / the poems you would / have written had / your life been good" (696). The poet does not deny the high quality of poetry produced by vice, but he adds that there is no necessary reason that poetry produced by a life of virtue should not be even better. Behind the moralizing, there is also the recognition implied by the subjunctive "may" that Auden is speaking hypothetically, and not from personal experience.

A few other late poems also refer to evil explicitly in terms of privation. Two of Auden's "Eleven Occasional Poems" are particularly worthy of note. One poem, "Epithalamium" (1965), reminds the newlyweds that "genders, married or not / . . . share with all flesh / a left-handed twist" (*CP* 761). "Left-handed" is the etymological sense of the word "sinister," while "twist" suggests the metaphor of crookedness that Auden frequently used to describe personal flaws. Both terms indicate that there is something abnormal about every person. All humans, regardless of gender or social relationships, share this abnormal characteristic, which is original sin described in terms of privation. In another poem, "Josef Weinheber" (1965), Auden comments that evil is ever present in the world: "never as yet / has Earth been without / her bad patch, some unplace with / jobs for torturers" (*CP* 758). Locating evil in an "unplace" does not suggest that evil is not really present, but only that evil necessarily deprives any location of its positive particularity. As Auden had argued at the end of *New Year Letter,* love acknowledges and accepts the differences and particularities in other people, while evil attempts both to deny the existence of particularities and to abolish them, a self-contradictory aspiration.

Another late poem that suggests the idea of evil as privation is "Song of the Devil" (1963), in which the Devil speaks in much the same voice he had in *New Year Letter,* and with many of the same connotations. Here the Devil's temptations are called "fiction" and are clothed "in up-to-date diction" that articulates the Freudian, liberal, and capitalist heresies that deny honor, honesty, and moral values (*CP* 782). The Devil's strategy is to maintain the delusion, to suppress real self-knowledge, as long as possible. The objective is to reduce each person to "a cipher of Hell's" (783). Auden explains the demonic psychology in *The Dyer's Hand* with characteristic humor: "One can conceive of Heaven having a Telephone Directory, but it would have to be gigantic, for it would include the Proper Name and address of every electron in the Universe. But Hell could not have one, for in Hell, as in prison and the army, its inhabitants are identified not by name but by number. They do not *have* numbers, they *are* numbers" (*DH* 274). The mark of the demonic is the privation of distinguishable names and faces, the reduction of particularity to identical and interchangeable units. The modern tendency toward the erasure of individual uniqueness is relatively easy to detect, Auden suggests, but he also warns against a more subtle temptation: "One of our greatest spiritual dangers is our fancy that the Evil one takes a personal interest in our perdition. He doesn't care a button about *my* soul, any more than Don Giovanni cared a button about Donna Elvira's body. I am his 'one-thousand-and-third-in-Spain'" (274). Hence, the speaker in "Song of the Devil" concludes, "Believe while you can that I'm proud of you, / Enjoy your dream: / I'm so bored with the whole fucking crowd of you / I could *scream!*" (*CP* 783). The Devil—who is still identified with the human tendency toward dualistic thinking that he took on in *New Year Letter*—is no more interested in individual humans than Mephistopheles is personally interested in Faust, but the final temptation is to believe, like Faust, that the Devil values him as an ally.

TO SPEAK OF EVIL AS A PRIVATION, as Auden learned to do from Augustine, is necessarily to raise the question, "Of what, precisely, is humanity deprived?" Auden had begun his spiritual journey by entertaining a series of ideologies, each of which conceived of evil as a privation or a corruption, but identified the missing element with very different aspects of human existence. Even Kierkegaard, whom Auden credited with making Christian faith meaningful to him, had his own blind spot that threatened to become yet another form of dualism. Although "few since St Augustine" had described the "unique 'existential' relation to God" as well as Kierkegaard had, Auden points out Kierkegaard's neglect of a further relation between God and humans: "every man has a second relation to God which is neither unique nor existential: as a creature composed of matter, as a biological organism, every man, in common with everything else in the universe, is related by necessity to the God who created that universe and saw that it was good, for the laws of nature to which, whether he likes it or not, he must conform are of divine origin. And it is with this body, with faith or without it, that all good works are done" (*Prose III* 579). In the modern, Western world, evil manifests itself as a privation of unity, often as a fallacious dualism that rejects either body or spirit as irredeemable. For both Auden and Augustine, the Manichean rejection of the goodness of the physical world was the most prevalent form of philosophical dualism, and it thereby warranted the most consistent denunciations.

This is not to say that Auden did not sometimes speak as though he believed that evil is a positive existence in the world. As in "The Sea and the Mirror," the mere fact of silence is an ambiguous sign, which may indicate either salvation or damnation, and the significance of silence depends not only on the motives for reticence, but on what specifically is believed to be essentially unspeakable. Both ecstasies and horrors may transcend the limits of language and render silent the person who has experienced them, and it is especially the unspeakable horrors that make Manichean dualism so intellectually attractive. In an essay on Kafka in *The Dyer's Hand*, Auden explains, "No one who thinks seriously about evil and suffering can avoid entertaining as a possibility the gnostic-manichean notion of the physical world as intrinsically evil . . ." (167). Later in the same volume, Auden asserts that the filth and grime of the modern, industrial world always tempt the artist to adopt a Manichean stance by condemning the physical world as unredeemably evil (460), and in a 1959 review of *The Image of the City*, a posthumous collection of essays by Charles Williams, Auden praises Williams because "he directed a lifelong polemic against the heresy of Manichaeism," and he proceeds to argue that "to think of spirit and matter as irreconcilably hostile, to attribute the evil we do and suffer to the weakness of matter, to think that a good God could not have created matter . . . must, after all seem to both our common sense and our moral conscience alike very plausible" (*Prose IV* 198).

Williams's and Auden's mutual insistence that evil is basically a privation of good does not deny the shocking ugliness of the modern world; nor does his Augustinian position on evil dismiss the destructive power of evil. On the contrary, the insistence that evil is a deprivation of goodness, especially in the human soul, implies that all humans have the capacity to commit great evils, and that the eradication of evil is not as simple as redistributing the means of production or undergoing psychotherapy. Auden came to believe what Augustine argued throughout his works, that humans are, by themselves, incapable of healing the flaws in their own souls and therefore must accept divine grace which alone can repair fallen humanity. Such grace penetrated the course of history as the Incarnation of Jesus Christ, who was, as Auden put it in *The Dyer's Hand*, "a real man who openly claims to be God" (207). But like Augustine, before he could fully accept the Christian faith, Auden had to examine the nature of moral evil as it appeared in himself first of all. His recognition that evil consisted of privation, and his consequent renunciation of dualism, was an initial step toward faith.

2. PHYSICAL EXISTENCE AS GOOD

In the midst of his gradual return to Christianity in the mid-1940s, Auden rejected two forms of philosophical dualism that he had found inadequate; the romantic dualism he associated with Rousseau, which exalted the primal, irrational urges above abstract reasoning; and the Platonic Idealism that he thought had overvalued abstractions at the expense of the human body and the physical world. He associated what he saw as false Platonic dualism with Manichacism, the dualistic religion against which Augustine directed much of his polemic in the fourth century. While the fourth-century Manichees were by no means Platonists—Augustine himself abandoned Manichaeism in favor of Neoplatonist philosophy before he became a Christian—Auden saw similarities between Platonism and Manichaeism, since both philosophies rejected the physical world as inherently evil and corrupt, and both philosophies offered to release their adherents' souls from their imprisonment in physical bodies. Plato, of course, did not go nearly so far as Manichean philosophy, which insisted that evil and physicality were roughly synonymous. The Manichees also strongly criticized the Christian and Jewish doctrine that God made all things good. They pointed out that, if God had created everything that exists, they must also believe that God created evil, since no one could deny that evil exists.

Auden followed Augustine in his response to the question: God did not create evil because evil is not an actual existence, physical or otherwise, but a real absence, a corruption or perversion of what was originally good. Evil did not and could not have any positive existence in its own right; evil was, instead, a deprivation, a loss of some good quality in those things that did have positive existence. Evil is thus parasitic; it depends entirely on good existences for its own existence. Working backwards from the idea that evil is a privation, Augustine concluded that existence as such must be fundamentally and intrinsically good, since it was created and sustained by a God who was himself fundamentally and intrinsically good. Since Augustine thought it better to exist than not to exist, he concluded that embodied human existence, however painful or corrupted, must therefore be a basically good thing.

During his return to Christianity, Auden consciously followed Augustine's logic from his intuition that evil was a privation into a sustained and repeated insistence that human existence in the body was good. For example, in 1939 Auden gave a couple of talks in which he argued for the veracity of what he called "monism," any philosophy that does not divide body from soul, against the false philosophy of dualism, which holds spirit to be good and body evil (see *Prose II* 481–82). But soon after Auden officially embraced Christianity by rejoining the Anglican communion, he dropped the term "monism" in favor of the language of orthodox Trinitarian Christianity. In 1944 Auden spoke before an organization of Anglican students at Swarthmore College, and the student newspaper there reported "The Christian concept of human nature [Auden] examined next. Contrary to Platonic doctrine, the existence of matter—the body—is good within itself" (qtd. in *Prose II* 483). Even before his full return to Christianity, this belief in the innate goodness of physical existence had become a central principle, and some have argued *the* central principle (see Replogle 49) of Auden's approach to poetics.

Despite his living to see the devastation and atrocities of two world wars and the national psychological trauma that resulted from them, he maintained throughout his post-conversion poetry and prose that human existence as souls in bodies, and indeed, the existence of the entire physical cosmos, was substantially positive. All evils, no matter how terrifying or pervasive, could be attributed to a corrupting disunity in the human soul and not to the fact of physical existence. The physical world, including the human body, suffers evil but was itself originally good. In *The Dyer's Hand*, Auden states that this Augustinian view of existence is the only tenable justification for the creation of art.

> Every poet, consciously or unconsciously, holds the following absolute presuppositions, as the dogmas of his art.
>
> 1. A historical world exists, a world of unique events and unique persons, related by analogy, not identity. The number of events and analogical relations is potentially infinite. *The existence of such a world is a good, and every addition to the number of events, persons and relations is an additional good.*
> 2. The historical world is a fallen world, i.e. though it is good that it exists, the way in which it exists is evil, being full of unfreedom and disorder.

3. The historical world is a redeemable world. The unfreedom and disorder of the past can be reconciled in the future. (DH 69–70, emphasis added)

Auden's first presupposition asserts that history is linear and that, as a result, truly novel events can occur. This view is implicitly opposed to cyclical views of history, whether ancient, like the Platonists',[1] or modern, like Yeats's. Auden maintains that, although physical reality and historical novelty are good in themselves, the historical (physical and temporal) world is afflicted by evil. Auden characterizes this evil strictly in terms of privation—or the lack of freedom ("unfreedom") and the lack of order ("disorder"). However, because the fallen world is fundamentally good, as Auden reasons in the third presupposition, it is possible to resolve conflicts, supply what is lacking, and thus redeem the historical world. As Auden would suggest in works such as "For the Time Being," God redeems the historical world through human beings.

AUGUSTINE AND CHARLES NORRIS COCHRANE

In the early 1940s, when Auden was drawing on Augustine's articulation of the nature of evil, he also began to borrow ideas about the nature of goodness from Augustine, but he would not begin to refer specifically to Augustine's articulation of the ideas until the late 1940s. But even in 1939, Auden was beginning to derive his views on the goodness of physical existence from Augustine, who sets out his position in the *Confessions* with characteristically straightforward logic: "it was manifested unto me, that those things be good, which yet are corrupted; which neither were they sovereignly good, nor unless they were good, could be corrupted: for if sovereignly good, they were incorruptible, if not good at all, there were nothing in them to be corrupted. For corruption injures, but unless it diminished goodness, it could not injure" (7.12). Augustine proceeds to argue that "all which is corrupted is deprived of good. But if they be deprived of all good, they shall cease to be," and he concludes that "each [thing] is good, and altogether very good, because our God made all things very good" (7.12). For Augustine, starting as he must with the premise that God is both all-powerful and absolutely good, whatever God created must be good insofar as it maintains its original created existence. Augustine then turns the logic of the Manichees back on itself. If Manichean philosophy holds that the physical world is corrupt, then, Augustine reasons, it must be good and not evil, for something that is totally evil cannot be further corrupted; only that which is initially good can become corrupt. As it turns out, the theory of evil as privation is embedded so deeply in his language that Augustine finds he cannot really conceive of evil as having a positive existence at all. Instead, as he announces later in the *Confessions*, "everything which in some degree has existence is good; for it derives from him who does not exist merely in some degree since he is Existence" (trans. Chadwick

13.31).[2] That is, God is the ultimate Existence from which every other existing thing derives its being, and since God's Existence is good, whatever else exists is also good inasmuch as it does exist.

Despite Augustine's repeated insistence that all bodily existence is intrinsically good, he has earned a reputation for suspicion of the body and its pleasures, especially sex. When he deplores public obscenity in the theaters, Augustine's rhetoric is strikingly harsh, and his many denunciations of the Pelagian heresy tend to emphasize the depravity of fallen human desires. But Augustine is careful never to denounce bodily existence or pleasure in themselves, and he is suspicious of extreme forms of Christian asceticism (see *Confessions* 10.31). Unlike many of his contemporary theologians, Augustine does not uphold asceticism as a normative model for the Christian life, chiding those who "perversely war on their bodies as though they were natural enemies. In this way they have been deceived by the words, 'The flesh lusteth against the spirit: and the spirit against the flesh; for these are contrary to one another'" (*On Christian Doctrine* 1.24, quoting Galatians 5:17). As he explains further in *The City of God*, the "flesh" spoken of in the Pauline epistles does not denote "body" as such, but rather denotes the corruption of the body, which corruption proceeds from a corruption of the soul (14.2–3). Similarly, Augustine understands "spirit" to mean not the human soul as opposed to the body, but rather the innate goodness of the intelligent soul that naturally desires to know and love God. In Augustine's eyes, it is the departure from this natural inclination toward God that produces sinful behavior.

Auden was certainly familiar with these Augustinian ideas, since he had read the *Confessions* by the late 1930s and may also have read *The City of God* by the mid-1940s, but he also absorbed many of Augustine's ideas through Charles Norris Cochrane's 1940 book *Christianity and Classical Culture*. In 1944, Auden published in *The New Republic* a review of the second, corrected edition of Cochrane's book, and he begins his review by claiming that he had "read this book many times," and that it had given him profound insights into his present day (*FA* 33).[3] Auden was occasionally given to exaggeration, but he did not often claim to have read a book "many times,"[4] and his statement suggests that Cochrane had by that time become an important influence on his intellectual development. Several of Auden's central theological ideas, including his belief in the innate goodness of the physical world, are explicitly bolstered by Cochrane's distillation of Augustine. Cochrane's work also offered a breadth and depth of knowledge of the classical and patristic epochs that surpassed even Auden's wide reading, and Cochrane's description of Augustine's philosophical triumph over both idealist and materialist dualisms could hardly have been more timely for Auden, who was engaged in his own struggles against modern dualisms when he read Cochrane for the first time in about 1940.

One of the major themes in Cochrane's book is Augustine's ability to offer a cogent articulation of the Christian doctrine of creation over the twin pagan dualisms of the fourth century, idealism and materialism. Augustine's rejection of pagan dualisms, Cochrane explains, was grounded in his early life experiences; he had spent his youth promiscuously indulging in a principle of physical gratification, but later in life, "Augustine's subsequent repudiation of this principle was complete and unequivocal" (390). But Cochrane adds that "it must not be supposed that, in rejecting it, he rejected in its entirety the life of sense. For, as against the Manicheans, he held tenaciously to the doctrine that there was no intrinsic evil in what is called 'matter.' And, with equal vigour, he denied the idealist contention that material exis- tence is involved in necessary ambiguities and contradictions, from which escape becomes possible only in the life of pure 'form'" (390). That is, Augustine did not escape from hedonistic materialism by embracing a stoic idealism. He ultimately rejected them both. And, while Augustine frequently stated that the Platonists were by far the best of the pagan philosophers because they were closest to Christianity, he still saw them as fatally flawed in their suspicion of human embodiment (see *City of God* 14.5).

Cochrane's reading of Augustine's corpus—he cites over twenty-five separate works—resoundingly emphasizes Augustine's affirmation of the goodness of em- bodied human life. In Cochrane's reading of Augustine, there is no original, inher- ent contradiction between the human body and the human soul: "That is to say, the roots of our nature as human beings strike deep into the physical world but they are not on that account any the less spiritual" (445). This is not to say that Augus- tine imagined the soul and body as equal partners in human life. Rather, Cochrane explains, "Augustine sees the life-process of human beings in terms of a body-soul complex in which body fulfills the requirements of an organ or instrument to soul, and this he applies no less to the elementary vital functions than to the highest manifestations of conscious and deliberate activity" (444). The body is an instru- ment of the soul, but Augustine does not identify the soul with consciousness and intellect. Instead, in an insightful anticipation of modern neuroscience, Augustine suggested that consciousness, rational thought, and willed choices do not operate independently of the body.

While Augustine had less to say about the innate goodness of the natural world than about the innate goodness of the human body, Cochrane explains that Augus- tine did object to the textbook science of his day that assumed that natural necessity operated in constant opposition to human freedom, so "it should be noted that Augustine's revolt was not from nature; it was from the picture of nature proposed by classical science; i.e. from a cosmology and an anthropology constructed in terms of form and matter as the basis for a 'formal' ethic and a 'formal' logic" (410–11). Against pagan science, Augustine asserted that the natural world is not a closed system governed solely by eternal and unchangeable laws, but is instead an order created by God who governs it from the outside and who makes it at least partially intelligible. Therefore, what is evil in the natural world only appears to be so because of human ignorance. Augustine's argument for the basic goodness of creation admits that the natural world frequently produces pain and calamity, but asserts that "natural" evils are often an element of a divine plan which humans cannot fully comprehend. While such explanations are often distasteful to the modern mind, Augustine considered them to be an improvement over a pagan science that had portrayed humans as helpless particles in an indifferent cosmos, and that had tried and failed to construct a philosophy that could relate the ethics governing human affairs to the natural laws governing the rest of the cosmos. From Augustine's point of view, Cochrane points out, "the problem of the Christian is not so much to read into nature the values of truth, beauty, and goodness as to detect those values in it" (481).

Both the natural world and the human being, body and soul, have fallen from their initial perfection and are now corrupted, though not beyond repair, so this potential renewal, or salvation, involves the restoration of the original goodness of matter. Cochrane explains that, for Augustine, "the problem of salvation is thus not to destroy or to suppress the affections; it is rather that they should be reoriented with a view to the supreme good. That good lies in God . . ." (342). Salvation, then, is a matter of reorienting one's will and one's love towards God. This love, "which, when directed to the pursuit of mundane ends, gives rise to moral confusion and ruin, is conceived by Augustine to yield the motive power necessary to a realization of creative peace, the Kingdom of God" (342). The possibility of salvation is predicated on the original goodness of that which is to be saved, namely the soul, the body, and the whole of physical creation. Today the term "salvation" is frequently used in Christian circles as a synonym for "conversion," but it is important to recognize that Augustine conceives of salvation in broader terms. As Cochrane presents Augustine's thought, "salvation" includes a past conversion event, but it also encompasses both a virtuous Christian life in the present world and eternal life after death in a resurrected body with God in the future. For Auden, who was sympathetic both to Freud and to Reinhold Niebuhr's pioneering of what would become known as the "social gospel," salvation was largely a matter of achieving a personally virtuous and coherent individual life, as well as a just and peaceful social order. For Augustine, the process of salvation consists of a continually novel acceptance of the knowledge of God in faith. Cochrane outlines Augustine's conception of the results of this salvation in distinctly modern terminology:

we may perceive the meaning of "justification by faith", i.e. the acceptance of Trinitarian Christianity as a condition for the eradication of intellectual and moral shortcomings as well as for the realization of those positive values to which mankind aspires. . . . *That goal is the integration of personality.* . . . That is to say, it makes possible, but in a significantly new sense, the classical ideals of freedom and detachment. In the second place it provides the technique necessary for the casting out of devils, *the expunging of congenital and habitual complexes which serve merely to inhibit constructive activity.* In doing so it points to *a realization of the classical ideal of peace,* not through the mortification but through the regeneration of the flesh. (454–55, emphasis added)

That is, Augustine viewed salvation as the means both to rid oneself of self-destructive impulses and habits and to restore the unity and concord that originally existed before the Fall. Cochrane's reading of Augustine in explicitly post-Freudian terms did not escape Auden's attention.

Reading these words in 1940, just after he had written a long poem (*New Year Letter*) that expressed his longing for an integration of consciousness and that vented his exasperation with modern "devils," Auden recognized that Augustine's theology offered plausible answers to his difficult psychological and philosophical questions. The direction of Auden's intellectual development had anticipated these answers. In his 1939 *The Prolific and the Devourer,* he had remarked that "Romanticism is right in asserting against [Catholicism and Protestantism] the goodness of the material world" (*Prose II* 446), but he was soon to find in Cochrane's book an ancient Catholic who insisted again and again that the material world was fundamentally good and redeemable, and who condemned the very same Platonic-idealist and romantic-materialist dualisms that he had firmly denounced in *New Year Letter* (see *CP* 234–35).[5] He had also written in *The Prolific and the Devourer* that "All existences are good, i.e. they are equally free and have an equal right to their existence. Everything that is is holy" (*Prose II* 426). Although Auden wrote this before he read Cochrane, he had already encountered Augustine's articulation of such ideas in the *Confessions,* but as other passages in *The Prolific and the Devourer* makes clear, Auden was not ready in 1939 to accept Augustine's Trinitarian theology as the basis of his rejection of dualism and his affirmation of the goodness of physical existence.

"IN MEMORY OF W. B. YEATS" AND "HERMAN MELVILLE"

For the first ten years of Auden's career as a poet, he said little about the nature of physical existence as such. Even in "The Composer," written in 1938, Auden comments that of all the arts music alone is "unable to say an existence is wrong," which implies that all other art forms can and do assert that certain existences are intrinsically evil, but the poem does not say whether such an assertion would be right or wrong (*CP* 181). His early poems appeared to be political or psychological allegories that alternately struggled with a divided self and prophesied an immanent political revolution. These were, at least, the conventional interpretations offered by early critics. Although Auden did flirt with a variety of dualistic ideologies, he had always assumed that the fact of his existence was basically a good thing. He wrote many poems expressing mental anguish, but he never wrote a suicidal poem. He never wished not to exist. But it was not until the late 1930s that Auden began to consider the broader philosophical questions behind his intuitions that existence in general and physical existence in particular were good. His conclusions appear explicitly in *The Prolific and the Devourer,* but because the work was not published in full during his lifetime, it was very difficult for any of his contemporaries to perceive the progression of his philosophical inquiries from Marxism and Freudian psychoanalysis to Augustinian Christianity. There were, however, anticipations of this transition in two of Auden's best-known lyric poems from 1939: "In Memory of W. B. Yeats" and "Herman Melville."

Just before he started work on *The Prolific and the Devourer* in mid-1939, Auden wrote an elegy, "In Memory of W. B. Yeats," in commemoration of Yeats's death in January 1939, and in that poem Auden remarks on the difficult relationship between the human person and the body. Initially the poem describes embodiment as integral to the human person. The poet says of Yeats's last day alive, "for him it was his last afternoon as himself" (*CP* 247). If the self is not exactly identified with the body, the line does suggest that the continuity between body and soul is necessary for the existence of the self.[6] At the same time, the poem also pictures the dead poet as "scattered among a hundred cities / . . . / To find his happiness in another kind of wood" (247). So, in some sense, the human person does maintain an existence after death, though perhaps only in the memories and imaginations of the living. But the poem makes no pronouncements on the question of life after death, and instead focuses on the legacy of the dead, now to be "modified in the guts of the living" (247).

As the poem's second section observes, the poet's legacy "survived it all: / The parish of rich women, physical decay, / Yourself" (*CP* 248). In the poem's imagery, the self is a kind of imprisonment, for each living person "in the cell of himself is almost convinced of his freedom" (247). There is a Platonic suggestion that the self, perhaps especially the body, is a prison for the soul, and in the middle section the poet briefly entertains a mind-body dualism that might have been attractive to Yeats, though Auden would quickly reject it. The poem returns to the image of self-imprisonment in its final lines: "In the prison of his days / Teach the free man how to praise" (249). The last three stanzas are an address to the poet, which begins, "Follow, poet, follow right / To the bottom of the night," and parallels the last line, "teach the free man how to praise," which is also in the imperative (248–49). It is never entirely clear exactly what the free man is to praise or why, and it is an ambiguity that Auden would revisit in subsequent poems, such as "In Sickness and in Health" (319) and "For the Time Being" (365). In the elegy, praise is a gratuitous act that should be performed, even if it is performed for no other reason than that one wishes to. For Auden it is an affirmation of the goodness of an existence whose purpose and nature the poet—Yeats in this case—could never fully understand.

While "In Memory of W. B. Yeats" addresses the nature of existence obliquely, another poem from the same year, "Herman Melville," explores the nature of evil and goodness more directly. The poem contrasts Melville's *Moby-Dick* and *Billy Budd, Sailor* in order to trace Melville's progression from a false, melodramatic view of good and evil to a truer, more moderate view. The poem is laced with allusions to Melville's life and works, and it appropriately opens by picturing Melville's intellectual development as a sea voyage ending mildly (*CP* 251). The second stanza relates Auden's own sense of the conclusions to which Melville eventually came: "Goodness existed: that was the new knowledge. / His terror had to blow itself quite out / To let him see it" (251). The following stanza makes it clear that this "terror" is a reference to *Moby-Dick*, with its "maniac hero hunting . . . / The rare ambiguous monster . . . / Hatred for hatred ending in a scream" (251). Auden suggests that Captain Ahab and Moby-Dick are mirror images of each other, and that to set up a novel on the basis of mutual hatred leaves little room for the necessary affirmation of goodness. Auden's sees this opposition as too melodramatic and concludes that Melville eventually realized, "All that was intricate and false; the truth was simple" (251). Auden's reading of *Moby-Dick* lacks the nuance of a scholarly treatment, but Auden's purpose is not a critical assessment of the novel. He uses the novel as an analogue for a falsely melodramatic view of good and evil. Auden implies that Melville learned, in contrast to Ahab, "Evil is unspectacular and always human, / And shares our bed and eats at our own table, / And we are introduced to Goodness every day" (251). Good and evil are not always distinguishable, as Ishmael found in his initial bedroom encounter with Queequeg, an incident to which Auden's poem clearly refers in the line, "shares our bed." The phrase also suggests sexual infidelity, and the line "eats at our own table" is an oblique reference to the Last Supper and Judas' betrayal of Jesus. Evil appears not as the dramatic, overwhelming malevolence of Moby-Dick or Captain Ahab, but as the always-possible infidelity of a friend or lover, not even as an intrinsically depraved being like Claggart, but as the potential in oneself for deceit and unfaithfulness.

For Auden in 1939, evil was thus always intermixed with good such that goodness is seldom encountered in its pure form, and evil never exists purely by itself. Auden said the same year in *The Prolific and the Devourer*, "Pure evil would be pure passivity . . . [which] is not possible even to electrons" (*Prose II* 426). Neither can we ever encounter pure goodness, though something close to it might at least be imaginable for Melville once he had exhausted the dramatic possibilities of evil in *Moby-Dick*. Auden suggests that the goodness to which we are introduced each day "has a name like Billy and is almost perfect, / But wears a stammer like a decoration" (*CP* 251). Of course, the reference is to Melville's novella *Billy Budd, Sailor*, which Melville never finished revising and which was only published in 1924 during the Melville Revival, a mere fifteen years before Auden wrote the poem. Auden indicates that the vision of good and evil in *Billy Budd* is more realistic than in *Moby-Dick*. Billy Budd is a Christ figure in the sense that he is condemned while remaining a perfectly innocent man. Billy embodies goodness as much as any fictional character can, and Claggart, Billy's accuser, represents evil as a devil figure (see *The Enchafèd Flood* 143). As the poem describes the situation, evil occurs through petty jealousy, false accusations, and an inflexible code of justice on the high seas that leads to Billy's execution. The story is a kind of parable about the parasitic nature of evil that destroys itself when it damages its good host. Billy inadvertently kills Claggart and is then himself executed, and in Auden's assessment, "It is the Evil that is helpless like a lover / And has to pick a quarrel and succeeds, / And both are openly destroyed before our eyes" (*CP* 252). The poem works toward an implicitly Augustinian position that holds that evil cannot exist independently of good, and that any victory for evil is merely Pyrrhic, revealing evil's parasitic nature and reaffirming the basic goodness of that which really exists.

The poem's conclusion considers the implications of Melville's Christ figure. If Billy can embody goodness, then even though he dies he suggests the possibility of hope for the rest of humanity. Auden indicates that Melville's final work opens up possibilities for redemption: "Reborn, [Melville] cried in exultation and surrender / 'The Godhead is broken like bread. We are the pieces.' / And sat down at his desk and wrote a story" (*CP* 252). The introduction of such explicitly Eucharistic imagery was a significant poetic development for Auden, though here in Auden's quotation of Melville's letter to Hawthorne (see Kirsch, *Auden* 107), he was resorting to Christian symbolism without necessarily invoking all the related Christian dogmas. In the same year, Auden wrote that he did not believe in "a creator who is distinct from and independent of the creation, an omnipotent free-willing immaterial agent" (*Prose II* 448). Instead, he had begun to use the name "God" to denote the totality of existence, such that "If anyone chooses to call our knowledge of existence knowledge of God, to call Essence the Father, Form the Son, and Motion the Holy Ghost, I don't mind: Nomenclature is purely a matter of convenience" (448). If this mythic nomenclature applies to the last lines of "Herman Melville," God (existence) has been broken up and is now divided into pieces (individual humans) who are always attempting to restore the divine unity of existence, and Melville makes his own attempt to restore it by writing a story, *Billy Budd, Sailor*. The story will not achieve an actual reunification of existence, but in Auden's view it has provided an analogy to reunification by revealing the fact that existence is good in itself and that even if reunification of the divided world is not possible, our knowledge of the nature of that division is an added good.

"Herman Melville" does not say whether reunification is possible, but "In Memory of W. B. Yeats" indicates that the poet's role is to praise what exists without attempting to use poetry as a vehicle for social or political change. Auden famously suggests that art is impotent to achieve anything, good or bad—"For poetry makes nothing happen" (*CP* 248). This line has occasionally been attacked without reference to its context in the rest of the poem, and the context suggests that the line should be read in the narrowest sense possible: poetry *makes* nothing happen, in the sense that the mere writing of a poem will not force humans to act against their own free will. Read in that narrow way, the line is axiomatic. Language can influence the human will, as the rest of the poem suggests, but it does not replace the human will and cannot make moral choices in its place. In contrast to the varied historical determinisms of Marx and Yeats, the line asserts that even if the course of history were predetermined—and in this poem Auden withholds judgment on that question—poetry has no power to force human society toward its predetermined end. Instead, the poem gives poetry a social role that is at once more modest and more liberating to the poet, who is under no obligation to produce political propaganda but is instead free to rejoice in whatever he finds praiseworthy. Poetry can help humans to understand themselves and to respond constructively to their negative circumstances in history. The poet's role, the poem implies, is to reassert the goodness of existence consistently, encouraging its audience not to give up hope.

About a year later Auden would suggest a similarly limited role for art in *New Year Letter,* in which he repeats his assertion that art cannot force a just society to exist, though it can exhort individuals to work for a more just social order. Auden warns that "No words men write can stop the war" (*CP* 206). Nevertheless, poets can "challenge, warn and witness," and "the Good Offices of verse" can sometimes help individuals to understand themselves and each other (202, 206). The poem itself enacts its assertion that poetry does have the power to challenge, warn, and witness as it quickly moves from its bleak outlook on politics and poetry to a general denunciation of false dualisms that "split creation into two" in order to reject one aspect of existence as irredeemably evil and embrace another aspect as unequivocally good (213), and the rest of the poem is concerned with revealing the sinister incoherence of various dualisms. Evil, Auden supposes, is not to be identified with any part of existence, but with disharmony between existences. But if one is to reject dualism, as the poem does, it is less emphatic about what exactly one ought to embrace instead. Auden emphasizes the need for "double-focus," but even in the double prayer that ends the poem, it is unclear what sort of unity that double-focus will reveal. The obvious logical corollary to accepting the Augustinian idea of evil as privation is an Augustinian affirmation of the goodness of all existences. But while Auden did entertain just such a logical step in *The Prolific and the Devourer* in 1939, he did not make any decisive statement on the question in *New Year Letter* in 1940, and he would not do so until "For the Time Being," which he began in the autumn of 1941.

Meanwhile, Auden more confidently affirmed the goodness of existence in his 1941 poem "Kairos and Logos." As Fuller and Mendelson both point out, the title derives from Paul Tillich's *The Interpretation of History*, which Auden had already cited in his notes for *New Year Letter* (Fuller, *Commentary* 389–90; Mendelson, *Later*

168). The "Logos" in the poem's title refers to Christ, the Word that appears in history as God incarnate, while "Kairos" refers to a decisive or propitious moment for a significant historical event, such as the Incarnation, to occur. The poem is composed of four sestinas, the first of which investigates the significance of the birth of Christ at the height of the Roman Empire. The poem's ideas would be refined and expanded in "For the Time Being," but here the poem clearly draws on Cochrane's analysis of Roman dualistic philosophy that "Besieged the body and cuckolded love" (*CP* 306), which is a reference to the various Gnostic cults as well as the Manichees, all of which denigrated bodily existence to some degree. The sestina ends on a laudatory note, praising "The just, the faithful and the uncondemned" saints of the early church, as well as their divine love that "never, like its own, condemned the world / Or hated time" (306). There is here at least the implication that the Augustinian Christianity described by Cochrane, defined by its belief in the Incarnation, affirms the goodness of the physical world, but as in *New Year Letter,* "Kairos and Logos" emphasizes Auden's rejection of Manichean dualism while only implicitly offering an affirmation of physical existence.

"FOR THE TIME BEING"

The Christian doctrine of the Incarnation holds that God, in the person of the Son, the second member of the Trinity, became human at a particular point in history, first gestating inside a mother's womb, then being born and growing to maturity as a man, Jesus Christ, who is recognized by the ancient creeds as both fully God and fully a man. In the centuries following the death of Christ, it was gradually acknowledged by theologians and clergy that the Incarnation upset the old Mosaic prohibition against images. Because God made himself visible in the incarnate Christ, Christians were now free to represent Christ artistically, along with all the rest of creation, in the physical medium of icons. Naturally, there were many dissensions about the extent to which iconography could be used in worship—the schism between Eastern Orthodoxy and the Roman churches was in part precipitated by differing views on iconography, and the Protestant Reformation included a strong iconoclastic element—but as Charles Williams explained in *The Descent of the Dove,* which Auden read in 1940, those who defended iconography always pointed to the Incarnation as the justification for religious art (see 93–94). If, as Augustine maintained, the physical world was innately good because God created it, and if redemption occurred through the physical world in the Incarnation, then physical portrayals of biblical stories, saints, and even God himself are both permissible and desirable elements of worship.

Hence Auden found it possible to experiment with overtly religious iconography in his Christmas oratorio "For the Time Being."[7] Auden's interest in iconography was longstanding—his famous 1938 poem "Musée des Beaux Arts" is an interpretation of the iconography implicit in Brueghel's *Icarus,* and in a 1960 review of an art history book he remarked that "what interests me most about a painting is its iconography" (*Prose IV* 303). "For the Time Being" draws on the conventions of medieval mystery plays, whose forms and purposes closely resemble medieval iconography, and Auden explains to his father in a letter why he chose to set the Christmas story in the modern era rather than attempt a "realistic" portrayal of a first-century nativity scene: "Perhaps you were expecting a purely historical account as one might give of the battle of Waterloo, whereas I was trying to treat it as a religious event which eternally recurs every time it is accepted. . . . I am not the first to treat the Christian data in this way; until the 18th Cent. it was always done, in the Mystery Plays for instance or any Italian paintings. It is only in the last two centuries that religion has been "humanized," and therefore treated historically as something that happened a long time ago; hence the nursery picture of Jesus in a nightgown and a Parsifal beard" (qtd. in Mendelson, *Later* 186).[8] Thus, Auden's poem on the Incarnation relies on a largely implicit acceptance of the iconographic demands of the genre he has chosen. With the exceptions of Joseph and perhaps Herod, the characters are flat types, not historical personalities, a narrative strategy that recalls both the flattened figures of pre-Renaissance paintings and the one-dimensional characters of medieval drama.

Fuller observes that "the oratorio is dedicated to [Auden's] mother and suffused with an eagerness to make the sort of difficult peace with the Flesh (and, interestingly enough, peace with the mother) that is found in Augustine's *Confessions*" (*Commentary* 346). Kirsch reports that Auden took notes on Augustine's *Confessions* in the back of the same notebook in which he drafted "For the Time Being" (*Auden* 59), so it is likely that he was reading the *Confessions* and writing the poem at about the same time. Kirsch also notes Auden's hostility to the Catholic doctrine of the Immaculate Conception, which states that the Virgin Mary was without sin, as well as his ironic ambivalence about the doctrine of the Virgin Birth (44–45), explaining that "the serious source of Auden's objections to both doctrines . . . was his antipathy to any attempt to deny the biological reality of human existence and his corresponding desire to affirm the importance of the body" (44–45). Kirsch represents Auden's ambivalence about the Virgin Birth as a clear rejection, citing Auden's recurring joke that everyone believes in a virgin birth because no one can imagine his or her parents having sex (44). Kirsch does not answer the obvious objection that, in "For the Time Being," Mary herself takes seriously the idea that her son has been miraculously conceived, and Gabriel's insistence that Joseph take a leap of faith is predicated on the divine origin of Mary's pregnancy. Auden can at least be credited with allowing his characters to struggle with the possibility that the Virgin Birth might really have occurred, and although his ironic jokes about the Virgin Birth may indicate a hostile dismissal, as Kirsch argues, they may also indicate a strategic reticence about a doctrine that was embarrassing to address openly, and that Auden preferred not to either defend or denounce explicitly. The tone of Auden's jokes suggests not flippant ridicule, but a jocular deflection of a topic he did not wish to talk about. While also possible that Auden grew more doubtful about the Virgin Birth in the years after he wrote "For the Time Being," Auden knew that the Virgin Birth is inextricably linked with the Incarnation in the Nicene creed, which he would have recited every time he attended church, and he was aware that an outright denial of the Virgin Birth would cast doubt on the doctrine of the Incarnation as well. Auden also knew that the doctrine of the Incarnation was historically cited to justify the iconographic approach to biblical narrative that he revives in the poem.

"For the Time Being" is about a singular event breaking in on an otherwise cyclical history. The event, the Incarnation, is almost impossible for its observers to accept, and yet its reality is undeniable, for it creates a reference point that makes both past and future meaningful. The Chorus that open the poem's first section, "Advent," suggests a monotonously cyclical history. All three stanzas spoken by the Chorus in "Advent" end with the same lines that began them, and the repetitious form reinforces the sense of endless cycles of history in which no event is truly unique. What the Chorus implies, the Narrator states outright, describing the way in which disasters "occur again and again but only to pass / Again and again into their formal opposites, / From sword to ploughshare, coffin to cradle, war to work," patterns which are "permanent in a general average way" (*CP* 351). Mendelson explains that the poem's sense of cyclical history in the pre-Christian world is derived largely from Cochrane's *Christianity and Classical Culture*, and Mendelson further identifies several places in the poem in which Auden directly borrows vocabulary from Cochrane (*Later* 184–86). But as Mendelson suggests, the poem's setting in the modern age is in part an attempt, sometimes unsuccessful, to make the historical past, the historical present, and Auden's personal life coincide (186).

It is sometimes a stretch to relate the historiography of first-century Rome to that of twentieth-century Western civilization, but Auden suggests some significant parallels between the modern, cyclical views of history which he hopes to discredit and the ancient, cyclical views of history denounced by Augustine. The Narrator's references to "sword to ploughshare" and "war to work" vaguely suggest the Marxist utopianism with which Auden had flirted in the 1930s and bears some surprising resemblance to the liberal utopianism espoused by Herod later in the poem in "The Massacre of the Innocents," but as Auden would point out later, neither Marxism nor Liberalism is based on cyclical views of history. On the contrary, he asserted in 1955 that the modern philosophies advanced by Marx, Freud, and others "were all Christian heresies" (*Prose III* 577). "That is to say," Auden continues, "one cannot imagine their coming into existence except in a civilization which claimed to be based, religiously, on belief that the Word was made flesh and dwelt among us, and that, in consequence, matter, the natural order, is real and redeemable, not a shadowy appearance or the cause of evil, and historical time is real and significant, not meaningless or an endless series of cycles" (577). So, while the opening of "For the Time Being" draws some superficial parallels between first-century Rome and twentieth-century Europe and America, Auden also suggests that the Incarnation irrevocably shifted the concept of history in the Western mind from a cyclical to a linear view. The monotonous cycles of history are rudely interrupted by the Incarnation, which the Narrator calls "an outrageous novelty," "this Horror," "the Abomination," and "the wrath of God" (351–52).

That a long poem on the Incarnation should be primarily focused on the nature of time bears some consideration. The poem relates time to the physicality of the Incarnation in a characteristically Augustinian way, since Augustine explores the relationship between time and the physical world in both the *Confessions* and the *City of God*. In what are perhaps the most theoretical and abstruse passages in the *Confessions*, Augustine inquires into the nature of time, suggesting that time is a created thing that exists along with the rest of the created cosmos, and that time consists of a distention or extension (10.17, 26). He hypothesizes that time is an expansion, a spreading out of the mind, since time is experienced primarily in the memory.[9] The present time, which is the only time that actually exists, is an infinitesimally thin line between the future, which has yet to exist, and the past, which has ceased to exist (10.15, 27). But, because Augustine links the mind with bodily existence (see Cochrane 444), time is also an extension of physicality, since time was created by God along with the physical world (*Confessions* 10.3, 12). As Augustine asserts in the *City of God*, "the world was not created *in* time but *with* time. An event in time happens after one time and before another, after the past and before the future. But at the time of creation there could have been no past, because there was nothing created to provide the change and movement which is the condition of time" (11.6). Time is not to be exactly identified with the motion of matter, but physical motion and change are contingent upon it. That is, for Augustine as for Auden, time is meaningful only in the presence of the unique, historical event.

Because the Incarnation is a unique event in history, and for the poem's Narrator it is also a horrifyingly undeniable event, the idea of strictly cyclical time proves untenable. In the poem, Christianity offers a radically different sense of reality as a linear movement out of a unique past into a unique future. The new sense of linear time established by the Incarnation subsumes the cyclical time in the natural world on the basis of which the pagan world had attempted to establish its philosophies of ethics and human government (e.g. Cochrane 411, 494), so for Auden's neo-pagans, the Incarnation represents the introduction of a completely new way of thinking about existence. "The Real," as the Recitative opines, "is what will strike you as really absurd," and it is absurd to both the leftist Narrator and the liberal Herod (*CP* 354, 394). It is also absurd to the Four Faculties, whose voices dramatize the inaccessibility of the Incarnation to the divided human consciousness. That there are four different faculties in the place of one coherent consciousness is a result of the Fall: "We were himself" before the Fall, but "His error became our / Chance to be" (355). Because they are divided, they are unable to see into "the garden of Being" in which the Incarnation has occurred (354). As it turns out, the Fall is a property of human consciousness, for as Gabriel tells Joseph, "There is one World of Nature, and one Life; / Sin fractures the Vision, not the Fact" (365). The Fall does not consist of embodiment, as the Manichees would have it, or of a lapse into subjectivity, as Herod thinks, but of an incapacity to apprehend reality as it really is. Thus the First Wise Man, representing the Baconian scientist, is unable to wring unequivocal data out of the natural world: "With rack and screw I put Nature through / A thorough inquisition," but "Her answers were disjointed / . . . / She is just as big a liar, in fact, as we are" (369). Such a dim view of empirical science would have sounded ridiculous just a few decades before Auden wrote the lines, but after Einstein's theories of relativity upset Newtonian physics, the natural world would never again yield perfectly coherent data. For the Wise Men, their visions of the natural world, of time, and of human society look hopelessly inadequate.

Nevertheless, the fact of corruption is itself a sign of hope. In the middle of the poem, Auden has a chorale sing to God, "for Thy Goodness even sin / Is valid as a sign" (*CP* 374). The Fall becomes an opportunity for redemption, as the chorale expresses hope "That from our incoherence we / May learn to put our trust in Thee" (374). Auden had said something similar in *New Year Letter,* though in less explicitly theological language. Here his statements recall Augustine's reasoning in the *Confessions*, where he explains that to claim that a thing is corrupt is to presuppose a perfect, uncorrupted state of existence that has become corrupted (7.12). The admission of sin as a fact assumes the existence of a standard of perfection by which sin is identified as a real failure and not just as a neutral fact of existence. As Augustine followed the logical trail from the definition of evil as privation into belief in the goodness of both nature and God, so "For the Time Being" identifies the moral failings of the twentieth century as evidence of the existence of an ultimate goodness.

A central feature of "For the Time Being" is "The Meditation of Simeon" in which Simeon is portrayed as a theologian/philosopher who is considering the philosophical and aesthetic implications of the Incarnation. The Fall, Simeon asserts, was not an illusion, nor a necessary progression from innocence to experience, nor is it reversible by mere effort (*CP* 385–86). Simeon then echoes the chorale's statement that the Fall does, nevertheless, provide an opportunity to recognize the existence of goodness. In Simeon's view, fallen humanity had to exhaust every hope of regaining coherence before it could be presented with the opportunity to accept or reject the Incarnation. Every dualism had to be weighed and found wanting: "Before the Positive could manifest Itself specifically, it was necessary that nothing should be left that negation could remove; the emancipation of Time from Space had first to be complete. . . ." (386). The word "emancipation" generally carries positive connotations, but in this case it bespeaks an inability to develop a coherent account of all elements of the cosmos—matter, time, space, energy, human will, and so forth. Likewise, every philosophical dualism that rejected some necessary aspect of existence had to be pushed to its unreasonable conclusion before humanity was ready to abandon dualism altogether in favor of an entirely different view of reality. Simeon does not identify specific pre-Christian philosophies but instead follows Cochrane's broad categorization of all pagan philosophies as either "materialist" or "idealist" (see Cochrane 390), both of which are false dualisms. One obvious example of a dualistic philosophy that produces an unreasonable result is Plato's *Republic.* Plato's scheme for a just society is based on idealism, which in Auden's and Augustine's view denigrates the body, and produces a tyrannical state that few sane people would want to live in.

The basic philosophical problem for pre-Christian Rome as described by Augustine and Cochrane, and for the modern world as Auden saw it, is the seemingly irreconcilable contradiction between the One and the Many. That is, the cosmos appears at times to consist of total unity such that all variation and difference is illusory, but at other times the cosmos appears to be the opposite, a chaotic collection of disparate parts in which unity and wholeness are illusory. The problem of the One and the Many is well illustrated by Raphael's painting, *The School of Athens,* which depicts Plato and Aristotle deep in an argument. Plato raises an index finger toward the sky, indicating his privileging of the One, whereas Aristotle gestures toward the earth with outspread fingers, suggesting his preference for the Many. Cochrane explains the problem as Plato articulated it (428). The Chorus of "For the Time Being" offers a tidy summary of the inevitable conclusion of the argument between the two philosophers: "*Promising to meet, we parted forever*" (*CP* 386).

To choose either view is to necessarily reject the other, and thus embrace an obviously false dualism, as Simeon explains. The road of philosophical inquiry inevitably "forks in opposite directions towards the One and the Many," at which point the philosopher is forced to "decide which is Real and which is only Appearance, yet at the same time cannot escape the knowledge that his choice is arbitrary and subjective" (*CP* 386). For Simeon, the problem of the One and the Many cannot be solved by reference either to unity or to diversity, so the decision to accept one and reject the other is irrational. Simeon's assessment is in some ways a caricature of philosophy, as few enough philosophers would admit that their *a priori* assumptions are purely arbitrary. But Simeon's point is a distillation of Cochrane's argument that Augustinian theology offers a resolution to the problem of the One and the Many in its doctrine of the Trinity in which both unity and plurality co-inhere. Neither the One nor the Many is illusory, and both can be accepted as fully existing. As Edward Callan points out, Auden replaces the Platonic aesthetic that relies on the metaphysical abstraction of "the Good" with "the Christian doctrine of the union of the material and the divine in the Word made Flesh" (31). As such, the Incarnation reveals that physical existence is not opposed to the abstract or the spiritual, but complementary to it.

However, not all critics recognize the aesthetic implications that Auden sees in the Incarnation. Rainer Emig, citing Mary's statement, "In human dreams earth ascends to Heaven / Where no one need pray nor ever feel alone" (*CP* 380), asks rhetorically, "If Heaven is a place where communication through prayer is no longer necessary because of the achieved proximity of souls and Creator, then what does Christ's presence on earth mean in terms of communication? Is not every word spoken about the Divine presence then superfluous? Does it not, indeed, show a misrecognition of the event? And where does that leave a 'Christmas Oratorio'? Even in its seemingly orthodox sections, Auden's text manages to undermine its very right to exist and argue its point" (139–40). Emig's identification of the Heaven of dreams with the historical Incarnation is questionable at best, but more importantly, he fails to recognize that Auden had anticipated such questions in "The Meditation of Simeon," in which Simeon explains the aesthetic consequence of the Incarnation: "Because in Him the Flesh is united to the Word without magical transformation, Imagination is redeemed from promiscuous fornication with her own images" (*CP* 388). Far from silencing art, the Incarnation unites the physical world with the world of abstract forms and legitimizes artistic depiction, even of God, such that the focus on the Incarnation is a defense of the poem's own existence as an iconographic representation.

Simeon's phrase "fornication with her own images" (*CP* 388) is a paraphrase of Augustine's famous phrase *fantastica fornicatio*, which Simeon uses to describe the tendency of art toward mere self-referentiality. Within a dualistic philosophy, Simeon suggests, poetry has no real place; Platonic idealism is suspicious of the physicality of language and the tendency of poetry to excite the passions and celebrate physical pleasures, whereas materialism is suspicious of the tendency of language toward generalization and equivocation. Only when the flesh is united with the Word[10] is space made for the paradoxical tendencies of art to both generalize and particularize. Simeon concludes this section saying, "Because in Him all passions find a logical In-Order-That, by Him is the perpetual recurrence of Art assured" (*CP* 389). For Simeon, as for Auden himself, Christianity establishes the only philosophically coherent justification for the production of art, "for the One and the Many are simultaneously revealed as real" (389). Simeon's speech is a defense not only of art in general, but also of this poem in particular. The poem as an icon is a kind of recurrence of the original event, a recurrence that is not bare duplication but a creative reenactment that is both a unique event in history and a repetition of a past event. With the reconciliation of Flesh and Word, of concrete thing and abstract sign, poetry need not be a closed system of self-referentiality, nor must it be banished from the just city as hopelessly carnal. Both the abstract and physical

qualities of language have an equal right to existence, and their fundamental goodness is most obvious when the two are accepted as equally legitimate.

However much "For the Time Being" wishes to affirm both the One and the
Many as real and non-contradictory, it also describes the difficulty of living consistently with the fact. After Simeon's triumphant speeches heralding the one solution to all philosophical problems, the next speaker is Herod, who dimly recognizes
the reality of the Incarnation but rejects it categorically and orders a massacre of
innocent infants to prevent its disrupting his utopian project. It is hard to affirm
the goodness of all existence when Rachel is weeping for her children. Even before
Simeon's meditation and Herod's massacre, the shepherds have related their own
mundane struggle to affirm existence as they know it. They are tempted by an existential angst that regularly asks why they want to go on existing at all, to which
they reply simply, "No, I don't know why, / But I'm glad I'm here" (*CP* 377). Emig
argues that there is a radical disjunction in the shepherds' identities: "at times it is
difficult to decide whether they are awaiting the birth of Christ as the redeemer,
or a proletarian revolution. Their main function is to remind the reader that the
search for salvation and redemption must never lose sight of the mundane issues of
daily practice" (139). On one level, Emig is right that the shepherds are concerned
with their own economic welfare. Auden has modeled them on the medieval shepherds in the *Second Play of the Shepherds*, who also complain at length about their
low pay and hard working conditions. Emig perceives a discrepancy between the
shepherds' symbolic significance as members of the working class and their status
as voices expressing a longing for redemption. The shepherds do indeed represent
their socioeconomic class, just as the wise men represent theirs, but as biblical characters who are dressed in modern clothing, as it were, there is no necessary conflict
between their desire for spiritual salvation and their desire for political or economic
salvation. For Auden as a socialist, the establishment of both social and economic
justice is an important component of the salvation of the whole human being, soul
and body.

Emig's misreading is rooted in his misapprehension of Christianity as a spirituality that aspires to pure abstraction: "Once more," Emig argues, "if there is a
Christian message in this text, it is by no means an orthodox one. Its vision of salvation encompasses physical needs, such as 'Light, water, and air,' as well as the end
of established 'Authoritarian/Constraint,' rather than projecting the fulfilment of
those demands into a metaphysical elsewhere" (139). Emig erroneously identifies
the Neoplatonic gnosticism of which Auden was so critical with orthodox Christianity. While Emig is correct that the shepherds' concept of redemption involves
the physical world, his description of Christian orthodoxy is irreconcilable with
the Christianity of the Apostolic and Nicene creeds, as well as with Auden's (and
Augustine's) repeated affirmations of embodiment as fundamental to human existence. The shepherds' own affirmation of existence is, admittedly, more tentative

than that advanced by Simeon, since it is not based on a rational extrapolation from the Incarnation, but on an intuition whose source they can never quite manage to trace. But a lack of philosophical certainty is not the same thing as a lack of faith.

Mary and Joseph are even more doubtful during "The Flight into Egypt," in which they attempt to evade the temptations of the bohemian desert by escaping into the crumbling civilization of Egypt. Yet temptations and dangers are everywhere along the route. Mary and Joseph have escaped Herod's dystopia only to descend into the anarchy of the desert on the way to the false security of a dead civilization in Egypt. There is no safe place where the Incarnation can flourish unhindered, only a constant pilgrimage through a wide variety of distractions and dangers. As the Narrator puts it, "To those who have seen / the Child, however dimly, however incredulously, / The Time Being is, in a sense, the most trying time of all" (*CP* 399). The Narrator uses the traditional church calendar to place the reader in the short interval of "ordinary time" between the seasons of Advent and Lent. Between the sudden, shocking vision of the Incarnation and the prolonged purgation of Lent and Good Friday lies a mundane existence during which it is easy to slip back into one tacit dualism or another, any of which will implicitly deny the Incarnation. The struggle to reenact the Incarnation every day, to keep natural, cyclical time contained within the all-encompassing linear time established by the Incarnation, requires more concentration and determination than anyone can muster.

As a kind of iconography, the poem naturally includes a didactic element, at which not a few critics understandably balk.[11] Yet the didacticism is intrinsic to the theological subject and iconographic form—icons are aids to contemplation, but also to formal instruction. The poem identifies Christ in the biblical language of "the Way," "the Truth," and "the Life," phrases that evoke the original context of those phrases in the Gospel of John, where Christ also announces, "No one comes to the Father except through me" (*CP* 400, John 14:6). Thus, it is appropriate that the Chorus ends the poem in the imperative mood: "Follow Him through the Land of Unlikeness; / You will see rare beasts, and have unique adventures" (*CP* 400). The phrase "Land of Unlikeness" is from Augustine's *Confessions*, as Fuller points out (*Commentary* 355). Auden would have found the phrase, as translated by Pusey, in Cochrane's *Christianity and Classical Culture*, and in its original context the phrase describes Augustine's pre-conversion forays into the bohemian culture of Carthage. Given Auden's earlier self-assessment in *New Year Letter* and other poems of the early 1940s, "For the Time Being" is addressing its exhortations to its own maker as much as to anyone else. The challenge for Auden was to particularize experience, to recognize the uniqueness of each historical moment. "In the meantime" between Christmas and Lent, the Narrator states, "There [is] . . . / . . . the Time Being to redeem / From insignificance" (*CP* 400). That is, the Incarnation must be reenacted by the individual in the historical moment, and whatever that may mean, the act of writing poetry with explicitly religious themes does not necessarily qualify. Auden would argue later in *The Dyer's Hand* that a Christian theme or image does not necessarily make a work of art any more or less Christian (458).

"THE SEA AND THE MIRROR"

"For the Time Being" was originally published in one volume with "The Sea and the Mirror," which began with "The Sea and the Mirror," even though Auden had written them in the reverse order. Auden's reasons for this arrangement are obvious enough: "The Sea and the Mirror" is a poem about the nature and limitations of art, and it ends by insisting that humans cannot give coherent, artistic order to their existence and therefore must accept God's intrusion into human affairs. "For the Time Being" then explores the implications of that divine intrusion. While "For the Time Being" advances an Augustinian articulation of the resolution of the question of the One and the Many, "The Sea and the Mirror" implicitly relies on a similar Augustinian resolution of spirit/body dualism. The poem is subtitled "A Commentary on Shakespeare's *The Tempest*," a play that Auden later referred to as "Manichean," as he said, "not because it shows the relation of Nature to Spirit as one of conflict and hostility, which in fallen man it is, but because it puts the blame for this upon Nature and makes the Spirit innocent" (*DH* 130). In response to these Manichean tendencies, Auden sets up his commentary to demonstrate the interdependence of body and spirit. The poem also explores the mutual culpability of body and spirit, and finally offers the possibility of resolving the spirit/body opposition, not through poetry but through the divine Word.

Nineteenth-century interpretations of *The Tempest* had tended to identify Prospero with Shakespeare, or artists in general, and to see Ariel as the artist's muse of spiritual inspiration—Auden later suggested that in an ideal staging of *The Tempest* Ariel should not appear onstage at all but rather speak from offstage so as to emphasize his (or its) identity as a voice without a body (*DH* 132–33). In contrast to Ariel, Caliban speaks mostly in prose rather than in verse, suggesting an inartistic disposition, and so was identified by nineteenth century critics with the body, largely unteachable and totally unartistic. Prospero was set between them as a figure of the artist who attempts to control the body with the help of his spirit of inspiration and with his magic art.

One problem with making such an allegory out of *The Tempest* is that it ignores the necessarily physical nature of art, poetry included. In the *Confessions*, which Auden was rereading about the same time he started work on the poem, Augustine points out that language exists as an entirely physical entity, since it involves the mouth, ears, and eyes, and Augustine argues further that spoken language is no less physical for its being transitory. For Augustine, the transitory nature of language emphasizes its belonging to the physical world of constant flux and change (see *Confessions* 11.22–23, 27). The written word exists largely in the physical world, and as would be discovered later, spoken language depends on physical vibrations in the air. Language cannot exist in a disembodied state. The idea that poetry is mainly "spiritual" rather than physical is an illusion that Auden's poem shatters.

Auden points up what he sees as Shakespeare's mistaken disembodiment of art by making Caliban, not Ariel, speak on behalf of the artistic process and on behalf of Ariel himself. Further, Caliban speaks in a Jamesian prose, which is paradoxically appropriate for several reasons (see Spears, *Poetry* 224; Mendelson, *Later* 230–32), not the least of which are its obvious artifice and tendency toward abstraction. Auden wrote in a letter to Theodore Spencer that in writing for Caliban he had tried to find "a style as 'spiritual', as far removed from Nature, as possible (Ariel's contribution) and James seemed to fit the bill exactly . . ." (qtd. in Kirsch, Introduction 31). Caliban's "spiritual" prose is in part an attempt to produce cognitive dissonance in the reader, for on one hand the style looks and sounds abstract and "spiritual," but on the other hand the speaker, Caliban, represents the body even to the extent that, as Auden told Spencer, Caliban is "the Prick" (qtd. in *Later* 230–31). Auden had associated the literary with the phallic as early as 1930, when he wrote to a friend, "Never write from your head, write from your cock" (qtd. in Schmidt 737). At the time, he may have meant that a writer should privilege the visceral while rejecting the abstract and intellectual—Auden made many such categorical pronouncements throughout his life, quite a few of which he subsequently contradicted—but in light of his later work the statement does suggest an early connection of poetry with the facts of human embodiment. For Auden, art could never truly be separated from the body.

At the same time, art is not the exclusive domain of the body. Auden is not denying the quasi-Platonic idealism of *The Tempest* in order to take up its mirror image, philosophical materialism. Rather, the connection between Ariel and Caliban becomes clearer when Caliban speaks specifically to aspiring poets and novelists about the troublesome relationship between the artist and the inspiring muse who, when "released" by the artist as Prospero releases Ariel, refuses to leave. At this point, Caliban says to the artist, one first begins to inquire into the nature of art itself and eventually sees in the mirror of Ariel's eyes an ugly, unfamiliar creature, "for this is the first time indeed that you have met the only subject that you have, who is . . . the all too solid flesh you must acknowledge as your own; at last you have come face to face with me" (*CP* 433). In his first moment of real honesty, the artist finds that his inspiration and his flesh cannot be separated and further, that his own flesh is the only subject he really has. "Subject" is a triple pun: the consciousnesses, which is rooted in the neurological physiology of the body, is a subjective perspective from which to view the world; the flesh is a subject for artistic depiction; and the body is a subject that is ruled by the will. Caliban chides the artist for not engaging in the fierce struggle with his own body but instead maintaining an aesthetic distance from himself in order to produce his art: "Had you tried to destroy me, had we wrestled through long dark hours, we might by daybreak have learnt something from each other; . . . we might both have heard together that music which explains and pardons all" (434). In this post-Freudian rereading of the biblical story of Jacob wrestling with the angel in Genesis 32, Auden pictures Ariel as the conscious Jacob wrestling with his shadowy double, Caliban, a mysterious stranger whom Ariel/ Jacob must subdue in order to achieve reconciliation.

Caliban's language echoes Auden's description of the contemplative mystic in his essay "The Protestant Mystics." "In the case of the Vision of God," Auden says, "it does not seem to be granted to anyone who has not undergone a long process of self-discipline and prayer, but self-discipline and prayer cannot of themselves compel it" (*FA* 55). Analogously, the moment of clear vision in which the artist sees reality as it is can come only after a difficult process of purgation. The "music" to which Caliban refers suggests the divine music of the spheres as depicted through-out Dante's *Paradiso*, which can be heard only by the blessed who have undergone a purgative process of fighting bodily desires, not in order to abolish them but in order to moderate and control them. But Auden's essay warns against developing too strict an analogy between an artistic inspiration and a mystical vision: "The vision of God cannot be a 'work' like a poem," Auden states, but is instead a gift given to some who through self-discipline have become able to receive it (*FA* 72). Barring the kind of wrestling with the flesh—the rigorous self-discipline required of the serious artist—that Caliban describes, the only other option that the artist has for developing a tolerable relationship with his flesh is "to keep our respective hopes for the future within moderate, very moderate, limits" (*CP* 435). It is not, perhaps, an ideal solution, but for an artist like Auden who found himself constantly dissoci-ated from and at odds with his bodily desires, expectations for co-existence had to be kept low enough to be easily met.

The struggle with Caliban that the artist has largely avoided is replayed in grander terms at the end of the poem, as Caliban describes the colossal failure of all human attempts to order life aesthetically. The moment of honest self-knowledge also reveals the absolute need for God, to whom Caliban refers as "the real Word," "that Wholly Other Life," and "the perfected Work" (*CP* 444). Yet the recognition of the "essential emphatic gulf" between the human and the divine does not result in a rejection of the human in favor of the divine, but in "the restored relation" between the divine and the human, and consequently a restored relation between Ariel and Caliban, spirit and body (444). Ariel's "Postscript," with an echo by the Prompter, briefly touches on the possibilities and problems inherent in accepting the restored relation. Ariel confesses to Caliban that he is "Helplessly in love" with Caliban as well as with "Elegance, art, fascination" but that he cannot be united to Caliban by collapsing the differences between them: "only / As I am can I / Love you as you are" (445). But neither can their differences ever completely sever Ariel from Caliban, so Ariel reminds his counterpart, "Never hope to say farewell" (445). The Prompter's echoing " . . . I," which implicitly opposes Antonio's earlier, ironic echoes insisting on total division and isolation, reinforces the possibility of the restored relation between Caliban and Ariel, a relation in which their differences are not erased, nor their unity divided.

As Cochrane explains, Augustinian theology envisions redemption as a restoration of unity between the elements of the human person: "the acceptance of Trinitarian Christianity [is] a condition for the eradication of intellectual and moral shortcomings as well as for the realization of those positive values to which mankind aspires. . . . That goal is the integration of personality" (Cochrane 454). Or, as Auden describes the process at the end of "The Sea and the Mirror," regardless of the existential struggles between them, Caliban and Ariel must co-inhere. In the more theological language that Auden borrowed from the debates leading up to the Nicene Council on which Augustine was a leading commentator, one must neither "confound the persons" nor "divide the substance" in defining the relationship between the body and spirit. Though they are frequently at odds, the existence of each one is always necessary to the existence of the other, and so each is intrinsically good in its own limited way.

"THE SHIELD OF ACHILLES" AND "HORAE CANONICAE"

In the poetry that Auden wrote after "The Sea and the Mirror," he continued to employ theological language to describe the elements of human existence that tend toward destructive binary opposition—body and mind, individual and society, past and present, sacred and secular—and he continued to insist that, while conflict between them was inevitable, such binaries should aspire to a dialectical harmony. From the beginning of his career, Auden had been seeking a unified vision of psychological and historical reality, but he would not accept a vision that achieved unity at the expense of particulars, nor individuation at the expense of unity. He saw in the political history of the twentieth century a dangerous tendency in political ideologies, fascism especially but also communism, that sought to dissolve human individuality into the state, and many of his later poems express a deep concern to reaffirm the goodness of the particularities of human existence. His 1952 poem "The Shield of Achilles," for instance, moves from a vision of an army composed of unindividuated "eyes" and "boots" (*CP* 597) to "A crowd of ordinary decent folk" watching a political execution (597), and finally to a "ragged urchin, aimless and alone" (598). The imagery of the poem moves from the collective to the individual, focusing the reader's attention more and more on the particular atrocities of modern tyranny. The "unintelligible multitude" (597) is ominous partly because its members have been deprived of individuality, but the "ragged urchin" is more obviously a victim of his social circumstances: "That girls are raped, that two boys knife a third, / Were axioms to him, who'd never heard / Of any world where promises were kept, / Or one could weep because another wept" (598).

Violence and injustice are the realities of his world, but these things also remind the reader that his world is ultimately a corruption of a human world that ought to be based on justice, fidelity, and empathy. To admit the ugly reality of the Fall is to admit that the world has fallen from a state of goodness that is still intrinsic to it.

In other poems of the 1950s and 1960s, Auden directly cites Augustine as a source of such a position, and these poems reveal a consistent recognition that ethics and a just civil order must be based on an acceptance of the body as an intrinsically good aspect of human existence. The poems of this period also show an increasing awareness that, since the body exists in time, the goodness of the body has social implications in the realm of human history. While Auden's later poems and prose maintain their implicit reliance on Augustine for their account of the goodness of the physical world, they also reveal a new tension between Auden's chosen role as a civic poet and his continuing doubts about the ability of poetry to directly affect history or politics. Despite his conflicted view of his own literary vocation, Auden maintained that the role of the poet is primarily to identify and praise whatever is good, even more than it is to denounce what is evil, though Auden did his share of denunciation too. When his later poetry sets out to be explicitly laudatory, the poems frequently identify embodied human existence as especially good and praise-worthy.

Auden's poem sequence "Horae Canonicae," which he completed in 1955, revisits many of the themes he had touched on in his first explicitly religious poem, "For the Time Being," in which he had indicated that the Incarnation, as a real historical event, must be reenacted by individuals within their own historical context. The poem's ending had not explored the possibilities for such reenactment in day-to-day life so much as commented on the difficulty of doing so. "Horae Canonicae" picks up at that point by investigating the ways in which the suffering and death of Christ might be reenacted at other points in history, focusing ironically on the ease with which the execution of Christ is often replayed in daily life. For some time Auden had been considering writing a poem sequence based on the canonical hours, and Mendelson reports that in a 1947 letter to Ursula Niebuhr "he explained he had 'a possible scheme in mind for a series of secular poems based on the Offices'; the word 'secular' was evidently a warning not to expect anything liturgical or devotional, although Auden's schemata, from the beginning, emphasized the liturgical and theological dimensions of the work" (*Later* 312). Auden eventually developed several detailed charts relating each of the canonical hours to particular historical events, biblical stories, personality types, and body parts, but the poems he actually produced bear little relation to the charts. Mendelson explains that one "chart portrays a linear sequence of events from Lauds to Compline, Creation to Apocalypse, dawn to dusk. But a strictly linear time ignores the repetitive physiology of the body. The finished sequence, with Lauds at the close, integrates linear history with cyclical nature . . ." (*Later* 313). While Auden's initial plans for the sequence changed significantly, it proved a logical successor to "The Sea and the Mirror" and "For the Time Being," in which he had struggled to articulate the necessity of the integration of opposites: nature and history, cyclical time and linear time, individual and society, conscious ego and unconscious self. Auden did retain one level of analogy with the canonical hours. Traditionally, each of the seven canonical hours was an occasion for meditation on a different event in the Passion,[12] so most of the poems in the sequence relate to the corresponding Good Friday event, if often obliquely. As Mendelson explains, "the event at their center is the specific historical act that was performed in first-century Jerusalem and, simultaneously, any apparently trivial act you may do that harms another person when you did not consciously intend to do harm" (*Later* 332). Mendelson's reading also identifies the body and its troubled relation to the consciousness as a central theme of the poem. The Incarnation as described in "For the Time Being" had emphasized the fundamental goodness of linear time and the goodness of the body by implication, and "The Sea and the Mirror" had pointed out the body's and the spirit's mutual responsibility for the conflict between them, but "Horae Canonicae" emphasizes the difficulties of embodiment and points out the necessity of redemption.

While "Horae Canonicae" revisits territory that had become familiar to Auden in "For the Time Being" and "The Sea and the Mirror," this sequence extends and expands his conception of the struggle between body and consciousness. The first poem in the sequence, "Prime," was also the first to be written—the rest are not arranged in order of composition—and it was begun in 1949, five years after "The Sea and the Mirror" was finished. The poem describes the first moment of undivided consciousness as "Without a name or history I wake / Between my body and the day" (*CP* 627). The speaker has, for a moment, returned to a pre-Fall Eden in which there is no division between what Auden generally referred to as the Ego, or the *I*, and the Self, or *me*.[13] In the moment the speaker calls "holy," there is no distinction between what one is and what one desires, so the speaker is "wholly in the right" (627). The speaker and his body are one, as "the will has still to claim / This adjacent arm as my own, / The memory to name me . . . / . . . / . . . and I / The Adam sinless in our beginning, / Adam still previous to any act" (627). R. A. York maintains that "the person at the first moment of consciousness is conceived as unfallen and the activities of the day as a fall" (234). But York is not quite right.

For Auden, the Fall does not occur in what follows the advent of self-consciousness; rather, the Fall is identified with the emergence of self-consciousness itself, and the subsequent activities of the day all occur east of Eden.[14] As Auden argues in *The Prolific and the Devourer*, the human race fell from innocence at the moment of self-consciousness in which the previously coherent self was split into competing and contradictory desires. In "Prime" the speaker momentarily recovers a sense of innocent wholeness, even to the extent that he senses no distinction between the body (the adjacent arm, for instance) and his self, but in becoming fully awake he reenacts the Fall. In a refined version of the ideas expressed in earlier works, the poem locates the Fall in the moment at which the self wished to be other than what it was, when identity and desire failed to coincide: "I draw breath; that is of course to wish / No matter what, to be wise, / To be different, to die and the cost, / No matter how, is Paradise / Lost of course and myself owing a death" (*CP* 628). The enjambment of "Paradise / Lost" contributes to the sense of ironic surprise, as the poem uses the innocent act of conscious breathing as an example of an emerging desire to be other than what one already is. The act is of no consequence in itself, but it signals the emergence of competing desires concomitant with the division of the *I* from the *self*, which has serious consequences for the body. "Death" is a pun on "debt," an Elizabethan commonplace that typically stated "we all owe God a debt" (e.g., see Shakespeare's *2 Henry IV* 3.2), but here the death debt is owed to the self, rather than to God. After the Fall, the body rebels against the *I* and introduces its own conflicting drives into the consciousness, so it becomes partially responsible for the ensuing divisions in the human person. Now fully awake and aware of his disparate and competing desires, the speaker refers to his body as "this ready flesh / No honest equal, but my accomplice now, / My assassin to be" (*CP* 628). Both body and mind had been equally good in their pre-Fall union, but the body will eventually become the agent of the speaker's own death, and the body is also an accessory to any sin that the ego commits. In the sequence, murder is a synecdoche for all sin, which Auden had defined in *The Prolific and the Devourer* as "consciously to act contrary to self-interest" (*Prose II* 427).

In the context of a sequence that reenacts Good Friday, the murder that the "assassin" body will commit is the execution of the innocent Christ. The next poem, "Terce," advances the association by contrasting the fallen, average man in "Prime" with "our victim who is without a wish" (*CP* 629). The victim, Christ, is sinless since he does not wish to be anything other than what he already is, the perfectly coherent person who knows that soon "we shall have had a good Friday" (629). Because Christ is innocent, there can be no rational reason for his execution, and the only "unforgivable" aspects of Christ that "Terce" identifies are his perfect understanding of fallen human nature and his ability to foresee the violent consequences of fallen humans' collision with the innocent man. The crucifixion is, indeed, an archetypal *acte gratuit*, a term that Auden defines in his review of Cochrane's *Christianity and Classical Culture*: "When a Christian, like Augustine, talks about ethics, therefore, he begins not with the rational act or the pleasant act, but with the *acte gratuite* [*sic*], which is . . . a pure assertion of absolute self-autonomy. . . . Man, that is to say, always acts either self-loving, just for the hell of it, or God-loving, just for the heaven of it; his reasons, his appetites are secondary motivations" (*FA* 36–37). The murder of the innocent victim may be ostensibly predicated on jealousy or pride, but such motivations are only pretenses. The murder is all the more atrocious because it is committed, finally, "just for the hell of it."

"Nones," a later poem in the sequence, begins just after the murder has been committed: "What we know to be not possible, / . . . comes to pass / Before we realize it . . ." (*CP* 634). Despite the speaker's disbelief in the possibility of the act, folklore and myth had long suggested that the impetus toward the murder of an innocent victim had always been implicit in fallen humanity, and now it actually happens. The mob that committed the murder has dissipated into the individuals of which it was comprised, individuals who cannot now give any rational explanation for their actions. Neither can they forget that their actions were real, for "the blood / Of our sacrifice is already / Dry on the grass" (634). Auden is not a particularly visual poet, as Richard Hoggart observed soon after this poem was published (17), so this image stands out as a reminder that the Fall and the consequent crucifixion were not abstract, mythical symbols of psychological complexes. Rather, the Fall and the crucifixion physically happened in real history, so each individual reenactment of Fall and sacrifice also happens physically in history. The fourth stanza suggests that all *acte gratuits*, even those that are innocent in themselves, like games, now evoke the crucifixion: "This mutilated flesh, our victim, / Explains too nakedly, too well, / . . . / The aim of our chalk-pit game . . ." (*CP* 635). Because of the unavoidable association of every *acte gratuit* with the crucifixion, "we shall always now be aware / Of the deed into which they lead, . . . / . . . / . . . wherever / The sun shines, brooks run, books are written, / There will always be this death" (635).

The poem suggests that all games are, in a way, reenactments of the crucifixion inasmuch as they are pursued for their own sake. A game is variation of the *acte gratuit*—and Auden considered art a kind of game too—so it can never appear to be wholly innocent to those who are already fallen. The poem notes the culpability of literary art at the end of the stanza, as it includes books along with the Arcadian landscape. Literature, being a game primarily for grown-ups, is perhaps especially implicated because, as the next stanza indicates, ". . . we have time / To misrepresent, excuse, deny, / Mythify, use this event / While . . . / . . . its meaning / Waits for our lives" (635). The poem identifies language as the primary means by which humans attempt to regard the murder as something other than what it was; the actions of misrepresenting, excusing, denying, and mythifying are executed by means of language. The poem specifically identifies mythologization as an illegitimate attempt to deny responsibility for the murder by claiming that the sacrifice is "just a myth" or that the innocent victim is "only a symbol."

The poem's layered associations link the physical repercussions of the Fall with the physicality of language itself. The end of the poem describes a dream in which the will begins to wander over a wide variety of freely associated landscapes until it reaches "a room, / Lit by one weak bulb, where our Double sits / Writing and does not look up" (*CP* 636). Mendelson identifies the doppelganger with the body, the external self from which the dreaming ego is dissociated, even though "the dream cannot say that the Double is the body, because the will has no way of knowing the meaning of dreams" (*Later* 345). That the Double, the body, is pictured writing emphasizes that the ego cannot express itself except through physical language. As Mendelson notes, "in the poetic world made up of words, the body does not look up from its work of making because, in dreams, the will cannot summon the body to act on the will's behalf" (*Later* 345). But the final stanza reveals that the Double's "writing" is a metaphor for the unconscious biological processes of the body that continue even during sleep:

> . . . while we are thus away, our own wronged flesh
> May work undisturbed, restoring
> The order we try to destroy, the rhythm
> We spoil out of spite: valves close
> And open exactly, glands secrete,
> Vessels contract and expand
> At the right moment, essential fluids
> Flow to renew exhausted cells,
> Not knowing quite what has happened. . . . (*CP* 636)

While the body is an "accomplice" to murder, as "Prime" indicated, it also resists the ego's arbitrary, self-assertive attempt to destroy innocent order "out of spite." The body acts as a willing instrument of the ego, and so it is always implicated in the Fall—after Nuremburg it is impossible to excuse oneself by claiming, "I was only following orders"—yet it also retains a commendable impetus toward order and coherence. Its orderly regularity and unity suggest that the body has not fallen so far as the ego, and if sleep cannot restore the unity of the ego and the self, it can at least postpone the ego's self-destructive acts and allow the body time to restore some of its original goodness.

The body also appears in "Vespers" to remind a Utopian and an Arcadian that their respective dreams are fictions that cannot accept all the contingencies of the physical world. The free-verse poem details a meeting between two antitypes, the speaker of the poem who is an Arcadian, and another man, a Utopian. In *The Dyer's Hand*, Auden explained that between the two "there is a characterological gulf as unbridgeable as that between Blake's Prolifics and Devourers" (409). There are many differences between them, but at base the Arcadian wishes to return to the lost world of the pre-Fall Eden while the Utopian looks forward to the perfect, political society of the New Jerusalem. As Auden put it, "Eden is a place where its inhabitants may do whatever they like to do; the motto over its gate is, 'Do what thou wilt is here the Law.' New Jerusalem is a place where its inhabitants like to do whatever they ought to do, and its motto is, 'In His will is our peace'" (409). That Auden himself had Arcadian leanings is obvious in many works, such as his poem "Under Which Lyre" and his essay "Dingley Dell & The Fleet" in *The Dyer's Hand*, so the first-person speaker of "Vespers" appears to reflect Auden's own aesthetic tastes. In "Vespers," the Arcadian speaker and the Utopian appear to have nothing in common, so they have nothing to say to each other as they walk through the city. Neither one can accept the totality of physical reality as it comes to him: "Passing a slum child with rickets, I look the other way: He looks the other way if he passes a chubby one" (*CP* 637). Both are dualists; their dreams deny that certain realities have any right to existence.

While the beginning of the poem draws attention to the sharp differences between the two positions, the Arcadian speaker wonders near the end whether the meeting was "simply a fortuitous intersection of life-paths, loyal to different fibs? / Or also a rendezvous between two accomplices who, in spite of themselves, cannot resist meeting . . . ?" (*CP* 639). Parenthetically he also asks, "do both, at bottom, desire truth?" (639). The obvious answer is "no," since both are committed to idealistic fictions and must therefore reject reality as it comes to them. Mendelson remarks that the phrase "at bottom" is a pun and "a comic reminder of the body," different aspects of which the Arcadian and Utopian reject (*Later* 355). The meeting between the two also forces both of them "to remember our victim (but for him I could forget the blood, but for me he could forget the innocence), / on whose immolation (call him Abel, Remus, whom you will, it is one Sin Offering) arcadias, utopias, our dear old bag of a democracy are alike founded: / For without a cement of blood (it must be human, it must be innocent) no secular wall will safely stand" (*CP* 639). Their own living bodies and the dead body of the victim are an embarrassment to each dreamer and reveal the sinister side of both fantasies. The Utopian reminds the Arcadian that the ritual sacrifice involves real blood; it cannot be reduced to a merely aesthetic spectacle in which no one really gets hurt. In *The Dyer's Hand*, Auden notes that, in every imagined Eden, "Whatever people do, whether alone or in company, is some kind of play" (411). So without the Utopian's presence, the Arcadian could go on pretending that the sacrificial murder—the *acte gratuit*—is only a symbolic game, not a physical reality. Likewise, the Arcadian's existence reminds the Utopian that the sacrificial victim is innocent. The Utopian would like to pretend that anyone who is excluded from the New Jerusalem deserves expulsion, and that those who die are manifestly guilty of capital crimes against his Utopia. But, like Herod in "For the Time Being," he finds that certain victims are innocent and that he must grudgingly go ahead with the execution anyway, violating the very principle of rational justice on which he wants to build his state. As Jan Curtis argues, "What unnerves the Arcadian and the Utopian and momentarily shatters their dreams of escaping history is the remembrance of the Paschal meal of evening prayer presided over by a powerless Messiah who experiences the ambiguities of history and falls into the abyss of death" (205). Both dreams are untenable fantasies that cannot acknowledge the reality of the crucifixion because they are unable to look at the fallen, physical world without either denying the most self-evident aspects of reality or questioning their own ideals.

Since neither regression to Eden nor progression to the New Jerusalem can resolve the conflicts between the *I* and the *self*, the next poem, "Compline," represents a personal attempt to address guilt through self-assessment and confession. The poem mirrors the first poem in the sequence, "Prime," in form and content. Both are written in a similar syllabic meter and stanzas of alternating longer and shorter lines,[15] and both examine the semi-conscious state between sleeping and waking, but while "Prime" is about waking up, "Compline" is about falling asleep. As the speaker falls asleep, the body escapes the control of the conscious will and enters the self-regulated state that the dream scene in "Nones" had depicted. However, "Compline" focuses on the ruminations of the ego as it struggles to remember a definitive past event that is now lost to conscious memory. As the speaker falls asleep, he expects "The instant of recollection / When the whole thing makes sense," but the memories come only in fragments, "And I fail to see either plot / Or meaning; I cannot remember / A thing between noon and three" (*CP* 640). In the context of the canonical hours, the event that the speaker cannot remember is the crucifixion and death of Christ, traditionally held to have occurred at noon and three o'clock, respectively. By implication, the speaker cannot remember his own guilty participation in a reenactment of that murder.

In his essay in *Modern Canterbury Pilgrims*, Auden comments on the relationship between memory and liturgical reenactment: "It is easy to forget, particularly if I do not wish to remember, what I thought or felt yesterday, but it is difficult to forget what I did. Even mere routine has its value, as a reminder" (*Prose III* 579). So, for example, "a man may go to confession in a frivolous state of mind, rattle off some sins without feeling any real contrition, and go away to commit them again, but as long as he keeps up the habit he cannot forget that there are certain actions which the Church calls sinful, and that he has committed them . . ." (579–80). A liturgy, Auden argues, requires active participation from everyone, so it serves as an aid to memory (579–80). The whole of "Horae Canonicae," despite Auden's initial plan to write "secular" poems, is an exercise in a liturgical recovery of memory that suggests the contrition of Augustine's *Confessions* as much as the free-association of psychoanalysis, hence the efforts of the speaker in "Compline" to recall what he did "between noon and three." In the second stanza the speaker is drifting further into sleep, and the ego has become almost completely unaware of his body, though what awareness he has left maintains the body's otherness. He is aware only of "A heart's rhythm, a sense of stars"; the phrase "*a* heart" rather than the expected "*my* heart" emphasizes the body's detachment from the conscious ego (*CP* 640). But in the next lines the speaker reclaims the heart as his own, suggesting that "maybe / My heart is confessing her part / In what happened to us from noon till three" (640). In phrasing reminiscent of Poe's short story "The Tell-Tale Heart,"[16] the speaker sup-poses that the sound of the heartbeat is itself a signal and admission of guilt, and further, that his heart is leading him to a Dantean Paradise among the stars. But the speaker immediately punctures what he calls such "vain fornications of fancy" (*CP* 640). The phrase is a translation of Augustine's phrase *fantastica fornicatio*, a version of which Auden had used previously in Simeon's speech in "For the Time Being." Here, the speaker uses the phrase to suggest that his imaginations, however pleasant, are perversions. He has imagined that his heart is automatically confessing with-out the ego's willing it to do so, implicitly absolving the ego of any responsibility to admit its own culpability. The speaker's fancy has taken a distinctly Manichean turn, since it makes the body solely responsibility for evil and releases the conscious mind from guilt. It has further implied that one's own body may become the scape-goat whose rejection merits the soul's ascent into Paradise among the stars. Such a thought, the poet says, is nothing but the imagination fornicating with itself.

The proper response to the body, and to the cosmos to which the body attests, consists of "blessing them both / For the sweetness of their cassations" (*CP* 640). Auden's technique of doubling is particularly thick here: "both" refers to the heart and the stars, and the word "cassation" has two meanings, both of which are relevant to the heart and the stars. According to the *Oxford English Dictionary*, the word "cassation" denotes the action of making null and void, but the word is also the name of a type of eighteenth-century instrumental music similar to a serenade. The heart's rhythm in the beginning of the stanza suggests music, and the heart has also, through its ostensible confession, nullified the ego's pride and reawoken its sense of guilt. The stars, on the other hand, are the source of the music of the spheres in the Ptolemaic cosmos, though the stars' distance from the ego suggests the possibil-ity of a blessedness available only through a contrition and confession that would nullify its guilt. The speaker rightly blesses his own physicality, represented by his heart, and the physical world outside himself, represented by the stars, because their manifest existence does not let him forget that there are things and people apart from himself whose existences are holy.

The third stanza edges closer to the total unconsciousness of sleep, which the speaker describes as "one step to nothing" (*CP* 641). "For the end," he says, "for me as for cities, / Is total absence: what comes to be / Must go back into non-being / For the sake of the equity, the rhythm / Past measure or comprehending" (641). Auden's language here recalls Augustine's description of the passage of time, as he details in the *Confessions*: "What then is time? Provided that no one asks me, I know. . . . I con-fidently affirm myself to know that if nothing passes away, there is no past time, and if nothing arrives, there is no future time, and if nothing existed there would be no present time. Take the two tenses, past and future. How can they "be" when the past is not now present and the future is not present? . . . If then, in order to be time at all, the present is so made that it passes into the past, how can we say that this present also "is"? The cause of its being is that it will cease to be. So indeed we cannot truly say that time exists except in the sense that it tends towards non-existence" (trans. Chadwick 11.14).[17] In this passage, Augustine attempts to make sense of his own existence in time, and while he eventually comes to some provisional conclusions about the nature of time, his hypotheses also involve a hesitancy that admits, in Auden's words, that the matter is "past measure or comprehending" (*CP* 641). Augustine recognizes, and Auden follows him here, that the existing present continually disappears into the non-being of the past, which then exists only in memory.

However, certain memories are not easily accessible to the consciousness. The speaker in Auden's poem cannot remember his guilty act until he learns to pray, even in the most pedestrian language, for himself, for his lover ("dear C," a reference to Auden's intimate friend and sometime lover Chester Kallman), "And all poor s-o-b's who never / Do anything properly . . ." (*CP* 641). It is a prayer for mercy, as the speaker asks, "spare / Us in the youngest day when all are / Shaken awake, facts are facts" (641). The speaker has shifted from the first-person singular *I* of the previous stanzas into the first-person plural *Us*, which indicates that he is learning to regard other people as equally important as himself, and in his identification with others in confession, he "shall know exactly what happened / Today between noon and three" (641). His confession now involves his full consciousness and volition, and it therefore results in the promise of redemption, which Auden pictures as "com[ing] to the picnic / With nothing to hide" (641). He ends the poem with a particularly Dantean image of redemption as a dance, which "moves in perichoresis, / Turns about the abiding tree" (641). "Perichoresis" is a theological term of Greek origin, literally meaning a turning or revolving but used figuratively to describe "the interrelationship or interpenetration of the Persons of the Trinity; the manner in which the three Persons are regarded as conjoined or interlinked without each one's distinct identity being lost" ("Perichoresis," *OED*).[18] It is analogous to Charles Williams's term "co-inherence," and the idea (though not by that name) was vigorously defended by Augustine, Athanasius, and a host of other patristic theologians. Auden's use here is appropriate given his association of the term's literal meaning with Dante's image of Paradise as a circular dance, and it evokes the idea, always attractive to Auden, of a peaceful unification without erasure of difference, not only at the divine level, but also at the human, social level, and most especially at the individual, psychological level.

Several important themes from "Compline" are reiterated in the last poem of the sequence, "Lauds," which Mendelson characterizes as a "naïve-sounding prayer for blessing, made possible by a free admission of guilt, [which] is phrased with Auden's subtlest skill" (*Later* 358). Mendelson observes that the people on whom the poet asks blessing are neither isolated individuals nor an anonymous public, but "a Realm—a *royaume*—ruled by a person, and . . . a People, a plurality made up of persons" (358). The poem reveals a peaceful consonance between the natural world, represented by the crowing cock and the singing birds, and the historical human world, represented by the mass bell and the mill wheel. The most prominent theme of the poem is the implicit resolution of social conflicts that were explored earlier in the sequence, especially in "Nones" and "Vespers," as the poet envisions the possibility that "Men of their neighbors become sensible," and that the public and private worlds might co-exist peacefully, an idea repeated in every stanza by the refrain, "*in solitude, for company*" (*CP* 642). While the poem uses the pastoral images of an Eden arranged to Auden's tastes—he had identified waterwheels as form of technology acceptable to the Arcadian in "Vespers"—it does not slip back into the blithe Arcadian fantasies that Auden had ironically portrayed in "Vespers." On its own the poem might sound merely sentimental, but following as it does a long, disquieting meditation on murder and guilt, it comes as the relieved denouement after the confessional climax at the end of "Compline." It reminds the reader that the whole sequence is based on a liturgical pattern, and "Lauds" is the doxology that both ends the sequence and offers a new beginning for the cycle.

"PRECIOUS FIVE"

It took Auden five years to finish all the poems for "Horae Canonicae." The first poems he wrote were "Prime" in 1949 and "Nones" in 1950, both of which he published in the volume *Nones* with no indication that he was planning to place them in a larger sequence. The rest of the poems for the sequence were written in the early 1950s, but while Auden was still developing his ideas for "Horae Canonicae" in the late 1940s, he wrote many other short poems, including two that are especially notable for their focus on the goodness of human embodiment: "Precious Five" and "Memorial for the City." The two, written within a year of each other, touch on the corrupted goodness of the human body that Auden was soon to examine at greater length in "Horae Canonicae"; they address the nature of human embodiment more directly and thus offer a clearer, though less intense picture of Auden's sense of the benefits of embodiment.

"Precious Five" is arranged as an address to the poet's own sensory organs—nose, ears, hands, eyes, and tongue—which are undergoing a process of recognizing the goodness that is always present in the surrounding world, knowledge of which is inaccessible to the conscious ego except through the mediation of the body's senses. At the same time, Auden is also addressing each of the sense organs as synecdoches of the body as a whole, which must assist the conscious ego's process of training and discipline in order to accept the intimations of goodness communicated by the body. The nose, for example, becomes a metaphor for the whole body's mediation between the physical world and the ego: "In anxious times you serve / As bridge from mouth to brow, / An asymmetric curve / Thrust outward from a face / Time-conscious into space" (*CP* 587–88). The nose is a reminder that the whole body is an extension in both space and time, an observation reminiscent of passages in book 11 of the *Confessions* in which Augustine contemplates the nature of time as extension of physical existence across temporal space, but it is also here a punning symbol of the connection, or "bridge," between the physical and the cognitive aspects of the person, between the appetites, represented by the mouth, and the consciousness, represented by the brow. At the end of the first stanza, the nose also becomes a sign of purgatorial hope: "Point, then, for honor's sake / Up the storm-beaten slope / From memory to hope / The way you cannot take" (*CP* 588). The poem returns to the image of Mount Purgatory that Auden had introduced several years before in *New Year Letter,* and the purgatorial climb retains the earlier poem's emphasis on the correction of the soul rather than the body. The fact that the body cannot follow the purgatorial way is an implicit rejection of Manichean dualism that Auden had attacked in "The Sea and the Mirror" for placing the blame for evil on the body. It is the conscious ego, not the unconscious body, that must undergo the process of purification through which it will become capable of apprehending the truth that the body constantly senses in the surrounding world. Like Augustine, Auden locates sin in the psyche and insists that the body itself is not responsible for sin, though it is necessarily corrupted by sin. Such ideas are consistent both with his Augustinian theology and with his theory of illness as psychosomatic, which he got from John Layard and Homer Lane in the 1920s and 1930s; Auden had always suspected that bodily diseases were products of psychological defects.

The second stanza, addressed to the ears, reemphasizes that human corruption is located primarily in the ego. The ears are called upon by "The paranoiac mind" to affirm its self-delusions, since "it cannot take pure fiction, / And what it wants from you / Are rumors partly true" (*CP* 588). The ego, retaining as it does a measure of its original goodness, does not wish to be completely deceived about the nature of reality, but it would like the body to misrepresent reality in accordance with its preconceived notions of what reality ought to be. In order to resist the temptation to misperception, the ears must "Go back again to school, / Drudge patiently" in order to perceive that all sounds are "natural, not one / Fantastic or banal" (588). The ears, being easy to deceive, must undergo a process of training. But this statement seems to contradict the indication in the previous stanza that the body cannot ascend Mount Purgatory. Either the body can participate in the redemption of the whole person or it cannot. The poem does not suggest any easy resolution to the question, but the different images with which Auden describes the redemptive process offer a clue. Auden imagines the purgation of the ego as a journey up Mount Purgatory, whereas he imagines the training of the body as a school. The two processes are analogous but not identical since the image of Mount Purgatory suggests that the ego requires a theological and ultimately spiritual reformation in order to reorder and reorient its passions, desires, and loves while the body needs information and technical training in order to do better that which it already does naturally. That is, the metaphor of purgation suggests a correction of the desires and the will whereas the metaphor of a school suggests a correction of defects in skill. Their training complete, the ears will "Dance with angelic grace, / In ecstasy and fun," an image that does suggest Dante's *Paradiso* in which the saints dance to the music of the spheres (588). It seems that the purgation of the ego and the training of the body are different but analogous means to the same paradisal end.[19] In the state of perfection, the ears, and by implication the entire body, may "do what you will" (*CP* 588), an echo of Augustine's famous statement, "Love, and do as you will" (*Homilies on the First Epistle of John* 7.8). That is, once the will is completely purified, what is willed is by definition identical with what is good.

Although all the senses, not just the ears, must undergo a similar training in order to convey the goodness of existence to the generally uncooperative ego, the senses have always been naturally predisposed to recognize goodness in the physical world. The mind is always tempted to solipsism by regarding only itself as real, but the eyes continually remind the mind that other objects also have real existence: "True seeing is believing / (What sight can never prove) / There is a world to see: / Look outward, eyes, and love / Those eyes you cannot be" (*CP* 590). As Augustine once remarked, "a man cannot love that which he does not believe to exist" (*On Christian Doctrine* 1.41). Once the ego through the eyes recognizes the existence of other people as legitimate and good, the whole person is enabled to extend unselfish love to those other people. While the eyes naturally recognize other objects, the tongue, like the ears, must undergo a process of training. The tongue—and here Auden revives a medieval trope of addressing this sensory organ according to its productive function rather than its receptive function—has to train itself to "Praise . . . the Earthly Muse / . . . / Praise Her revolving wheel / Of appetite and season" (*CP* 590). Several years before in "In Memory of W. B. Yeats," Auden had asserted that the poet should "teach the free man how to praise" without saying what exactly should be praised (249). Here the poet clearly identifies the object of praise as physical existence. The attempt to praise is more important than an achieved perfection, for "Although your style be fumbling, / Half stutter and half song, / Give thanks however bumbling" (590). The injunction recalls what Auden had said at the end of "For the Time Being," that in the ordinary time between the initial vision and the final consummation, "the Spirit must practice his scales of rejoicing" (400). Here in "Precious Five" the poet is more specific about the content of that rejoicing, since the tongue must praise even human appetites, including the sexual appetite represented by "his twin, your brother / Unlettered, savage, dumb, / Down there below the waist" (590). No natural aspect of the body, no matter how corrupted or difficult to live with, is excluded from the tongue's halting hymn.

It is not necessary that the self, or the ego for that matter, know *why* it should give thanks for existence. The final stanza urges, "Be happy, precious five, / So long as I'm alive / Nor try to ask me what / You should be happy for" (*CP* 590). The poem suggests that purely physical reasons for happiness, such as sex, alcohol, and material comforts, are mere rationalizations, since the ego is incapable of offering a compelling reason to do that which it intuits is right and good to do. The ego could also rationalize anger and despair, but the poem's speaker admits that the physical world outside himself merely reasserts "That singular command / I do not understand, / *Bless what there is for being,* / Which has to be obeyed . . ." (591, emphasis in original). One early Auden critic has identified this command as one articulation of Auden's poetic center of gravity, maintaining that "*the* central Auden belief . . . , beyond any doubt, would be 'Life remains a blessing', or '*Bless what there is for being*'" (Replogle 49). The line "Life remains a blessing" comes from "As I Walked Out One Evening" (*CP* 135), written in 1937, though Auden reiterates the injunction on several other occasions. In the 1940 poem "In Sickness and in Health," the speaker insists that there "comes a voice / Which utters an absurd command— Rejoice" (319), and in "The Temptation of St. Joseph" from "For the Time Being," the Narrator states, "To choose what is difficult all one's days / As if it were easy, that is faith. Joseph, Praise" (365). The command to praise the goodness of embodiment lies at the core of Auden's convictions, even though the attempt to obey it is always problematic, first because the conflicting desires of the fragmented consciousness make consistency in action and motive impossible, and then because the reason for the command is incomprehensible to the rational mind. But in "Precious Five," the ego must finally ask, "What else am I made for, / Agreeing or disagreeing?" (591). The poet may accept or reject the command, but he cannot finally dismiss the recognition that he has been created with a natural inclination to praise what is good. The passive voice subtly obscures the theological implications of the poem; it suggests that "I am made" by somebody who is not named in the poem but whose presence is implied by the very existence of the physical world and by the goodness that is perceptible in it.

Fuller suggests that in the poem's ending "the theological position is one of Leibnizian optimism" (*Commentary* 430). The optimism of Leibniz—that the present world is the best of all possible worlds that God could have created—seems to be the rational basis of the imperative praise. But surely this is almost the opposite of what Auden is saying, for the poem indicates that the existence of any compelling reason for praise is inscrutable and inaccessible to human reason. It is an act of pure faith to assert that there is a reason at all, just as it is an act of faith to believe "What sight can never prove," that the objective world of matter and sense really exists and is not just an illusion (*CP* 590). Further, the fact of the Fall, which the poem takes for granted, means if nothing else that the present world could have been better than it now is. Given the poem's reliance on distinctly Augustinian conceptions of the goodness of the physical world and its reference to a central principle in Augustine's thought, "Love, and do as you will," the poem's final, tentative optimism remains closer to Augustine than to Leibniz.

"THANKSGIVING FOR A HABITAT" AND LATER POEMS

Mendelson explains that "Horae Canonicae" and other poems of the late 1940s and early 1950s had "emphasized the body but said nothing 'coolly realistic' about the facts of bodily needs" (*Later* 443), so in the late 1950s Auden set out to write a series of poems about his new home in Kirchstetten, Austria, in which he had recently settled. The house was a natural subject for a sequence in which he wished to explore the facts of corporeal existence; as Mendelson observes, "A house is a frame and an extension of the body . . ." (443). Auden said something very similar in a 1971 essay in which he remarked on the difference between the conscious *I* and the *self,* the latter being "both physical and mental, which I am inhabiting like a house or driving like a motor car" ("Pride and Prayer" 7). Auden's meditations on his house in "Thanksgiving for a Habitat" represent a reinvigorated interest in human embodiment, so it is fitting that explicit references to Augustine's ontology of good and evil appear throughout the sequence, reinforcing Auden's belief in the innate goodness of physical, created things despite their corruption. As Callan suggests, "An alternative title for this cycle might be 'Against the Manichees'; for it provides a poetic counterpart for the thesis against the Manichean-Gnostic imagination that pervades his criticism . . ." (241). The sequence contains several direct references to Augustine's ideas about the nature of good and evil—we have seen previously that the postscript to one of these poems, "The Cave of Making" (*CP* 695), refers to the Augustinian definition of evil as a privation. Another poem in the sequence, "For Friends Only," written about the guest room, contains a pun on Augustine's definition of evil. In the poem, Auden comments on the necessity of maintaining friendships through frequent visits and regrets the frequent good-byes: "absence will not seem an evil / If it make our re-meeting / A real occasion. Come when you can" (707). The statement that "absence will not seem an evil" is a witty reversal of the Augustinian theory that evil consists of an absence of good.

The correlative Augustinian position on the goodness of the physical body most clearly underpins the sixth poem of the sequence, "The Geography of the House."[20] The poem is about the toilet, and it draws comparisons between artistic production and the production of the bowels. After citing Martin Luther's inspirations in the privy and the posture of Rodin's *The Thinker,* Auden states, "All the Arts derive from / This ur-act of making, / Private to the artist: / Makers' lives are spent / Striving in their chosen / Medium to produce a / De-narcissus-ised en- / -during excrement" (*CP* 699). Defecation parallels the process of artistic making on a number of Freudian levels—the production of an object out of oneself, the preference for privacy, the socially unacceptable fascination of the maker for the product. This stanza develops the analogy further, as the physical nature of artistic production and the biological facts of embodied existence both prevent the poet's work from slipping into the total abstractions of Manichean dualism that would denigrate the body and, by implication, the act of artistic production. The artist must never forget that he lives in a physical body and in a physical world inhabited by other people with physical bodies. Even in the early 1960s when this poem was written, electronic communication devices like radio, film, and television, as well as hygienic technology from washing machines to deodorants, were making it increasingly easy to act as if the body were a superfluous accessory to the mind. In earlier ages, Auden notes, it was harder to forget the less attractive aspects of embodiment, as he suggests in a parenthetical stanza near the end of the poem: "(Orthodoxy ought to / Bless our modern plumbing: / Swift and St Augustine / Lived in centuries / When a stench of sewage / Ever in the nostrils / Made a strong debating / Point for Manichees)" (700). Before modern innovations in sanitation, the claim that human embodiment was good was hard to support with concrete evidence, but Auden points out that Augustine's insistence that the body is fundamentally good, though now corrupted by the Fall, should be easier to accept now that modern technology has made embodied life more pleasant and comfortable. At least, physical comfort appears to have made it easier for Auden personally to accept Augustine's doctrine of the body's goodness, despite his often squalid living conditions.

Auden's exposition of the goodness of the body extends into a later poem in the sequence "The Cave of Nakedness." The poem is not about sex, as the title might imply, but about the way in which the bedroom reveals the difference between the public and private selves. The bedroom signifies the absolutely private realm where a person can "switch from personage, / with a state number, a first and family name, / to the naked Adam or Eve. . ." (*CP* 711). In a scene that resembles "Lauds" from "Horae Canonicae," the poem ends in the morning twilight when a sleeper awakes as songbirds "express / in the old convention they inherit that joy in beginning / for which our species was created, and declare it / good" (712). The declaration that creation is "good" refers, of course, to the creation story of Genesis 1 in which God repeatedly calls his creations "good." The sleeper in the poem offers his own compliment to the body: "We may not be obliged—though it is mannerly—to bless / the Trinity that we are corporal contraptions, / but only a villain will omit to thank Our Lady or / her hen-wife, Dame Kind, as he, she, or both ensemble, / emerge from a private cavity to be re-born, / re-neighbored in the Country of Consideration" (712). While "Prime" in "Horae Canonicae" had pictured the process of awakening as a reenactment of the Fall, "The Cave of Nakedness" pictures the same process as a positive re-creation that enables neighborly love. "Dame Kind" is Auden's name for the natural world of causal necessity, and "Our Lady" and "Dame Kind" represent the spiritual and physical sources of human identity, respectively. The aphoristic "Postscript" to the poem does hint that the Fall continues to occur: "Only look in the glass to detect a removable blemish: / As for the permanent ones, already you know quite enough" (713). The "permanent blemishes" include interior flaws that do not appear in a mirror because they are spiritual rather than physical. The body's flaws, by contrast, are not permanent, nor are they detrimental to the soul's aspirations to virtue. As another aphorism in the "Postscript" says, "Our bodies cannot love: But, without one, / What works of love could we do?" (713). The body is the necessary instrument by which the person makes contact with the world.

Some time later, Auden revisited the themes of "Thanksgiving for a Habitat," and particularly "The Geography of the House" in another poem, "Ode to the Medieval Poets" (1971), in which he expresses his amazement that poets like Chaucer and Langland achieved so much given their limited resources: "how on earth did you ever manage, / without anaesthetics or plumbing, / . . . / . . . to write so cheerfully, / with no grimaces or self-pathos?" (*CP* 863). One would expect that an age of physical danger and political turmoil would produce literature whose main topics would include wars, plagues, pain, corruption, and despair, while an age of physical comfort would produce literature praising the beauties and comforts of the physical world, but Auden finds that the reverse is true. "Our makers," he says, referring to modern writers and artists, "beset by every creature comfort, / immune, they believe, to all superstitions, / even at their best are so often morose or / kinky, petrified by their gorgon egos" (863). In "Thanksgiving for a Habitat," Auden had identified the fourth and eighteenth centuries, the ages of Augustine and Swift respectively, as eras when physical discomforts made Manichaeism attractive, but in this later poem he depicts the Middle Ages as a time when the poetic celebrations of the physical world coincided with notably harsh living conditions. A younger Auden might have tried to account for the fact by referencing some theory of historical development, but here he accepts it as an impenetrable historical mystery. He does suggest that the artistic neuroses of the present age may be linked to the mechanization of the modern world, but as in "Thanksgiving for a Habitat," Auden observes that modern technology has had some benefits as well. He admits that he could not own printed books were it not for the mechanized age in which he lives, for "Without its heartless / engines, though, you could not tenant my book-shelves, / on hand to delect my ear and chuckle / my sad flesh . . ." (863). Although Auden had been fascinated by mining technology as a child, his later attitudes toward technology were mixed. He did object strongly to certain forms of technology—atom bombs and jukeboxes were favorite targets—but he also recognized some of the potentially dehumanizing effects of the modern machine age. Like the body, technologies for Auden were generally neutral instruments that could be used for good or evil purposes.

Despite all manner of physical comforts, modern artists and writers display profound discomfort with everything around them. When Auden refers to contemporary authors as "morose," "kinky," and "petrified," he may or may not have been including himself in such categories; throughout his prolific career he had written poems which might well be described in just those terms. But during the last few years of his life, he continued his conscious efforts to defend the innate goodness of physical existence against what he saw as an ever-present tendency in the modern world toward Manichean dualism. Just a few months before his death in 1973, Auden wrote in "No, Plato, No," "I can't imagine anything / that I would less like to be / than a disincarnate Spirit, / unable to chew or sip / or make contact with surfaces / or breathe the scents of summer / or comprehend speech and music / or gaze at what lies beyond" (*CP* 888). Auden had sharply criticized Platonism many times, perhaps most clearly in *New Year Letter,* for its suspicion of bodily existence and its trajectory toward disembodiment as an intellectual ideal. Earlier, he had gone further in *The Dyer's Hand,* asserting, "If we were suddenly to become disembodied spirits, a few might behave better than before, but most of us would behave very much worse" (99).

The language of the poem is very similar to a statement that Augustine made in *On Christian Doctrine* debunking desire for disembodiment: "that which some say, that they would rather be without a body, arises from a complete delusion: they hate not their bodies but the corruption and solidity of their bodies. They do not wish to have no bodies at all but rather incorruptible and most agile bodies, and they think that no body could be so constituted because then it would be a spirit" (1.24). Auden's poem also follows Augustine's critique of Platonism in the *City of God,* in which Augustine declares, "anyone [e.g. a Platonist] who exalts the soul as the Supreme Good, and censures the nature of flesh as something evil, is in fact carnal alike in his cult of the soul and in his revulsion from the flesh, since this attitude is prompted by human folly, not by divine truth" (14.5). Auden tended to conflate Platonism and Manichaeism in his writings, and while Augustine also saw some similarities between the two, he did make a clear distinction between Platonism and Manichaeism in a subsequent passage: "The Platonists, to be sure, do not show quite the folly of the Manicheans. They do not go so far as to execrate earthly bodies as the natural substance of evil . . ." (14.5). But Auden recognized that both Platonism and Manichaeism arose from a similar supposition that the immaterial was inherently superior to the physical, and since the term "Platonist" did not have quite the derogatory connotations of "Manichean" in the modern world, Auden seems to have preferred the latter term as a general epithet for any dualism, including Platonism, that involved a suspicion of human embodiment.

Another late reference to Augustine also touches on the nature of human embodiment. The reference appears in "Aubade," written in 1972 and dedicated to Eugen Rosenstock-Huessy, the historiographer whose work Auden had championed and whose ideas also appear in some of the charts Auden constructed in preparation for "Horae Canonicae" (see Mendelson, *Later* 311–13). "Aubade" returns to the subject matter which "Prime" had treated, the process of waking up. Despite the similarity in subject, the tone of "Aubade" is less intense and treats the event positively. The poem records the moment at which the speaker is "expelled from the padded cell / of Sleep and re-admitted / to involved Humanity" (*CP* 881). Waking up is now pictured as a release from an insane asylum of sleep, in which the ego has been imprisoned, powerless to command the body, and the waking human is now capable of entering into meaningful relationships with other people. Such relationships are predicated on both embodiment and self-consciousness, which Auden describes with a quotation from the *Confessions*: "as wrote Augustine, / I know that I am and will, / I am willing and knowing, / I will to be and to know" (*CP* 881, c.f. *Confessions* 13.11). As Augustine asserts in the *City of God*, "it is as certain that no one would wish himself not to exist as it is that no one would wish himself not to be happy. For existence is a necessary condition for happiness" (11.26). Both Augustine and Auden believed that there is within the human person a natural impulse toward continued existence and toward knowledge and happiness, and "Aubade" views those impulses as positive starting points for healthy relationships with the world outside the self.

BETWEEN THE BEGINNING of Auden's return to Christian faith in the late 1930s and the composition of his long poems in the early and mid-1940s, his use of Augustine's ideas and language appears frequently when he discusses the nature of evil. But when he turns to an examination of the goodness of the created world, an idea he clearly affirmed at that time, his affirmations of embodiment as good are more obliquely related to Augustine's thought, as they rely on intuitions that predate his return to Christianity. Shortly after his conversion, Auden did write some poetry that affirms physical existence as good, but he seldom stated the idea in Augustine's language, as he did with the definition of evil as privation. By the late 1940s, the situation reverses itself. Auden's references to evil become less explicitly Augustinian, even though his views on the subject did not change substantially between 1939 and his death in 1973, but his poetic references to the intrinsic goodness of physicality become far more frequent and also tend to include clear and direct references to Augustine. The reasons for this shift in emphasis are complex, but some of the change may be attributed to the simple fact that, once Auden felt that he had satisfactorily resolved a philosophical question, he tended not to write about the issue extensively afterward. But Auden's historical situation suggests an additional reason. The years during which Auden's poetry focuses most on the nature of evil coincide almost exactly with Hitler's reign in Germany—he came to power in 1933 and died in 1945. Soon after the end of World War II, Auden's theological poems contain many more clear affirmations of the goodness of created existence. Once the political threat of Nazi Germany disappeared, Auden relaxed the psychological tensions that fascism's presence had urged him to maintain, and that relaxation is reflected both in his shift from metrical feet to syllabic lines, and in his shift in emphasis from examining the nature of evil to praising the goodness of physical existence.

During the war, Auden had been interested in the immediate political ramifications of his newfound Christianity, and after the war he continued his inquiry into Christianity's relationship with the world of civic responsibility and physical necessities. In an essay in *The Dyer's Hand*, published well after World War II ended, Auden remarked, "The wicked man is not worldly, but anti-worldly. . ." (205). In his 1966 review of E. R. Dodds's book *Pagan and Christian in an Age of Anxiety*, Auden observed that orthodox Christianity always includes an implicit affirmation of the goodness of physicality: "Despite appearances to the contrary, the Christian faith, by virtue of its doctrines about creation, the nature of man and the revelation of Divine purpose in historical time, was really a more this-worldly religion than any of its [classical] competitors, so that, when its opportunity came in the following centuries with the collapse of civil government in the West, it was the Church which took on the task of creating such social order and of preserving such cultural heritage as there was. On the evidence of its history, it would seem that Christianity has always been more tempted by worldliness, by love of money and power than, say, Islam or Buddhism" (*FA* 47). Auden recognized from the beginning of his return to the church that Christianity affirmed the existence of the physical, temporal world, and as he told Clement Greenberg in a 1944 letter, the Christian faith is the opposite of "a withdrawal from the world. (Jesus said My kingdom is not of *this* world. He did not say of *the* world.)" (qtd. in Kirsch, *Auden* 21). Auden's theological forays sometimes indulged in abstractions, but he was always attracted to theology that had strong implications for honest, physical engagement with the world.

Augustine bolstered Auden's assertion that it was primarily the body's extension of the human person in space and time that allowed for a rich variety of contacts with the world of nature and of other persons. As Auden asks rhetorically in "Thanksgiving for a Habitat," "Our bodies cannot love: / But, without one, / What works of Love could we do?" (*CP* 713). It was impossible, Auden found, to take moral responsibility for one's actions without asserting that the body was a good and necessary instrument for those actions. The command to love one's neighbor, which Auden always took very seriously in both his writings and his personal life, was rooted in the recognition that human embodiment was created by God to be good in every way. At the same time, human life as we know it is terribly marred and requires redemption, which humans cannot effect for themselves. In his last poem, "Archaeology," Auden comments on archaeological discoveries unearthing an ancient record of human destruction and cruelty: "From Archaeology / one moral, at least, may be drawn, / . . . / What they call History / is nothing to vaunt of, / being made, as it is, / by the criminal in us . . ." (896–97). The historical record is primarily a fragmentary account of broken humanity, but history is not the last word, either in human existence or in Auden's poem. Instead, the last line of his last poem states simply, "goodness is timeless" (897).

3. EROS AND AGAPE

Some of Auden's best-known poems are love poems. From his first major poetic efforts in his 1928 verse play *Paid on Both Sides,* which involves a struggle between family loyalty and marital love, to his lyrics of the late 1930s such as "Lullaby" and "As I Walked Out One Evening," to post-conversion poems like "In Praise of Limestone" and "'The Truest Poetry Is the Most Feigning,'" Auden's poetry repeatedly returns to the conflicts between different kinds of love.[1] His poetry is often concerned with the troubled relationship between friendship and sex, and after his return to Christianity, the question of how God relates to them both vexes and energizes his poetry. From the beginning, Auden did recognize a difference between the selfish love epitomized by sexual desire and the altruistic love epitomized in friendship between equals, and his poetry from the 1930s exhibits regret and guilt that the two forms of love never manage to coexist permanently. In the early 1940s, he aspired to a purified form of love inspired by his reading of Denis de Rougemont, who mediated an Augustinian view of love that Auden was also encountering in Charles Norris Cochrane. Auden's homosexuality complicated his theological aspirations considerably, and he eventually became doubtful about his ability to live up to his early, post-conversion enthusiasm about the possibilities of transforming his erotic desire into divine love. By the time he reached middle age, he had largely given up his attempts to reconcile his sexuality and his religion, although both remained significant elements of his personality.

Auden's early poetry uses the word "love" ambiguously, though the context in which he uses the word typically suggests a distinction between "love" in the sense of selfish, acquisitive desire and "love" in the sense of a self-giving, reciprocal relationship, which might or might not include sex or even the close friendship of philia. As he began his return to Christianity at the end of the 1930s, Auden began to use the Greek terms *eros* and *agape* to distinguish between these two different types of love. In his 1944 review of Cochrane's *Christianity and Classical Culture,* a book that heavily emphasizes Augustinian theology as a corrective to late classical philosophy, Auden defines these terms: "The doctrine of the Trinity is the theological formulation of the Christian belief that God is Love, and that by Love is meant not Eros but Agape, i.e., not a desire to get possession of something one lacks, but a reciprocal relation, not an everlastingly 'given' state, but a dynamic free expression; an unchanging love is a continually novel decision to love" (*FA* 35–36). As Auden used the term after about 1940, *eros* designates a basically acquisitive desire that seeks its own gratification and, consequently, its own cessation, for once desire is satisfied, it ceases to exist. Eros is a form of love that very often expresses itself as sexual desire, even though it can just as easily be a desire for fame, possessions, or power. As Auden would describe it, eros is rooted in the biological survival instinct, which drives an organism to acquire sustenance and to reproduce. It is quite different from agape, which is more difficult to define exactly, but which Auden generally describes as a conscious and deliberate attempt to do good to another person, and for Auden it is always based on the recognition that the other person is equal in value to all other human beings, oneself included. For Augustine no less than Auden, the willfulness of agape is of vital importance, as Cochrane explains: "Translated into terms of psychology, the doctrine of grace resolves itself into the doctrine that 'my love is my weight' and that the greater love is ultimately irresistible. As such, the working of the spirit emerges, not as magic but, in the deepest and truest sense of the word, as 'natural law.' Accordingly, it may be described as *ardor caritatis,* or *ignis voluntatis,* the 'heat of love,' or the 'flame of will.' Its efficacy as a means of salvation thus depends upon the assumption that the image of God, i.e. of the creative and moving principle, has not been wholly effaced from the hearts even of unbelievers" (453).[2]

Cochrane's description of Augustine's view of love alludes to one of Augustine's most famous statements on the subject, which comes near the end of the *Confessions* and emphasizes the necessity of proper motivation for love by likening love to physical weight—Augustine always thinks of love in terms of the physical world, never as a pure abstraction. Augustine states, "In Thy Gift we rest; there we enjoy Thee. Our rest is our place. Love lifts us up thither. . . . The body by its own weight strives toward its own place. Weight makes not downward only, but to his own place" (13.9). Here Augustine refers to the conventional physics of his day, in which it was supposed that each of the four elements—earth, water, air, and fire— naturally gravitated toward its proper place in relation to the other three, moving up or down as its own nature compelled it. Augustine explains, "When out of their order, [the elements] are restless; restored to order, they are at rest. My weight is my love; thereby am I borne, whithersoever I am borne" (13.9). In Augustine's view, it is as true of the human soul as it is of physics that an object out of place will naturally seek its proper place until it comes to rest—a continuation of his statement addressing God at the opening of the *Confessions,* "Thou madest us for Thyself, and our heart is restless, until it repose in Thee" (1.1).[3]

Thus, Augustine explains at the end of the same work, "We are inflamed, by Thy Gift we are kindled; and are carried upwards; we glow inwardly, and go forwards. . . . We glow inwardly with Thy fire, with Thy good fire, and we go; because we go upwards to the peace of Jerusalem. . . . There hath thy good pleasure placed us, that we may desire nothing else, but to abide there for ever" (*Confessions* 13.9). In this passage, which Auden included in the *Viking Book of Aphorisms* (see Spears, *Poetry* 244), Augustine does not distinguish self-interested love from altruistic love, but rather implies through the metaphor of fire that love (Latin *amore*) is both a natural appetite for self-fulfillment (*eros*) and a willful giving of self to the object of affection (*agape*), since fire both consumes fuel and rises to its proper place above the other elements. For Augustine, desire (Latin *cupiditas,* similar to common use of the Greek *eros*) is neither right nor wrong in itself, but when desire operates alone and unchecked it becomes an acquisitive form of self-interest that results in the vices of pride, greed, and lust; desire that is directed and controlled by agape naturally attracts the human person to love God, which results in the love of neighbor. According to Anne Fremantle, Auden was well aware of Augustine's ideas about love when he had a conversation with her that she relates in *W. H. Auden: A Tribute,* which was compiled by Auden's friend Stephen Spender in 1974, a year after Auden's death. Fremantle, with whom Auden eventually edited *The Protestant Mystics,* recalls that Auden at first told her,

> "I avoid the word mystical." "Yet," I countered, "you wrote that '. . . all actions and diversions of people, their greyhound races, their football pools, their clumsy acts of love . . . what are they but the pitiful, maimed expression of that entire passion, the positive tropism of the soul for God'." "Yes, yes," he said, "but Augustine said it first, and better." So I quoted irrequietum est cor nostrum donec requiescat in te ["our heart is restless until it rests in you"] and went on to ask if he agreed with my favorite of all Augustine's remarks, that Virtus est ordo amoris ["virtue is rightly ordered love"]—wasn't that absolutely true for a writer above all? "I think," Wystan said, "that the ideal for the writer is to find that he has a view of reality he shares with everyone else, but knows he sees it uniquely and can express both the unique vision and the shared view and feel he knew this all the time. And the writer must remember—as Augustine also said—'that the truth is neither mine nor his nor another's but belongs to us all, and that we must never account it private to ourselves, lest we be deprived of it'."
> (Spender 91)

This conversation occurred in the early 1960s, and at that point Auden had come to believe that the human soul did naturally and ultimately desire God. It was to this concept of love—eros transformed by agape—that Auden aspired after his return to Christianity. From the beginning of his career as a poet in the late 1920s, he had suspected that his homosexuality was a deceptive and isolating form of self-love. Many of his poems from the late 1920s and 1930s allude to his sexual relations with a variety of short-term partners at Oxford, Berlin, and elsewhere, but those poems also reveal a frustrated desire to reconcile his promiscuous sexuality with his need for friendship. During his return to Christianity in the late 1930s and early 1940s, Auden met and fell in love with a younger man named Chester Kallman, and partly because of that relationship, Auden intellectually settled on a Christian view of love drawn from Augustine, both directly and through some crucial mediating sources.

In 1940, the same year in which he reentered the Anglican communion, Auden read Denis de Rougemont's *Love in the Western World,* which had just been published in an English translation.[4] Auden favorably reviewed Rougemont's book in June 1941, and Donald Pearce, who took a class that Auden taught at Michigan in the fall of 1941, reports that Auden assigned "a new book which he was enthusiastic about by Denis de Rougemont called *Love in the Western World*" (138). The book begins with a close analysis of the legend of Tristan and Isolde, in which Rougemont argues that the two lovers constantly seek out obstructions to their love, so as to heighten their emotional passion at the expense of consummation. Rougemont concludes that the eros that Tristan and Isolde experience is not ultimately desire for companionship or sex, but for disembodiment in death; hence eros is a form of perpetually suffering desire, an idea implicit in the word "passion," or "askesis" as Rougemont sometimes calls it. Rougemont links the Tristan myth to the courtly lyrics of the Troubadours, which share with the Tristan story a prolonged passion without consummation. Such lyrics, Rougemont argues, emerged from the allegorical hymns of the Cathars, a heterodox mystical sect that flourished briefly in southern France during the early Middle Ages but was fiercely persecuted and eventually wiped out by the Roman church.[5] Rougemont argues further that the passionate eros of twelfth-century French lyrics, which began with the Cathars, extended in various forms into the modern novel and nationalist politics of his present day, and that such valorization of mystical eros remains consistent with the principles of ancient Gnostic mysticism,[6] which has always been starkly opposed to the Christian idea of agape as demonstrated in Christian marriage.[7] Rougemont explains that Gnostic mysticism seeks the realization of the mystic's own divine nature, whereas orthodox mysticism aspires to an "epithalamic" union between the mystic and God in which the distinction between creature and creator is maintained (143–44, 147). The Greek word agape is used frequently in the New Testament but seldom in other ancient Greek literature and is now usually translated as "love," or as "charity" in older translations, and for Rougemont it denotes a love analogous to God's love for human beings. Agape is a matter not only of fidelity—eros can exhibit fanatical fidelity (290–94)—but also of the recognition of equality, and so God's choice to become a man in the Incarnation becomes the model of "a truly mutual love [that] exacts and creates the equality of those loving one another" (296).

Rougemont mediated and modified certain Augustinian ideas which Auden then absorbed.[8] On its surface, Rougemont's *Love in the Western World* does not appear particularly Augustinian, yet Rougemont stands in the Augustinian tradition for several reasons. First, he fits into Auden's definition of an "existential" thinker who "begins with man's immediate experience as a subject, i.e. as a being in need, as interested being whose existence is at stake" and who "does not assert, as he is usually accused of asserting, the primacy of Will over Reason, but their inseparability" (*Prose II* 214). Auden places Augustine at the beginning of the Christian "existential" tradition, and Rougemont's analysis of the ways in which the will can collaborate with reason to produce either redemption or despair places him squarely in the existential tradition as Auden understood it. Rougemont closely follows Augustine in his argument that eros is not the basis of human desires but rather a sign of a fundamentally spiritual desire that the individual translates into sexual behavior. In opposition to the Freudian idea that "spiritual" desires are the expression of repressed sexual energies, Rougemont expands on Augustine's argument that disordered sexual activity is an attempt, sometimes conscious and sometimes unconscious, to satisfy an ultimately spiritual desire.[9]

Rougemont also uses the term "Manichaeism" to refer to the heterodox Gnostic mysticism that he identifies with the Cathars and denounces throughout his book. It might have been more accurate to refer to this broad phenomenon merely as "Gnosticism," but Rougemont is convinced that the medieval Cathars, the various Gnostic sects of the late Roman Empire, and a wide variety of cultic religions from the Near East, including Zoroastrianism, are all versions of the same secretive, mystical religion, and he suggests a rough-and-ready genealogy: "a kind of Indo-European unity may be seen looming out like a watermark upon the background of medieval heresies. As early as the third century, there spread over the geographical and historical area that is bounded by India on the one hand and by Britain on the other, a religion that syncretized all the myths of Night and Day, a religion which had been elaborated first in Persia and then by the Gnostic and Orphic sects. This religion actually spread underground, and it is known as Manichaeism" (78). In his overview, Rougemont collapses some major differences between the various mystic sects. He might have used any number of other terms, since no medieval or modern mystic identified by Rougemont ever explicitly claimed to be "Manichean," but his use of the word "Manichaeism" seems calculated to evoke Augustine's denunciation of Manichean dualism in the *Confessions*, *The City of God*, *Against Faustus*, and elsewhere. Against the Manichees, Augustine insists on one God as the creator of both soul and body and on the intrinsic goodness of the created body, despite its obvious corruption by sin.

Augustine's denunciations of Manichaeism thus provide the theological and polemic background for Rougemont's own critique of what he believes is a Western outgrowth of Manichean mysticism. Rougemont draws his definition of eros directly from Augustine: "To love love more than the object of love, to love passion for its own sake, has been to love to suffer and to court suffering all the way from Augustine's *amabam amare* down to modern Romanticism" (61). The phrase *amabam amare*, "I longed to love," comes from the *Confessions,* where Augustine relates his experiences as a young man in Carthage: "To Carthage I came, where there sang all around me in my ears a cauldron of unholy loves. I loved not yet, yet I loved to love [*amabam amare*]. . . . I sought what I might love, in love with loving . . ." (3.1). From this and similar passages in the *Confessions,* Rougemont reasonably links what he calls by the Greek word *eros* with Augustine's *cupiditas,* which for Augustine is a love directed primarily at self-gratification.[10]

Rougemont has been criticized for setting up an absolute division between eros and agape,[11] but that characterization is not quite fair. While Rougemont's book does begin by setting up eros and agape in strong opposition to each other, he does so with an eye toward reconciling them in the end. In the final chapters of *Love in the Western World,* he explains that, while eros tends to isolate itself from agape and to lead ultimately to death, Christian agape seeks to redeem eros and return it to its proper subservient place. Before Christianity, Rougemont argues, the "natural man," or humans under the control of eros, found that death was the only escape from servitude to eros: "thus Eros could lead him but to death. But a man who believes the revelation of Agape suddenly beholds the circle broken: faith delivers him from natural religion. Now he may hope for something else; he is aware that there is some other release from sin. And thereupon Eros in turn has been relieved of his fatal office and delivered from his fate. In ceasing to be a god, he ceases to be a demon.[12] And he finds his proper place in the provisional economy of Creation and of what is human" (321, emphasis original). Here Rougemont sets himself in opposition to the Swedish Lutheran theologian Anders Nygren, who had published the second volume of his monumental work *Agape and Eros* in 1936. The book argues that eros, desire that seeks its own satisfaction, has no place in Christianity and that Augustine and the medieval theologians had perverted Christian agape, a totally selfless love, by attempting to recover eros as a valid element of Christian experience. Against this background of a Protestant theology that views eros and agape as diametrically opposed, Rougemont contends that eros has a legitimate if minor place within the rightly ordered loves of Christianity.

In his 1941 review of the book, Auden was quick to emphasize this crucial point, and he chides Rougemont for not being clearer on the matter all along: "my only

criticism of Mr de Rougemont's profound and brilliant study is that I find his definition of Eros a little vague. He sometimes speaks as if he meant, which I am sure he
does not, that Eros is of sexual origin and that there is a dualistic division between
Agape and Eros rather than—what I am sure he believes—a dialectical relation. For
Eros, surely, is 'amor sementa in voi d'ogni vertute, e d'ogni operazion che merta
pene,'[13] the basic will to self-actualization without which no creature can exist, and
Agape is that Eros mutated by Grace, a conversion, not an addition, the Law ful-
filled, not the Law destroyed" (*Prose II* 139). Auden's clarification links Rougemont's
work to the Augustinian tradition. In *City of God*, Augustine argues that, according to Scripture, charity (*caritas*), love (*amor*), fondness (*diligis*), and even desire
(*cupiditas* or *concupiscentia*) may have good or bad connotations in Scriptural use
depending on what is loved or desired and for what reasons[14] (14.7). Augustine concludes, "a rightly directed will is love in a good sense and a perverted will is love in
a bad sense" (14.7). For Augustine, the rightness or wrongness of a passion is always
judged primarily by the motive for the passion, and then by the object of the passion, and not by the fact of desire itself. Desire (*cupiditas*) for Augustine, and for
Auden as well, might be properly directed toward God himself and therefore cannot
be in itself sinful.

According to the Gospels and to the longstanding tradition of the church of
which Augustine is a significant part, the love of God is the basis of a rightly ordered
love, and out of that love of God comes a love of one's neighbor. After all, the second
greatest commandment, according to Jesus Christ, is "you shall love your neighbor
as yourself" (Matt. 22:39), the wording of which does imply a valid love of self. Once
eros or *cupiditas*[15] ("desire," or the survival instinct, as Auden saw it) is put into its
proper place within the orderly loving of God and neighbor, Augustine finds himself free to speak of his relationship to God using erotic imagery. For example, he
exclaims in the *Confessions*, "Thou hadst pierced our hearts with Thy charity . . ."
(9.2), and in a later passage, "Not with doubting, but with assured consciousness,
do I love Thee, Lord. Thou hast stricken my heart with thy word, and I loved Thee"
(10.6). These are references to the arrow of Cupid/Eros, in which Augustine envisions the pagan god as a type of Christ. Augustine's justification for this identification of the erotic love of Cupid/Eros with the divine love of God is also derived from
a long mystical tradition—both Jewish and Christian—in which the erotic imagery
of the Song of Songs was interpreted allegorically so as to picture the love between
God and humans. Augustine thereby develops the idea of agape's redemption of
eros in ways that Rougemont's analysis can only suggest.

AMBIGUITIES OF LOVE IN THE 1930S

During Auden's early career in the late 1920s and 1930s, the word "love" appears
regularly in his poetry, but its meaning is never fixed. It can refer alternately to the
sexual act, to close friendship, to political camaraderie, or even to a vague altruism.

Before 1940, Auden's poems never address divine love, since he was a tacit atheist for much of this period, but one of his chief concerns in his poetry is the distressing fact that sex and friendship never quite align. At times, Auden draws on Freud and associates sexual love with death (see Mendelson's analysis in *Early* 6, 78, and 139). Auden's early poetry displays various subtle changes in opinion about love, thoroughly tracked in Mendelson's *Early Auden*. In the first ten years of his career, Auden remained uncertain about the nature of love, and his search for a coherent account that would reconcile sex and friendship led into the first major shift in his thinking about love in 1939, in which he regained some hope that eros and philia could co-exist in a long-term relationship.

Shifts in Auden's thinking, however, were never abrupt or unprecipitated. In a 1933 poem, which Auden later titled "Summer Night,"[16] the speaker reflects on a moment of newfound equality with casual acquaintances. It is an autobiographical poem set in a summer evening during Auden's tenure as a teacher at Downs School, and it begins by establishing a sexually charged atmosphere in "the sexy airs of summer" in which "The bathing hours and the bare arms / . . . / Are good to a newcomer" (*CP* 117). As in Auden's other poems of the period, eros is not a product of the will, but of arbitrary circumstance that the poet here calls merely "lucky." But despite the erotic overtones of the first few lines, the poem takes an unexpected turn: "equal with colleagues in a ring / I sit on each calm evening / Enchanted as the flowers / The opening light draws out of hiding / With all its gradual dove-like pleading, / Its logic and its powers . . ." (117). Against a background of eros the speaker has found companionship with not one person but several people, all equal in status and by implication in regard for each other. The metaphoric language of the stanza suggests that the poet considers his recognition of equality to be a kind of spiritual experience, which involves "opening light" that is "dove-like" and possesses both logic and power. While the moment is fleeting, the effect remains, and the speaker holds out hope that the participants "May still recall these evenings when / Fear gave his watch no look" (117). The erotic opening of the poem is redirected toward an unexpected equality from which sexuality is simply absent, leaving eros behind for a more fulfilling experience of neighborly equality.

About thirty years after writing the poem, Auden gave a prose account[17] of this experience:

> One fine summer night in June 1933 I was sitting on a lawn after dinner with three colleagues, two women and one man. We liked each other well enough but we were certainly not intimate friends, nor had any one of us a sexual interest in another. Incidentally, we had not drunk any alcohol. We were talking casually about everyday matters when, quite suddenly and unexpectedly, something happened. I felt myself invaded by a power which, though I consented to it, was irresistible and certainly not mine. For the first time in my life I knew exactly—

because, thanks to the power, I was doing it—what it means to love one's neighbor as oneself. . . . My personal feelings towards them were unchanged—they were still colleagues, not intimate friends—but I felt their existence as themselves to be of infinite value and rejoiced in it. (*FA* 69)

In the same essay, Auden classifies this experience as a mystical vision of agape and describes it as a recognition of the equality and value of other people that transcend one's personal feelings about them (69). Auden notes that this love of neighbor was not a product of intellectual intimacy, sexual attraction, or inebriated affection—it is in no sense a Platonic climb up the ladder of loves from eros to friendship to wisdom. Rather, he describes it as a sudden invasion of a benevolent power, language that more commonly describes the eros associated with "love at first sight," though Auden insists that the "power" was not eros at all.

Mendelson suggests that the stanza's metaphors of doves and light, "with their distant echoes of the Annunciation, suggest religious resonances Auden was not yet prepared to acknowledge more directly" (*Early* 167). Indeed, the religious imagery is a gesture toward Christian spirituality, but Auden himself suggested later that he associated the experience not with the Annunciation but with the coming of the Holy Spirit at Pentecost. Just before he describes his experience, Auden notes that "the classic Christian example of [the vision of agape] is, of course, the vision of Pentecost," (*FA* 69), an association that explains why the description of the light in "Summer Night" is "dove-like," though doves do appear in many paintings of the Annunciation. Mendelson also notes that "for the first time in Auden's career he associates love with conscious choice rather than simple instinct. The worlds of Eros and responsibility coincide as never before . . ." (*Early* 164). Paradoxically, Auden says that the experience occurred with his full consent even though he says the "power" was "irresistible" (*FA* 69). The experience was neither a product of his own idealization of his companions, nor was it traceable to his own physical desires.

The rest of the poem tries to work out the implications of the poet's vision of agape. The poet watches the moon rise over the English landscape of "churches and power-stations," noting that the moon is obedient to the natural law of gravity, whereas the speaker and his colleagues look up from their garden and "endure / The tyrannies of love" (*CP* 118). The juxtaposition of the moon's gravity and humans' love evokes a parallel with Augustine's statement in the *Confessions* that "My weight is my love" (13.9). Auden was already familiar with the *Confessions* even at this early date (see introduction), and given the Christian imagery of doves and wedding rings which he used to describe his vision of agape early in the poem, it is possible that he had Augustine's work in mind as he drafted this stanza. Auden's rhyming of "move" and "love" suggests a similarity between the two words that evokes a long Augustinian tradition that includes Dante's *Paradiso,* in which the love of God is identified with the primum mobile that sets the cosmos in motion—"The love that moves the sun and the other stars" (33.145). But in this poem the moon, along with the whole of the natural world, operates according to strict causal necessity, in this case gravity, while humans are not entirely subject to natural necessity, since the poem shows them unmoved by the natural force of hunger. And yet, they obey a seemingly irresistible but wholly mysterious love. The characterization of love as tyrannical would have fit well in Auden's other poems of the period, where love is often equated with the sex drive, but the use of the word "tyrannies" is strange in this poem where, for once, agape has temporarily superseded eros. Auden's language in his prose account implies that agape itself may be a kind of benevolent tyranny: "I felt myself invaded by a power which, though I consented to it, was irresistible and certainly not mine" (*FA* 69). Even in this early vision of agape, Auden cannot quite abandon the idea that love in any form is beyond the lover's willful control.

Mendelson is surely correct in suggesting that the word "tyrannies" also "acknowledges the existence of more painful tyrannies elsewhere" (*Early* 169). The comfortable colleagues sitting in their ring of agape are apathetic toward political turmoil in Poland, and the speaker acknowledges that this vision of agape has been made possible in part by injustice and oppression elsewhere in Europe. The original version of the poem then embarks on several stanzas of political hand-wringing which, however immediately appropriate to contemporary current events, detracted from the poem's investigation of the ramifications of the vision of agape. The later, shorter version of the poem maintains the uneasy tone in the final stanzas, and it retains the implication that the setting for the vision of agape depends on injustice elsewhere in the world, but the elimination of the stanzas removes much of the overtly personal guilt from the poem. The last four stanzas, which Auden left relatively intact, picture a coming deluge that will break "through the dykes of our content" and reveal the "vigors of the sea" (*English Auden* 138), an almost apocalyptic image that suggests the emergence of politics, perhaps fascism, based purely on the unconscious physical drives of which the sea is a constant image in Auden's early poetry. However, the poem looks toward a renewed, post-diluvian world that will support agape: "May this for which we dread to lose / Our privacy, need no excuse / But to that strength belong" (138). Auden later changed the lines to refer more clearly to the vision of agape, changing "this for which" to "these delights" (*CP* 118), a change that prioritizes the "delights" of agape rather than the unnamed thing for which privacy was the necessary condition in the earlier version. This agape, the poem concludes, may "calm / The pulse of nervous nations; / Forgive the murderer in his glass" (119). Even for the Auden of the mid-1940s, who kept these lines in the poem, agape has particular political consequences, though they are less urgent than the Auden of the early 1930s might suggest.

The vision of agape, as "Summer Night" describes it, was important to Auden's future for another reason. He says at the end of his prose account, "among the various factors which several years later brought me back to the Christian faith in which I had been brought up, the memory of this experience and asking myself what it could mean was one of the most crucial, though, at the time it occurred, I thought I had done with Christianity for good" (*FA* 70). Auden does not mention his 1933 vision of agape in his essay in *Modern Canterbury Pilgrims,* where he lists many other factors in his eventual return to Christianity, including his service in the Spanish Civil War, his acquaintance with Charles Williams, his experience with Nazi sympathizers in New York City, and his reading of Kierkegaard, to name a few. Auden's 1933 vision of agape was not in itself a decisive turning point. The fact that the original version of the poem attempted to merge agape into sexual intimacy on the one hand and into patriotism on the other suggests that Auden was not able to allow his vision to exist on its own terms until he began to explore Christianity seriously. Even in its final, revised form, the poem remains an isolated example of pure agape among the other poems of the period that are concerned almost exclusively with eros.

Perhaps the best-known example is "Lullaby," also known by its first line, "Lay your sleeping head, my love." Written early in 1937, it underwent relatively few revisions—Auden later changed four words—and it describes a scene that he must have repeated many times throughout his life. The speaker lies in bed talking to a sleeping lover with whom he will soon part. Mendelson accurately characterizes the poem's tone: "He is grateful for the pleasures of the body, but his post-coital sadness is felt as ethical self-reproach" (*Early* 230). The poem represents love as imposing high ethical demands on the lovers. Venus has replaced the god Love (Eros), and her vision "of supernatural sympathy, / Universal love and hope," a vision of agape in Auden's pre-Christian vocabulary, is "grave" (*CP* 157), a pun that evokes the poem's obvious Freudian perspective in that it associates eros both with the love of humanity as a whole and with a subconscious death wish. The hermit's ecstasy emerges from a vision of universal love, though Auden was well aware of Freud's view that universal love is an expression of repressed sexual desire. The line originally read "sensual ecstasy" (*English Auden* 207) rather than the later "carnal ecstasy" (*CP* 157). If the hermit's ecstasy is merely "sensual," the line is ambiguous. The hermit's spiritual experience may or may not be authentic; many mystics have used highly erotic language to describe a vision of the divine, though in the context of the poem's open admission of infidelity, the language of eros is already suspect. Auden's later change to "carnal ecstasy" more strongly indicates that the hermit's ecstasy is indeed "a quite straightforward and unredeemed eroticism," as Auden once called his own pseudo-devout phase in adolescence (*Prose III* 575). The certainty and fidelity that pass "on the stroke of midnight . . ." (*CP* 157) belong to the self-deceived hermit as much as to the faithless lovers. Love as desire seeks its own satisfaction and therefore its own demise, so not even the universal love that Venus introduces can escape the transience that pervades the poem.

The last stanza confirms the transience of the vision offered by Venus, as the speaker offers a benediction to the beloved as the vision of Venus dies: "Noons of dryness find you fed / By the involuntary powers" (*CP* 158). With the dying of the vision of universal love, the poet hopes that day will bring some blessing in the mortal world, beyond which he will not seek for beatitude. The poem does not explain what "the involuntary powers" are that feed the abandoned lover, but given Auden's earlier identification of unconscious human drives with eros, it is reasonable to conclude that the speaker hopes that future experiences of love, whether sexual or otherwise is not clear, will sustain the beloved. The poem ends with a wish that the abandoned lover will be "watched by every human love," a line that suggests that there is real value in expressing eros as universal love (158). The conclusion is not altogether hopeless, although the speaker's abdication of personal responsibility to love another person also implies that he is finally irresponsible in love. Eros, in this case, does not lead the individual lover to the neighborly agape that Venus offered in the middle of the poem. Nevertheless, the poem does represent "another of Auden's innovations in love poetry," as Mendelson explains: "It is the first English poem in which a lover proclaims, in moral terms and during a shared night of love, his own faithlessness. . . . Innovative as it is in the history of poetry, 'Lullaby' represents a transitional stage in the history of Auden's work. He admits faithlessness, but here he blames it on the human condition. Later he will blame it on himself" (*Early* 233). In fact, it was less than one year later that he wrote his famous lyric "As I Walked Out One Evening," in which he places all the blame for infidelity on the lover himself.

Auden wrote "As I Walked Out One Evening" in November 1937, and unlike his other popular poems from the 1930s, this one underwent no revision whatsoever in later collections. The poem reenergizes many images and themes that Auden's earlier poems had used, though often with less poignancy. The mirror as a place of self-assessment, the sea as a symbol of primal desires, the hyperbole of the lyric tradition, the mixture of pastoral and urban imagery, the inevitability of unfaithfulness, and the overwhelming feeling of guilt all coincide to achieve a unified critique of the love-lyric tradition of which the poem is a part, but more specifically of a tendency toward infidelity that permeates relationships based exclusively on eros. The poem juxtaposes a lover's hyperbolic love song with a response by the city's clocks, which point out lovers' ignorance of the real effects of time on an erotic relationship. As in all of Auden's love poems, the greatest threat to the relationship is infidelity, and while infidelity is not explicitly mentioned, several stanzas strongly suggest it. While some of Auden's other poems from the 1930s frankly celebrate the ephemeral nature of his sexual encounters, few if any of these poems entirely lack the sense of regret and guilt that would be foregrounded in "As I Walked Out One Evening," where the lover is fully culpable in the disintegration of the relationship.

This poem reflects Auden's personal situation at the time which, though homosexual, was not far removed from the position in which Augustine found himself as a young man. As he records in the *Confessions*, he had been cohabiting with a woman with whom he had a son, but he was persuaded to get married and so dismissed his mistress in order to be free to marry, and in the meantime he procured yet another mistress with whom he could satisfy himself while he waited to be married (6.12–15). Augustine says of his sexual addiction, "bound with the disease of the flesh, and its deadly sweetness, [I] drew along my chain, dreading to be loosed . . ." (*Confessions* 6.12). Augustine's descriptions of his own struggles with sexual infidelity were strikingly familiar to Auden, as they articulate an acute distress that approximates much of the erotic angst that permeates Auden's poetry and reaches what seems to be a final impasse in "Lullaby" and "As I Walked Out One Evening." Both are important poems in Auden's corpus, since they summarize much that Auden believed about romantic love and since they offer an honest assessment of human nature. But by themselves the poems do not come much closer than Auden's earlier works to resolving the continual problem of eros and agape. The resolution of such opposites vexed Auden in the late 1930s, and in his 1938 essay "Jehovah Houseman and Satan Houseman," he writes: "Heaven and Hell. Reason and Instinct. Conscious Mind and Unconscious. . . . Yes, the two worlds. Perhaps the Socialist State will marry them, perhaps it won't. . . . Perhaps again the only thing which can bring them together is the experience of what Christians call Charity. . ." (*Prose I* 438–39). By his own testimony, Auden hoped for a marriage of opposites through the agency of charity, but it would take a radically new personal experience to flesh out Auden's hopes.

LOVE AND MARRIAGE: 1939–1941

In April of 1939, just a few months after he had immigrated to America with Christopher Isherwood, Auden met a young Jewish man named Chester Kallman in New York City, and the two quickly became close friends. The development of the relationship between Auden and Kallman is well documented in several books, particularly in Carpenter's biography, in Richard Davenport-Hines's *Auden*, and in Dorothy Farnan's *Auden in Love*. By all accounts, Kallman was bright and well read, and Auden found him attractive both physically and intellectually. It was Kallman who introduced Auden to opera, a genre to which Auden had previously paid scant attention but about which he was enthusiastic ever afterwards. The two would go on to collaborate on several libretti, including *The Rake's Progress*, set by Igor Stravinsky, and a translation of *The Magic Flute*. Only a few weeks after the two first met, Carpenter says, Auden was contemplating entering into "a marriage with all its boredoms and rewards" (261). By May of 1939, Auden's friends found him referring to his relationship with Kallman as a marriage, and he had begun to wear a wedding band (262). With considerable relief, Auden now believed that sex and friendship could harmoniously coincide within his ad hoc marriage to Kallman, and it was against the background of this relationship that Auden began his long trek back to the church.

From 1939 on, Auden would address many poems to Kallman, explicitly or implicitly. One of the first is "Every eye must weep alone," which bears a dedication to Kallman and which Mendelson dates "? 1939," though it must have been written after he met Kallman in April of that year (*English Auden* 456). The poem uses language from Augustine's *Confessions* to explore the implications of selfless love within a marriage, "Every eye must weep alone / Till I Will be overthrown." at which point "all I's can meet and grow" (*English Auden* 456). The poem appropriates Augustine's explanation in the *Confessions* of the three aspects of the self: "To Be, to Know, and to Will. For I Am, and Know, and Will: I Am Knowing and Willing: and I Know myself to Be, and to Will: and I Will to Be, and to Know" (13.11).[18] In this passage, Augustine is comparing the unity of the three persons of the Trinity with what he identifies as the three basic faculties of the human being, but Auden's use of Augustine's language discards the original theological context—at the time of writing it is unlikely that Auden was even a theist, much less a Christian—and focuses instead on the way in which these three aspects of the human being interact in a loving relationship.

In this poem, the phrase "I Will" suggests the self-centered eros described in Auden's earlier poetry; Lucy McDiarmid explains that "I Will" is synonymous with "what I want, what I insist on, what I determine" (67). In that egotistical sense the "I Will" "can be removed" and "overthrown," presumably in order to subject it to the agape of "I Love." The poem aspires to a condition in which "I Am" becomes "I Love," a strange aspiration since being would seem to be a prerequisite to loving. The phrase "I Am" recalls God's self-identification to Moses in Exodus 3:14, but when spoken in a human voice the phrase suggests a pretended self-sufficiency. The human who says "I Am" is playing at being a god and is thus likely to say "I Will," a phrase that the poem uses to designate exploitative desire that regards its object only as something to be possessed. While Auden's earlier poems had frequently used the word "love" to designate eros, here he is beginning to describe eros as an act of sheer willfulness and to contrast eros with what he now calls "love," which is redefined as an event in which "all I's can meet and grow." That this newfound "love" corresponds to agape is suggested by the clause "all I's can meet"; rather than limit the love to an exclusive relationship between two people, the poem says "all," opening the possibility of mutual love to a potentially infinite number of other people. The poem's third stanza indicates that the agape inherent in reciprocal love ("I Love . . . I Am Loved") replaces the desire to possess inherent in "I Have Not," which is the defining characteristic of the narcissistic "I Am" that isolates itself in its own sorrowful weeping.

Randall Jarrell, who objected strongly to Auden's penchant for abstraction and personification, cites this poem as a particularly egregious level of abstraction: "In

Another Time there is one thirteen-line menagerie in which the capitalized abstractions I Will, I Know, I Am, I Have Not, and I Am Loved peer apathetically out from behind their bars" (49–50). Jarrell is unaware of the phrases' origin in Augustine, and he misses the poem's use of puns and double-meanings, in which abstract language suggests concrete images. For example, the "eye" that weeps alone is also the "I" in "I Will" and "I Am" that must be overthrown by agape. The eye is a synecdoche for the whole person, the "I," that emphasizes the tendency of the eros-driven person to objectify other persons. The phrase "I Know" suggests the carnal knowledge of sexual intimacy, which the poem says the faculty of the will does have the sense to resist. The phrase "I Will" may even be a mockery of wedding vows, in which the traditional "I do" is sometimes replaced by "I will," at least in some American ceremonies. The poem's "I Will" suggests that eros is not automatically checked by a wedding; on the contrary, two people may very well marry for entirely selfish reasons. The poem also uses opposing concrete images of organic growth and crying to illustrate the difference between agape and eros, respectively. This, then, is a more physical poem than Jarrell allows.

It was not only Auden's personal relationships that fixed his writing so intently on love in the late 1930s. The political situation in Europe was quickly worsening, and war with Nazi Germany already seemed inevitable to him. Soon a rapid series of personal and political events in 1939 and 1940 would concentrate Auden's poetic attention on the nature of human relationships. In the summer of 1939, the same year in which "Every eye must weep alone" was written, Auden and Kallman took a bus trip to New Mexico and California, partly to visit Christopher Isherwood, but also to celebrate what Auden was calling their "Honeymoon" (Carpenter 266). Kallman, as would later become obvious even to Auden, was more ambivalent about the marriage, but at the time he seems to have been content to play along. It was during that summer that Auden wrote *The Prolific and the Devourer,* in which he sets out his political and aesthetic beliefs at the time and in which he also maintained his dissatisfaction with all forms of organized Christian religion. That same autumn, Auden wrote "Heavy Date" and "Law Like Love." In the fall of 1939, as the Nazis invaded Poland, Auden had his startling experience with Nazi sympathizers in a Manhattan theater, where he found that his longstanding middle-class liberalism could not offer a compelling rationale for his own sense of ethics that he had heretofore taken for granted. About the same time he also met Elizabeth Mayer, to whom he would soon dedicate *New Year Letter,* which he began in January of 1940. As he was finishing the poem in the first part of that year, he read Charles Williams and Kierkegaard and perhaps Cochrane as well. In the fall of 1940, Auden met the Niebuhrs, and it was about this time that his friends began to notice that he was slipping away on Sunday mornings to attend church.

Love had been especially prominent in the few poems Auden had written at the end of the 1930s, so it is hardly surprising that "September 1, 1939" contained the line "We must love one another or die" (*English Auden* 246). It is arguably the best-known line Auden ever wrote, though the poem contains several other frequently quoted lines such as "a low, dishonest decade" and "Those to whom evil is done / Do evil in return" (245). Auden's repudiation of the poem has become almost as famous as the poem itself, and the provenance of this poem has been ably traced by Mendelson (*Early* 325–26) and Gottlieb (223n). It has been irrepressibly popular despite Auden's eventual renunciation of its most famous line as "a damned lie" (qtd. in *FA* 326), and it achieved notable prominence among New Yorkers after September 11, 2001. The poem's view, however, is characteristic of Auden's vague and shifting ideas about love in the 1930s. Eros appears in the poem, this time not in sexual terms, but as a general self-centeredness. The desire "to be loved alone" is "bred in the bone"; that is, the lines suggest that the will to deny love to others is inherent in the very physical nature of all humans (*English Auden* 246). The last stanza returns to this account of human nature. The poet says he is "composed like them / Of Eros and of dust" (247). "Dust" is a reference to the story of the creation of man in Genesis, where God "formed the man of dust from the ground" (2:7), and "Eros" here suggests the natural impetus toward self-actualization that Auden's earlier poems, such as "Meiosis," attribute to all forms of organic life. It is in this biological sense that Auden used the word "love" in the infamous line, "We must love one another or die" (*English Auden* 246).

This love is not the agape of "Summer Night" in which love generates mutual respect and kindness, but as Mendelson explains in his analysis of the line's context in the stanza, "His lines say we must love one another because hunger allows us no choice. This is a statement of necessity: love is a biological need which must be satisfied lest we die. Auden had said as much repeatedly during the past five years" (*Early* 326). At the same time, as Mendelson points out (327), Auden had also characterized love as an act of the will, as "voluntary love," three years earlier in a poem that became the fifth of "Twelve Songs" (*CP* 139). Eventually, Auden recognized that the poem's use of the word "love" in the sense of eros made nonsense of the line "We must love one another or die," and he came to suspect that eros is a love of self, not a love of another person, so it is a contradiction in terms to imply that eros can impel us to "love one another." The love of the other is not eros, but agape, which, to be fair, Auden did suggest could also be an irresistible compulsion that nevertheless elicits the lover's assent. The word "love" is constantly ambiguous in Auden's poetry: in "As I Walked Out One Evening," the lover sings "I'll love you dear, I'll love you" (133), and in "Lullaby" the speaker hopes his lover will be "Watched by every human love" (159), but Auden also hopes in "Every eye must weep alone" that "I Am [will] become I Love" (*English Auden* 456). In his poems from the late 1930s, Auden never seems exactly sure what he means by the word "love."

Between the time Auden met Kallman early in 1939 and his decision to regularly attend church late in 1940, Auden wrote very few poems that could be called love poems. This was partly because he had spent much of 1939 and 1940 writing *The Prolific and the Devourer*, "New Year Letter," and "The Quest," a sonnet sequence that would be published in the same volume as "New Year Letter" in March 1941. "The Quest" does, however, touch on the nature of love. It is an apt companion piece for *New Year Letter* since it begins in metaphysical uncertainty and ends with a tentative affirmation of Christian hope. A later poem in the sequence, titled merely "XVIII" in the *Collected Poems* but in other editions titled "The Adventurers," pictures the Desert Fathers attempting their own quest to escape the temptations of the flesh through the *via negativa,* a subject Auden likely derived from Charles Williams's description of these early Christian ascetic mystics in *The Descent of the Dove* (see esp. 57–59). These mystics recall the ecstatic hermit of "Lullaby," though while the hermit of "Lullaby" achieves a "sensual" or "carnal" vision and is ultimately self-deceived, the mystics of "The Quest" do not achieve the desired spiritual vision at all. Auden describes them as "Spinning upon their central thirst like tops" and following "the Negative Way towards the Dry" (*CP* 294). The "thirst" that paradoxically drives them to the asceticism of "the Dry" suggests a desire akin to the hunger that "September 1, 1939" established as a biologically necessary eros. But the result, in the case of the Desert Fathers, is almost comically paradoxical: "yet, / Still praising the Absurd with their last breath, / They seeded out into their miracles," and both married and single women visit their shrines to "wish for beaux and children in their name" (294–95). While the Desert Fathers rejected both art and sex, the poem shows their asceticism enabling both pictorial art and sensual pleasure as their memories are invoked on behalf of painters, would-be lovers, and those who hope to bear children. Individually, the ascetics' rejection of eros, though that rejection is itself identified as a form of eros, is absolute, but when their lives are merged into the larger, catholic community, their personal barrenness enables fruitfulness in others.

Just as the poem shows the asceticism of the *via negativa* being subsumed into a broader whole of Christian experience, the poem itself is but one aspect of the larger "Quest" sequence in which a set of average people undertakes a heroic search for significance that turns out to be impossible. The penultimate poem of the sequence, numbered "XIX" in the *Collected Poems* but elsewhere titled "The Waters," describes a generally unsuccessful quest, as "Poet, oracle, and wit / Like unsuccessful anglers by / The ponds of apperception sit" (*CP* 295), lines that evoke a similar image at the end of Eliot's *The Waste Land.* But the poem's final couplet suggests that it is the fishermen themselves, not the water, that are to blame for the lack of vision: "The waters long to hear our question put / Which would release their longed-for answer, but" (295). The poem ends with the unfinished sentence, which parallels Auden's use of tetrameter rather than pentameter lines, all suggesting a continued deferral of closure. Since the philosophical fishermen do not know what question to ask, they can only "tell the angler's lie" and pretend that their pronouncements are the products of genuine insights instead of concocted fish stories (295).

The last poem of "The Quest," sometimes titled "The Garden," envisions a state of renewed innocence[19] where "all opening begins" and "flesh forgives division as it makes / Another's moment of consent its own" (*CP* 295). The poem continues, "All journeys die here: wish and weight are lifted" (296). In this garden, the demands of eros ("wish") "are lifted" along with "weight." Auden's use of "weight" in the context of love clearly draws on the *Confessions,* in which Augustine describes his love for God using the metaphor of physical weight (13.9). According to Augustine, he is raised to God, or "lifted" as Auden's poem puts it, by his love, which he likens to fire that seeks its proper place above the other elements. The poem's last lines reiterate the identification of deliberate love with weight: "The gaunt and great, the famed for conversation / Blushed in the stare of evening as they spoke / And felt their center of volition shifted" (*CP* 296). Kirsch notes that the phrase "center of volition" is derived from Charles Williams's description of Augustine's conversion in the garden (*Descent* 37). So while the poem does not actually use the word "love," the sense of agape is unmistakable in the connections it establishes between "wish," "weight," and "volition." The last line implies that the movement of the "centre of volition" is itself prior to the conscious will, that what moves the will cannot itself be willed but must be an outside agent that the poem leaves unnamed, but which the allusion to Augustine's conversion suggests is divine. Similarly, *New Year Letter* names the agent, also using a line from Augustine, "O da quod jubes, Domine" (*CP* 242), or, "O give what you command, Lord" (c.f. *Confessions* 10.29). An earlier poem in the sequence, "XVII" or "Adventure," wryly points out the futility of attempting "to see the face of [an] Absconded God" (*CP* 294), and the last poem of the sequence is content merely to imply the necessity of divine grace rather than name it explicitly.

As the poems of "The Quest" demonstrate, after 1939 Auden's view of love becomes more consistently linked with an Augustinian sense of love as a volition. Before that year, Auden had never sounded quite sure in his poems whether the various thoughts, emotions, and desires he called "love" were biological impulses or conscious choices, but he was coming to define love more and more in terms of volition. Since the tension and anxiety that had marked his earlier erotic relationships was not initially present in his relationship with Kallman, his love poems of 1939 and 1940 replace the anguish with anticipation of the difficulties of committed love. It was that erotic tension and uncertainty that appears to have been the emotional impetus behind much of Auden's early love poetry—as he had said in the notes to *New Year Letter,* "poetry might be defined as the clear expression of mixed feelings" (119). But having achieved what he said was a "happy personal life" (qtd. in Carpenter 290), Auden's inner conflicts now arose from the demands that his renewed Christian faith was making on him. By the end of 1940 Auden felt that his "marriage" to Kallman had set his sexual life in order, and that his sexual fidelity might be energized by a newfound fidelity to God.

About this time, Auden's reading of Rougemont confirmed his inclination to maintain the marriage. While it not clear exactly when in 1940 Auden read Rougemont, it is clear that he first read the book in the summer or early autumn. Rougemont does not appear in *New Year Letter,* which Auden finished in April of 1940, even though the denunciation of Rousseau near the end of the poem anticipates Rougemont's own critique of romanticism, but references to Rougemont begin to appear in other poems from later in 1940. Richard Davenport-Hines even mentions that Rougemont visited the Middagh Street house in Brooklyn where Auden lived from October 1940 to July 1941, though Davenport-Hines is not clear as to whether the two actually met (207). Given that Rougemont and Auden were in some of the same social circles in New York City, and that Auden had greatly admired his book, it is possible that they met at some point. Auden references Rougemont in a 1941 letter to Ursula Niebuhr (see Spender, *Tribute* 106), and he favorably reviewed Rougemont's book in June 1941.

One of Auden's earliest direct references to Rougemont appears in "In Sickness and in Health," which Edward Mendelson dates "? Autumn 1940" (*CP* 320). The poem replicates Rougemont's reading of the Tristan myth exactly: "Tristan, Isolde, the great friends, / Make passion out of passion's obstacles, / Deliciously postponing their delight, / Prolong frustration till it lasts all night . . ." (*CP* 318). The stanza reworks "The hermit's carnal ecstasy" in "Lullaby" (157) while neatly summarizing Rougemont's argument in the first chapters of *Love in the Western World* that Tristan and Isolde intentionally obstruct the consummation of their illicit relationship. Auden had been familiar with the legend of Tristan since childhood, when his mother taught him to sing Isolde's part in a duet from Wagner's opera (Osborne, *Life of a Poet* 11). But the myth took a serious hold on his imagination only after he read Rougemont's book, which he did just as Kallman was reintroducing him to Wagnerian opera. Rougemont identifies the Tristan legend as quintessentially Gnostic, or, to use the term that Rougemont prefers, Manichean, and from 1940 on, Auden would repeatedly use Tristan as an example of the archetypal suffering lover who is in love, not with another person, but with love itself and ultimately with his own destruction. Following Augustine's *amabam amare,* Rougemont explains, "Tristan and Iseult do not love one another. They say they don't, and everything goes to prove it. *What they love is love and being in love.* They behave as if aware that whatever obstructs love must ensure and consolidate it in the heart of each and intensify it infinitely in the moment they reach the complete obstruction, which is death" (33, emphasis original). Poetic associations of eros with death are common enough in the lyric tradition, and Auden had added his own example of asexual reproduction by cellular fission ("Meiosis," *CP* 125) to the tradition well before he read Rougemont, but Rougemont offered Auden a compelling mythic and historical explanation of the entire history of the association.

The rest of "In Sickness and in Health" both recalls the "praise" of "In Memory of W. B. Yeats" and anticipates the admonition to "praise" directed at Joseph in "For the Time Being": "Rejoice, dear love, in Love's peremptory word," and the stanza announces that the couple will "Describe round our chaotic malice now, / The arbitrary circle of a vow. (*CP* 319). Until the last line, the most concrete word in the stanza is "flesh." The last line, which evokes the "ring" of companions in "Summer Night," refers to a wedding ring, a concrete object that symbolizes a permanent commitment. In the context of marriage, Auden owes the word "arbitrary" to Rougemont, who argues that the decision to marry "must always be arbitrary" (313), by which he means that a Christian marriage must be entered into with the understanding that it is a free but irrevocable choice that is not based on any calculation of the likelihood of future happiness. As Ursula Niebuhr points out in her contribution to Spender's *Tribute* volume, Auden understood the word "arbitrary" to mean not "random" or "capricious" but "free" and "gratuitous." When during a discussion Auden referred to grace as "arbitrary," Niebuhr mentions that "someone who obviously did not know Latin, questioned the word 'arbitrary.' I hastened to translate it into the English word 'free.' Wystan, rather like a school master, gave his approval" (Spender, *Tribute* 106). Thus, one does not choose a marriage partner at random; rather, one enters into marriage uncompelled by any sense of necessity, consciously making a free choice to love one person uniquely, which is the intended connotation of the "arbitrary" vow.

It is possible, Carpenter indicates, that Auden and Kallman had actually sworn marriage vows (312). Carpenter cites this poem as the only substantial evidence of real vows between the two (312), and he notes that the poem does express hope "That this round O of faithfulness we swear / May never wither to an empty nought, / Nor petrify into a square" (*CP* 320). The "round O" is both the vow and, presumably, the wedding band that symbolizes the promise of fidelity. Although Auden frequently used autobiographical material in his poetry, he did sometimes modify details significantly, making it difficult to use the poems to establish biographical facts that are not corroborated elsewhere. Auden and Kallman began their relationship in earnest in 1939, a full year before Auden had read *Love in the Western World*, but the book certainly validated the relationship in Auden's mind, and if he and Kallman did make explicit vows to each other, Rougemont may have suggested the idea.

Another poem from 1940, "Leap Before You Look," takes up an image from Kierkegaard to describe both marital agape and religious faith. The last stanza states, "A solitude ten thousand fathoms deep / Sustains the bed on which we lie, my dear: / Although I love you, you will have to leap" (*CP* 314). The poem is generally read partly as an encouragement to Kallman to convert to Christianity, though

Kallman never did. Auden drew the image of floating over thousands of fathoms from Kierkegaard, who uses the image to characterize the "religious stage" of life which one can inhabit only by a "leap of faith." Most of Kierkegaard's works had not been translated into English until some years later, but Auden was reading Kierkegaard's journals in 1940, as well as Rougemont, who explains the connection between Kierkegaard's three stages and romantic love: "Kierkegaard . . . extolled passion as being the highest value in the 'aesthetic stage' of life; then rose above passion by extolling marriage as being the highest value in the 'ethical stage' . . . ; and finally condemned marriage as the highest obstruction in the 'religious stage,' since marriage fetters us to time where faith requires eternity" (Rougemont 309). Since Kierkegaard saw marriage as an obstruction to the religious stage, Auden's use of Kierkegaard's flotation metaphor to refer positively to marriage appears to be drawn from Rougemont's modification of Kierkegaard, which is somewhat less negative about the value of marriage.

Rougemont argues, "Everything to be urged against marriage is true, and therefore should be urged against it," but once all the difficulties are acknowledged, "I adopt an open mind towards the imperfect poise of marriage and—happily or unhappily—live in wait of perfection. I realize that it is a wild attempt I am making (although at the same time an altogether natural one) to live perfectly in imperfection" (310–11). Auden's invitation in his poem to abandon the "dream of safety" and "leap" into faith, both faith in God and fidelity to each other, owes something to Rougemont's suggestion that marriage might be a "wild attempt." In his 1941 review, Auden indicates that he took seriously the book's argument on marriage: "In the last few chapters of his book Mr de Rougemont states the Christian doctrine of marriage, which will seem absurdly straitlaced to the hedonist and shockingly coarse to the romantic," and he added that "perhaps the unpleasant consequences of romantic love and romantic politics are making thoughtful people more willing to reconsider it than they were while a bourgeois convention, which professed to be Christian but was nothing of the kind, was still à la mode" (*Prose II* 140–41). Auden was certainly among those "thoughtful people" who had been reconsidering, and in his case embracing, Rougemont's account of Christian marriage, inasmuch as it was possible for him as a homosexual.

It was to this Augustinian conversion of eros into agape that Auden aspired in his attempt to form a marriage with Kallman at the same time that he was in the process of returning to Christianity. But by Auden's own account in *Modern Canterbury Pilgrims,* his conversion to Christianity was not complete until "I was forced to know in person what it is like to feel oneself the prey of demonic powers, in both the Greek and the Christian sense, stripped of self-control and self-respect, behaving like a ham actor in a Strindberg play" (*Prose III* 579). Auden refers to his furious and almost violent reaction to his discovery in July of 1941 that Kallman had taken a lover besides Auden, and that Kallman had never really intended to remain faithful to Auden in the first place (see Carpenter 311–12). As Carpenter describes it, their relationship had never had the equality of status that Auden's poetry had hoped for, but instead "Auden tended to treat [Kallman] as a schoolmaster treats a clever pupil, showing him off to friends when it was convenient and pleasant to do so, but brushing him aside or leaving him in the background when there was serious conversation to be had" (312). Once Auden discovered Kallman's infidelity, the two stopped having sexual relations, even though they remained close friends and even occasionally lived together for the rest of Auden's life. After the marriage dissolved, Auden's love poetry reflects a subtle shift away from the celebrations of difficult but obligatory fidelity that had characterized the few love poems from the early 1940s. Some of his post-Kallman poetry reflects a sad indulgence in ephemeral eros that is similar to the regret of his earlier poems but lacks even the wish for permanence. But other poems of the same period celebrate the difficult development of agape through care for one's neighbor.

L'AFFAIRE C: THE EARLY 1940S

Even before Auden had brought Augustine's thought to bear on his love poetry in the late 1930s, he had expressed doubt about the conventions of such poetry in the Western tradition. His love poetry had never been "conventional" in the sense of offering unqualified praise to the beloved, and he generally avoid the unrequited love that energizes many medieval and Renaissance lyrics. He had openly attacked the hyperbolic conventions of love lyrics in "As I Walked Out One Evening," and he would again satirize those conventions in the 1953 poem "'The Truest Poetry Is the Most Feigning.'" Yet his early love poems had been conventional in one crucial regard: they all focused on obstacles to love. Auden's thematic innovations had mainly to do with ways in which such obstacles were viewed. Love lyrics of the Renaissance tended to identify obstacles that are, strictly speaking, external to the lovers—class differences, physical distance, death, and even marriage to someone else—but the obstacles to love in Auden's early poetry are almost wholly internal to the lovers themselves. While internal obstacles to love are not wholly novel to the Western lyric tradition, Auden explored them in far greater depth than had any English poet before him. In Auden's lyrics from the 1930s, the main obstacles to lasting commitment are the lovers' own acquisitive desires and their consequent propensities toward infidelity. Then in 1940 Auden read Rougemont's *Love in the Western World*, which told him that the entire history of love poetry, from the "courtly love" of the troubadours to the repressed passion of the modern novel, was rooted in the same Manichean dualism that he had just finished denouncing in *New Year Letter*. Rougemont's book also argued that love poetry focused on obstacles to love because eros was not really a desire for gratification, though it often seemed so, but was actually a desire to go on desiring eternally. Therefore, according to Rougemont, eros seeks to prolong itself indefinitely and is thus always desiring the final obstacle to gratification, which is death. As such, eros seeks disembodiment in death as its ultimate good and so denies the goodness of the material world.

Since Auden's works in the late 1930s and early 1940s had appropriated Augustine's critique of Manichean dualism and, like Augustine, affirmed the goodness of the material world, it was understandable that Auden would take very seriously Rougemont's argument that lyric love poetry was the direct descendent of a heterodox mysticism that grew out of Manichaeism. The connection between Manichaeism and eros appears in a few of the poems that Auden wrote in the immediate aftermath of his discovery of Kallman's infidelity. One such poem, written in July 1941, titled "VIII" in the sequence "Ten Songs" from the *Collected Poems,* but better known by its first line, "Though determined Nature can," warns of the dangers even of committed love. In several ways the poem is a continuation of "In Sickness and in Health" (1940), which had anticipated the difficulties of commitment to fidelity in marriage and had yet acknowledged "an absurd command—Rejoice" (*CP* 319). But "Though determined Nature can" implicitly views the rejoicing in painful retrospect: "Hearts by envy are possessed / From the moment that they praise," and so "To rejoice, to be blessed" is highly dangerous (270). Fidelity always risks infidelity, and analogously, to be happy always opens up the possibility of misery. The lovers "cannot follow how / Evil miracles are done / Through the medium of a kiss" (271), and the poem goes on to suggest that "Aphrodite's garden" is haunted, so even the unspoken vows of lovers invite the demon eros. The "evil miracles" that come through a kiss evoke Judas' betrayal of Christ with a kiss in the Garden of Gethsemane, but also, more obliquely, the death of Auden's namesake, St. Wystan, who was murdered when his uncle Bertulph, "while giving Wystan the kiss of peace, . . . drew a sword from beneath his cloak [and] struck Wystan on the head, and killed him" (Osborne, *Life of a Poet* 9). The treacherous kiss is associated with "Aphrodite's garden," and in Greek myth, Aphrodite is the mother of the god Eros. In the poem, every romantic kiss is potentially a traitor's kiss.

The lovers "register their vow" with looks and sighs, rather than concrete objects such as the wedding ring to which "In Sickness and in Health" alludes. They do not even use words; the "vow" is entirely implicit in the relationship, and it becomes an explicit vow only as it is articulated in the poem. The tokens of the vow, the look and the sigh, suggest that the underlying motivation for the relationship is an acquisitive eros unmitigated by a self-giving agape. Vows motivated by eros in turn invite "Legion," the collective name of the many devils who are exorcized by Christ in the Gospels (see Mark 5:1–20). The legion of devils also recalls sections of *New Year Letter,* in which the Devil is a personification of conflicting and irreconcilable desires that compete for dominance within the human mind. But in this poem, the choice to satisfy the desire for a stable fidelity inevitably stimulates contrary desires, the legion of demons, the divided and contradictory desires of the fallen human mind. Despite the presence of the demonic in the relationship, the last stanza indicates that the failed relationship has nevertheless produced empathy, since "We, my darling, for our sins, / Suffer in each other's woe." That shared suffering becomes a not-very-reassuring plea: "O my love, O my love, / In the night of fire and snow / Save me from evil" (*CP* 271). The poem had initially placed the blame for the relationship's failure on the eros of both lovers, but the end of the poem somewhat ingenuously places the hope of restoration on only one of them.

Soon after he wrote "Though determined Nature can," Auden began writing his Christmas oratorio. It is widely acknowledged that Auden's crisis with Kallman, or "l'affaire C" as Auden sometimes called it, provided the emotional energy behind several passages in "For the Time Being," which he began writing in October 1941 (see Mendelson, *Later* 175, 179–83, and Carpenter 312–13). One section of the poem, "The Temptation of St. Joseph," is frequently pointed out as one of the best parts of the oratorio, and its emotional intensity resembles the lover's anxiety that had characterized Auden's earlier love poems. The passage depicts Joseph as a cuckolded lover whose demands for a divine explanation go unanswered:

> Where are you, Father, where?
> . . . .
> Answer me, Father, how
> Can I answer the tactless wall
> Or the pompous furniture now?
> . . . .
> All I ask is one
> Important and elegant proof
> That what my Love had done
> Was really at your will
> And that your will is Love. (*CP* 363–64)

Gabriel's answer is emphatic if not reassuring: "No, you must believe; Be silent, and sit still" (*CP* 364). The passage recalls the whole tradition of the theological "complaint," from Job and Jeremiah to Milton's "When I consider how my light is spent," in that it emphasizes the necessity of faith without empirical proof that God has the speaker's best interests at heart. While the existence of eros is easily evidenced by greedy and acquisitive behavior, the existence of agape is much more difficult to prove. As Auden would explain years later in *The Dyer's Hand*: "When a lover tells his beloved that she is his mistress and that he desires to be her servant, what he is trying, honestly or hypocritically, to say is something as follows: 'As you know, I find you beautiful, an object of desire. I know that for true love such desire is not enough; I must also love you, not as an object of my desire, but as you are in yourself; I must desire your self-fulfillment. I cannot know you as you are nor prove that I desire your self-fulfillment, unless you tell me what you want and allow me to try and give it to you'" (139). Auden's interpretation of the honest lover's offer to be the servant of the beloved suggests that in a romantic relationship eros and agape always coexist and that even the hypocritical lover must pay lip-service to agape. The honest lover clearly desires to possess the beloved (*eros*), but he also desires the beloved's own self-fulfillment (*agape*), and he hopes that these two desires will not be contradictory. But the honest lover cannot prove the existence of agape unless the beloved expresses her desires. Joseph's dialogue with Gabriel in "For the Time Being" illustrates the point. Joseph may demand "proof / . . . / that your will is Love" (*CP* 364), but God will reject such demands to prove that he desires Joseph's self-fulfillment. Instead, it is God who gives a command to believe silently, obedience to which will be the proof of Joseph's own agape love for both God and Mary. As far as the metaphor goes, God will be the beloved who gives commands (typically the female), but never the lover who obeys commands (typically male), hence the further reversal of gender roles when Gabriel tells Joseph, "To-day the roles are altered; you must be / The Weaker Sex whose passion is passivity" (365).

Other parts of "For the Time Being" provide a more encouraging account of the transformation of eros into agape. For example, Mary says in "The Annunciation,"

> My flesh in terror and fire
> Rejoices that the Word
> Who utters the world out of nothing
> As a pledge of His word to love her
> Against her will, and to turn
> Her desperate longing to love,
> Should ask to wear me,
> From now to their wedding day,
> For an engagement ring. (*CP* 360)

The stanza is perhaps the clearest expression in all of Auden's poetry of the way in which eros, or the "desperate longing" of the world, can be transformed into love, specifically agape, and as Anthony Hecht points out, "This 'choice' or assent of Mary's symbolizes St. Augustine's declaration, quoted by Auden in *Secondary Worlds*: 'God, who made us without our help will not save us without our consent'" (259). Through Mary's personal assent to the Incarnation, God's grace can express itself in human history. While the divine love expressed in the Incarnation opposes the general will of the world—Herod speaks for those who take the rejection of divine love to extremes—Mary's willful acceptance of God's love makes possible the alteration of the corrupted loves of others. Gabriel reemphasizes the fact that Mary's consent is freely willed: "child, it lies / Within your power of choosing to / Conceive the Child who chooses you" (*CP* 360). Adam's free choice to sin greatly diminished human freedom, but Mary's free choice to do right restores the possibility of agape within human history. Simeon's speech offers a further explanation of the relationship between freedom and love. He asserts that "the course of History is predictable in the degree to which all men love themselves, and spontaneous in the degree to which each man loves God and through him his neighbour" (388). Simeon indicates that in the world of natural necessity driven by eros, the selfish will to self-actualization, is the "natural" state of all living creatures, including humans; so just as animal behavior is predictable because based on the drives of self-preservation and reproduction, all human actions based solely on eros are conditioned behaviors and therefore not truly free acts at all. Human actions based on agape, however, are not conditioned behaviors but are freely willed, and thus they are not predictable but always novel and surprising.[20]

Mendelson reports that an early draft of Simeon's speech paraphrased a passage from Augustine's *Confessions* in which Augustine comments on his excessive response to the death of a close friend (*Later* 214). Auden's draft has Simeon saying, "At eighty bereavement has become a familiar experience / But every time some dear flesh disappears / What is real is the arriving grief" (qtd. in *Later* 214). The idea of bereavement being more real than a human friend derives from Augustine's statement that, after the death of his friend Nebridius, "I wept most bitterly, and found my repose in bitterness. Thus was I wretched, and that wretched life I held dearer than my friend. For though I would willingly have changed it, yet was I more unwilling to part with it, than with him; yea, I know not whether I would have parted with it even for him . . ." (*Confessions* 4.6). Augustine castigates himself for allowing his grief to overwhelm him with a fear of death and for loving his friend without being aware of their mutual mortality (4.6–7). In Auden's draft version of this sentiment, Simeon is an old man who is still tempted by seductive griefs as Augustine was. The death of a friend can still lead to a disordered preference for grief, which is itself a kind of eros. Auden later discarded the passage, but as Mendelson observes, he eventually incorporated some of the ideas in the draft into the beginning of Prospero's speech in *The Sea and the Mirror* (*Later* 214). Prospero says to Ariel, "every time some dear flesh disappears / What is real is the arriving grief; thanks to your service, / The lonely and unhappy are very much alive" (*CP* 404). Prospero holds Ariel, the inspiring muse, responsible for making grief seem more real than the dead friend, but Ariel is also prone to encouraging the artist to indulge in what Simeon calls the imagination's "promiscuous fornication with her own images" (388), *fantastica fornicatio* in Augustine's language. Even grief can be a form of unredeemed eros.

Nevertheless, in the early 1940s, Auden identifies eros with the general survival impulse in all sentient life, without which no life would exist, and he explores the idea of eros as the "natural" state of humans in "Mundus et Infans," which Auden wrote about a month after finishing "For the Time Being." The poem describes the tyrannical eros of a baby: "Kicking his mother until she let go of his soul / Has given him a healthy appetite . . ." (*CP* 324). The line evokes the Roman emperor Nero, who kicked his own mother to death, and the political language of the next few lines suggests further parallels between dictatorships and the autocratic desires of the infant, who demands that his desires be met immediately and without regard to the well being of other people. The poem implicitly extrapolates from Augustine's account in the *Confessions* of the jealous baby, who for Augustine demonstrates that the human will is corrupted from birth (1.7). "For the Time Being" makes use of this passage in the voices of human embryos, whose primal cell divisions are analogous to the divided consciousness that is already arising in them before birth. But the use of Augustine's description of the jealous baby in "Mundus et Infans" even more closely approximates the context in which Augustine's discussion appears. In both the *Confessions* and "Mundus et Infans," the baby's angry cries are reminders that, as Auden's poem puts it, "we had never learned to distinguish / between hunger and love . . ." (*CP* 325). Selfish desire, or eros, which in the baby is primarily expressed as hunger, is the initial motivation of every human being, though as Augustine remarks, "the very same tempers are utterly intolerable when found in riper years" (*Confessions* 1.7). Childish selfishness is intolerable in adults, though both Augustine and Auden recognize that the loves expressed even by adults more often approximate childish eros than mature agape. As Prospero muses in "The Sea and the Mirror," "seducers / Are sincerely puzzled at being unable to love / What they are able to possess" (*CP* 405). In these poems, the unbridled expression of eros, whether as hunger, as libido, or as any other natural desire, precludes the expression of agape.

Because eros is the natural condition of all humans—"natural" in the sense of existing from birth as a result of the Fall, rather than in the sense of being part of the originally good creation—the transformation of eros into agape is never easy. For instance, "Canzone," written soon after "Mundus et Infans," struggles to articulate the strained relationship between the demands of eros and agape in what Mendelson calls "the cramped, knotted style Auden favored when writing in the first person about emotional agonies he did not want to identify" (*Later* 215). Gottlieb explains at some length Auden's use of the Dantean form of the canzone and points out the ambiguities of the poem's use of the word "will," one of the five rhyming words in the poem (164–71, 176–82). "Will" may appear as either sheer volition or as possessive desire, and is complicated by the presences of two individuals, each with their own "wills," within the relationship. Gottlieb also explains that Auden's later essay in *Modern Canterbury Pilgrims* repeats phrasing from the poem's third stanza (177), which reads "In my own person I am forced to know / How much must be forgotten out of love" (*CP* 331); the essay states, "I was forced to know in person what it is like to feel oneself the prey of demonic powers . . ." (*Prose III* 579). While the poem itself never positively identifies its own subject, the obscurity fits the mood of the speaker, who is not sure of his own feelings about the unidentified crisis of love.

However, at the outset of "Canzone," the demands of agape are clearly stated: "When shall we learn, what should be clear as day, / We cannot choose what we are free to love?" (*CP* 330). The question sounds like a contradiction in terms, but it indicates that we are existentially free to give or withhold love, but we are not morally free to choose to love one person but not another. The Christian is morally obliged to love everyone, even though free will allows the Christian to disobey. The poem's premise as stated in the first two lines is that the speaker knows he has a moral obligation to love (in the sense of *agape*) all other humans, but genuine agape cannot be coerced, but must be given freely. The next stanza states that "we are required to love / All homeless objects that require a world" (330). The word "objects" suggests the insentient, but Auden seems to have in mind all other human beings, whom the subjective self views as objects. The key word is "homeless," which, thanks to Reinhold Niebuhr, Auden identified with Augustine's "restless" heart, which is anxious or "homeless" in the world and only at home in God.[21] The poem holds out little hope that eros can be redeemed, since "Our claim to own our bodies and our world / Is our catastrophe" (*CP* 330). Possessiveness, even of one's self, is a feature of eros, which may express itself in acquisition or, conversely, by withholding agape: "What we love / Ourselves for is our power not to love . . ." (*CP* 330). Gottlieb points out that the word "power" is the syllabic center of the poem (171), so the vindictive refusal to love selflessly is not just another manifestation of eros but its very essence. In the speaker's case, agape recognizes "how much must be forgiven, even love" (*CP* 331), a statement which makes little sense outside the context of Kallman's betrayal of Auden, which necessitated Auden's forgiveness of Kallman for loving someone else.

At the same time, the poem hints that the self-willing eros is redeemable because, as a desire, it points out the possibility of divine agape. The poem characterizes eros as "blind monsters" who reside "in the depths of myself" and who are afraid of "Love / That asks its images for more than love" (*CP* 331). If the capitalized "Love" is God—an inversion of 1 John 4:8 in which "God is love"—then Love's "images" are humans, who are made in God's image. As it appears in Auden's poem, human nature correctly fears that God demands "more than love," that is, agape and not just eros, love freely given rather than appetites selfishly satisfied. The demands of agape, however, also provoke eros: "The hot rampageous horses of my will, / Catching the scent of Heaven, whinny" (331). But the poet immediately reminds himself of his responsibility to keep eros on a tight rein, since "Love / Gives no excuse to evil done for love" (331). The proper response to the temptation to indulge in eros is to "praise our God of Love / That we are so admonished, that no day / Of conscious trial be a wasted day" (331). The exhortation to praise in the midst of a relational crisis appears again and again in Auden's poetry, and almost always, as here, against a background of emotional pain and insecurity. The last line reminds us, "There must be sorrow if there can be love," that agape always involves personal risk (331), but even in the event of unrequited agape, the poet says that he can at least be grateful that his experience has taught him a lesson.

But what lesson did Auden learn from what he called a "day / Of conscious trial"? (*CP* 331). In "Canzone" he is honest about the ethical demands that Christian love has begun to make on him, and he is also honest about his own failure to exercise agape in response to Kallman's infidelity. Agape, he recognized, was a sacred duty, but after he and Kallman broke off their marriage, it was no longer clear to Auden how the demands of eros that his sexuality made on him could be reconciled with the demands of agape that his renewed faith made on him. He had thought that, by entering into what he considered to be a Christian marriage, he could express his sexuality within the confines of a monogamous relationship, which would moderate eros and keep it subjected to the agape that was expressed by his vow of faithfulness. It is a testament to Auden's strength of character that he was able to maintain his fidelity to Kallman for two years, and but for Kallman's infidelity, Auden might have remained monogamous indefinitely. But after the crisis, Auden gave up the idea that his homosexuality could be reconciled with his Christianity. For Auden, sex was an addiction that had to be regularly satisfied. Like many addicts, he occasionally regretted and resisted it, and often he happily indulged in it. According to Christopher Isherwood, Auden's "religion condemned it and he agreed that it was sinful, though he fully intended to go on sinning" (249). Isherwood's statement is, perhaps, an oversimplification of Auden's complex and conflicted attitudes about his own sexuality, but whether he was unable or unwilling to give up his homosexuality, it eventually entered into an uncomfortable coexistence with his faith.

In "The Sea and the Mirror," Auden is quite likely referring to his own conflicted attitudes toward his homosexuality when Caliban, as the voice of the body, says, "Had you tried to destroy me, had we wrestled through long dark hours, we might by daybreak have learnt something from each other; . . . we might both have heard together that music which explains and pardons all" (*CP* 434).²² The subjunctive "had you tried" presumes, of course, that this has not happened. The poet to whom Caliban addresses this segment of his monologue has not wrestled with the eros of his physical desires, but neither has the poet allowed his eros total liberty "to be drunk every day before lunch, to jump stark naked from bed to bed, to have a fit every week or a major operation every other year, to forge checks or water the widow's stock . . ." (434). The only option left for him, Caliban says, is "to forgive and forget the past, and to keep our respective hopes for the future within moderate, very moderate, limits" (435). While it is not immediately obvious that this passage refers to Auden's personal life at all, much less to his difficulties with his homosexuality, Auden did say in a letter to Stephen Spender, "I'm extremely pleased and surprised to find that at least one reader feels that the section written in a pastiche of James is more me than the sections written in my own style, because it is the paradox I was trying for, and am afraid hardly anyone will get it" (qtd. in Kirsch, Introduction xxxii).

Auden's claim that Caliban's voice is "more me" than the other voices in the poem is most clearly applicable to the view Caliban expresses about the nature and limitations of art, but in an earlier essay titled "Jacob and the Angel," Auden uses the same image of Jacob wrestling with the angel to describe the Freudian relationship between the conscious self and unconscious drives, arguing that "the daemon creates Jacob the prudent Ego, not for the latter to lead, in self-isolation and contempt, a frozen attic life of its own, but to be a loving and reverent antagonist" (*Prose II* 39). He adds that "it is only through that wrestling bout of which the sex act and the mystical union are the typical symbols that the future is born, that Jacob acquires the power and the will to live, and the demon is transformed into an angel" (39). In "The Sea and the Mirror," the sex act still symbolizes the struggle to achieve the "mystical union" of body and spirit, which have largely replaced the Freudian id and ego, but the settlement Caliban describes is only a stalemate, not marriage. Caliban's final statement about his relationship with the unnamed poet whom he addresses is an exact description of the uneasy settlement to which Auden came with his homosexuality; he kept his expectations for reconciliation between his faith and his sexuality within very moderate limits.

After Auden's marriage fell apart, he continued to write some poems about love, although in the direct aftermath of "l'affaire C," he wrote comparatively fewer lyric poems than he had in the past, and he spent the rest of the 1940s composing several long poems: "For the Time Being," "The Sea and the Mirror," and "The Age of Anxiety." While each of these touches on the nature of romantic love, Auden's poetry returns to a serious consideration of the continuously problematic relationship between eros and agape only in the late 1940s, but few of Auden's poems of this period make any attempt to reconcile eros and agape. Most of them treat the two loves separately. Quite a few of Auden's later love lyrics picture a self-conscious indulgence in Manichean eros in that they portray an occasionally successful attempt to cordon off the poet's active sexuality from his religious beliefs. Other poems from the same period make serious attempts to discuss the obligations and rewards of neighborly agape, though they often focus on the ultimate failure of humans to express genuine agape. Nevertheless, the few poems that address agape do develop a nuanced account that connects it theologically with the goodness of the material world and the freedom of the will. Such poems stand in stark contrast to Auden's poems on eros, even though both strains of poetry continue paradoxically to rely on Augustine's understanding of love.

AFTER L'AFFAIRE C: SELF-CONSCIOUS MANICHAEISM

A conspicuously Manichean poem is Auden's "The Love Feast" (1948), which is rife with ironic references to rituals of Christian worship. The poem describes "an upper room at midnight" where revelers gather in the name of "love" (*CP* 613). The references to the Last Supper are obvious, and the poem's title refers to the communion service as well (which is still referred to as a "love feast" in some Christian traditions), but in the poem's first stanza, the "love" on whose behalf the group is gathered is not Christ's self-sacrificial agape, but the eros as celebrated by popular culture and mass media. Like the Last Supper, the feast includes unfaithful companions. The poem's middle stanzas shift away from a parodic treatment of the Last Supper toward a more general parody of religious language, and with this subtle shift in metaphor comes a shift in tone. While the first stanzas are irreverently funny, the next few stanzas take on a surprising moral seriousness while maintaining their humorous veneer: "Steep enthusiastic eyes / Flicker after tits and baskets; / Someone vomits; someone cries" (613). The party, while pleasurable, is not an idyllic aesthetic experience. The wide-eyed eros of neophyte revelers co-exists with sickness and sadness, and each named person in the poem is undergoing some kind of emotional pain. Troubled family relationships remind the poet of his own guilty relationship with God from whose gaze he cannot escape: "The Love that rules the sun and stars / Permits what He forbids" (614).

The juxtaposition of the pain-causing eros with the divine agape that will not violate free will is poignant, as is the contrast between a dog that is incapable of sin and the sinner who gratuitously gives the dog pleasure by petting it: "Drunken absent-minded fingers / Pat a sinless world" (*CP* 613–14). The petting of the dog is perhaps the only example of human agape in the poem, since the fingers that pet the dog are "absent-minded," suggesting that the dog is being given pleasure freely, without being expected to offer any in return. The last two stanzas of the poem replicate the structure of the poem's fourth stanza, in which the first two lines describe the revelers and the next two lines offer a theological commentary of sorts. The speaker watches a woman lying to someone over the telephone and remarks, "The Love that made her out of nothing / Tells me to go home" (614); he plans to make advances toward a coy "Miss Number" as he says " I am sorry I'm not sorry . . . / Make me chaste, Lord, but not yet" (614). The last line of the poem quotes from Augustine's *Confessions* to at once acknowledge the ethical demands the poet's faith makes on him and temporarily resist those demands. Auden's reference to Augustine is apt; in the original context in the *Confessions,* the phrase is part of Augustine's explanation of his early struggle between his emerging sexuality and his awareness of divine disapproval: "I wretched, most wretched, in the very commencement of my early youth, had begged chastity of Thee, and said, 'Give me chastity and continency, only not yet.' For I feared lest Thou shouldest hear me soon, and soon cure me of the disease of concupiscence, which I wished to have satisfied, rather than extinguished. And I had wandered through crooked ways in a sacrilegious superstition, not indeed assured thereof, but as preferring it to the others which I did not seek religiously, but opposed maliciously" (8.7). Auden's "prayer" at the end of "The Love Feast" exactly represents Augustine's early preference of sexual indulgence to a morally coherent life. Both Auden and Augustine frankly acknowledge the incoherence of their aspirations, based as they are on irreconcilable desires, and they openly admit their intention to persist in their sin.

Augustine's immediate connection of his adolescent incontinence with his foray into Manichaeism—the "sacrilegious superstition" referred to above—is also significant in this context, since Auden explicitly links unrestrained sexuality with Manichaeism in a 1969 poem, "Doggerel by a Senior Citizen." The poem contrasts the poet's Edwardian upbringing that inculcated staunchly middle-class values with the more permissive world of the late 1960s, noting that, while sex has always been an enticing mystery, the newsstands of the Edwardian age "did not yet supply / Manichaean pornography" (*CP* 852). The lament that the twentieth century was more sexually permissive than the nineteenth century had already become a commonplace in the 1960s, but the connection between pornography and Manichaeism requires some explanation. At one level, the connection recalls Augustine's youthful preference for Manichaeism over Christianity because the former allowed him to be sexually promiscuous. But at a deeper level, pornography is "Manichean" because it reduces individual humans to objects of physical desire, treating them as mere bodies rather than as whole persons. The objectification of the body as separate from the soul denigrates the person as a whole, but also justifies aggression and violence against the body, an attitude that is generally consistent with the Manichean denunciations of the human body as intrinsically evil. Auden later wrote, "all pornography is Manichean. Its purpose is to throw shame on the bodily functions" (qtd. in Bridgen 3). Yet another reason for Auden to connect pornography with Manichaeism is Rougemont's attempt to link the eros, or passion, of Manichean mysticism with the development of erotic literature in Western culture. Auden had ample reason for calling pornography "Manichean."

A poem that treats Manichean eros more seriously is "Pleasure Island" (1948), which Auden wrote about the social atmosphere at Fire Island, an island near New York City where Auden had rented a summer cottage two years earlier. Carpenter reports that Fire Island suited Auden not only because the beach offered cooler weather in the summer than did the city, but also because it was becoming a local magnet for homosexuals (345). The poem describes a locale surrounded by an indifferent ocean, a place where the only socially unacceptable activities are those that render one unavailable for revels. It is a place wholly unsuited to literary work especially, and the poem follows a once-busy writer (apparently not Auden) who soon finds himself relaxed on the beach where he watches "As bosom, backside, crotch / Or other sacred trophy is borne in triumph / Past his adoring by / Souls he does not try to like . . ." (*CP* 344). In this environment, the writer is faced with an irresistibly Manichean temptation to abstract the soul from the body, or even body parts from the body as a whole. He begins to objectify body parts and even revere them as "sacred trophies," and in doing so he separates bodies from the souls that animate them, an activity that makes artistic production impossible for the writer. Auden would later comment on the ultimate irreconcilability of Manichaeism and artistic production in *Secondary Worlds*, where he claims, "Whatever heresies they fall into, by the very nature of their work, an artist cannot become a gnostic Manichee, nor a scientist a Pelagian" (137). On one hand, Auden did admit that some works of art could be Manichean, since he accused Shakespeare of writing one (*The Tempest*; see *DH* 130). But the artist as a person, Auden said in *The Dyer's Hand*, could not degrade the physical world per se, since the work of art must exist as a physical entity (69–70). Thus, the writer in "Pleasure Island" finds he must abandon his art when he allows himself to adore bodies divorced from souls, an ironic acquiescence to the Manichean devaluation of bodies.

The Manichaeism of "Pleasure Island" ultimately leads to isolation as friendships do not last longer than a weekend. The poem momentarily returns to the sadness of ephemeral relationships that characterized Auden's poems in the 1930s, but there is no praise for the momentary pleasures of promiscuity as the speaker watches "some decaying / Spirit" wandering down the beach, "excusing itself / To itself with evangelical gestures / For having failed the test . . ." (*CP* 345). The figure walking away from the lively bar is merely a "spirit," though not exactly a disembodied one since it is "kicking idly at driftwood and dead shellfish" (344). Yet, the language of the passage depicts the person as an abstracted spirit to such an extent that it obscures even the person's gender. The poem's connection of isolation with Manichean abstraction of the soul from the body recalls Rougemont's argument that eros is ultimately a form of morbid, narcissistic isolation (32–38, 291–92). The poem's title, "Pleasure Island," with its Arcadian overtones, is therefore highly ironic, since Fire Island is a "Place of a skull, a place where the rose of / Self-punishment will grow" (*CP* 344). The lines allude to the hill of Golgotha outside Jerusalem, the "place of the skull" where Christ was crucified, but they also evoke a trope in several seventeenth-century paintings in which Arcadian shepherds gather around a newly discovered human skull that has disrupted their idyllic existence.[23] The association of eros and death had already been made commonplace by Freud, but it took on theological significance once Auden appropriated Rougemont's Augustinian critique of the cult of eros.

Later in life Auden wrote a few more self-consciously Manichean poems, which were circulated among his friends but not published until after his death. Three of these from the 1960s were collected under the heading "Three Posthumous Poems." All three frankly celebrate the poet's homosexual relationships, but the second, titled "Aubade,"[24] looks forward with some apprehension to the time when he will have to give up sex and "put on / The Widow's Cap" (*CP* 747). The other poems express unreserved gratitude for lovers whom the poet names, "Hugerl" who "for a decade now" has been "An unexpected blessing / In a lucky life" (746), and "Bert," whose visit has made it possible for the poet to "listen to the piercing screams / of palliardising cats / without self-pity" (748). These poems are relaxed, both formally and emotionally, and represent Auden's later work in its most complacent Manichaeism in which his sex life has been largely isolated from the rest of his existence, and so has ceased to be a source of either emotional or literary tension. He tells Hugerl that he is "Glad our worlds of enchantment / Are so several / Neither is tempted to broach" (746). According to Mendelson, Hugerl was an auto mechanic in Vienna whom Auden paid for sex (*Later* 375). The partners inhabit totally separate worlds: "I cannot tell a / Jaguar from a Bentley, / And you never read" (*CP* 746). The relationship consists of pure eros in that each partner participates from purely economic motives, to get something he needs from the other. In contrast to his early love poems, the speaker has no illusions that this sexual relationship could ever become a friendship.

However, Mendelson points out another significant difference: Auden's "idealizing or animalistic moods of the 1930s, when he addressed his beloved impersonally as 'my dove, my coney' or as 'you, my swan,' were gone, and not regretted" (*Later* 375). So in one sense the poems are Manichean in their indulgence of eros, but at least the first poem in the series "Glad," which is addressed to Hugerl, resists becoming fully Manichean because it recognizes the particularity of the relationship and describes it as a good thing in all its physicality. It could hardly be called a "Christian" poem, except in the broadest sense that it presumes the fundamental goodness of physical existence. It has been suggested that, in these poems in which Auden frankly celebrates his own sexuality, Auden is working in the Platonic-Catholic tradition of Dante in which erotic love becomes a ladder to love of God, but such a reading ignores both Auden's earlier critiques of Platonism and the fact that none of the poems show any hint of aspiration to divine love. When it came to relating his homosexuality to his faith, Auden had learned to keep his expectations within very moderate limits.

AFTER L'AFFAIRE C: ASPIRATIONS TO AGAPE

Partly because of his homosexuality, and partly because of the ambiguity of the terms, Auden's various statements about the exact relationship between eros and agape are not entirely consistent with each other. Monroe Spears plausibly argues that Auden's views changed in the 1940s, during which time "Auden shifts from this initial tendency to regard Eros and Agape as wholly distinct (in the manner of Kierkegaard, Barth, Nygren, and extreme Protestants in general) to the view that they are conjoinable in the Catholic concept of Caritas. This trend away from Gnostic or Manichean tendencies is very much in the spirit of Dante" ("Divine" 60). But Spears claims elsewhere, "The classic Protestant exposition of the radical distinction between Agape and Eros is Anders Nygren's *Agape and Eros*," whereas "the Roman Catholic position is that the two are united in Caritas," and Spears cites D'Arcy's *The Mind and Heart of Love* as an example, adding that "Auden's attitude has always been

Protestant in this respect" (*Poetry* 164n). Whether Auden had ever fully agreed with Nygren's total denunciation of eros is questionable since Auden read and absorbed Rougemont almost as soon as he had formally rejoined the Anglican Church. He had always aspired to a reconciliation of eros with other kinds of love, but the actual possibility of achieving such a reconciliation remained elusive, either in his poetry or in his personal life. But there can be no doubt that Auden was indeed attracted to the Catholic[25] and specifically the Augustinian concept of caritas as a fusion of agape and eros.

In a favorable 1947 review of *The Portable Dante,* Auden also praised D'Arcy's book, recommending that a modern reader of Dante should, "in view of the infinite distance between the common modern meaning of the word *love* and the *amor* of Dante, . . . read a first-rate study of the subject . . . , *The Mind and Heart of Love*" (*Prose II* 325). As it happened, D'Arcy and Auden had known each other for some time. D'Arcy knew of Auden when the latter was an undergraduate at Oxford, though Auden did not yet know him. Auden attended a lecture on Christian love that D'Arcy gave in New York in 1940, and they began corresponding when Auden wrote to D'Arcy asking for clarification on certain points of the lecture (Harp 13). D'Arcy's book offers a much more nuanced treatment of Western ideas of love than does Rougemont's *Love in the Western World,* but essentially the book, as Spears states, "joins Eros and Agape in the concept of Caritas" ("Divine" 60n). D'Arcy's work refutes Nygren's hypothesis of an irreconcilable difference between eros and agape, but it also argues that Rougemont's account of the conflict is not historically warranted and overlooks other kinds of love, such as friendship, or philia (D'Arcy 40–41). D'Arcy also notes that Nygren's and Rougemont's respective accounts are not wholly inconsistent with each other in that they articulate differing perspectives on the same basic conflict (199). D'Arcy argues that eros and agape are the acquisitive and sacrificial impulses, respectively, or as he calls them, "centripetal" and "centrifugal" loves, and he explains that the two loves can peacefully coexist within the Christian life (200).

Auden had made a very similar argument in his 1941 review of Rougemont's book that eros and agape could reconcile within a dialectical relationship (*Prose II* 139). Auden found in D'Arcy's book a Christian account of love that went much further than Rougemont in explaining in detail how agape and eros, along with other forms of love, such as philia, could exist side-by-side with each other, maintaining their differences without conflict or violence. It may seem strange that Auden was attracted both to Rougemont's ideas and to D'Arcy's, since Spears suggests that they represent polar opposites in a Protestant/Catholic debate, but in theological matters Auden liked to find continuities between different traditions, a habit of thought that was reinforced by Williams's *The Descent of the Dove,* and he was able to admire both Rougemont's and D'Arcy's works as different articulations of the Christian concept of caritas (charity) that is traceable to their mutual source in Augustine.

Rougemont emphasized the conflict between eros and agape, and D'Arcy emphasized their union, but Auden's praise of both books suggests that he interpreted
them as fundamentally in agreement with each other, despite differences in details
and emphases.

One of D'Arcy's many significant contributions to the debate on eros and agape
is his opening up a consideration of more than two forms of love. The book is subtitled *Lion and Unicorn, a Study in Eros and Agape,* but instead of allowing Nygren
and Rougemont to set the terms of the discussion as a debate between only two
opposing loves, D'Arcy explores the ways in which other loves, such as friendship
(philia), relate to centripetal eros and centrifugal agape. Auden's early poetry had
also endeavored to relate friendship to other forms of love, but after his breakup
with Kallman, the term "love" never appears in his poetic discussions of friendship,
even though friendship continues to be an important element of his later poetry.
He dedicates many of his later poems to various friends and acquaintances, and
in "Thanksgiving for a Habitat," he includes several poems on friendship, such as
"The Cave of Making," which is addressed to his deceased friend Louis MacNeice;
"For Friends Only," which explores the implications of the guest room; and "The
Common Life," which comments on the relationship between common living space
and friendship. But these poems are not about what Auden would call "love," for in
his mind, the word "love" never entirely lacks sexual connotations. In this respect,
Auden's later work continues to rely less on D'Arcy than on Rougemont, for whom
Christian charity exists primarily in Christian marriage, an institution in which
Auden found he could not participate.

It is unfortunate that Auden never wrote a review of D'Arcy's book, although
it is not surprising since most of his book reviews were commissioned. But the
book's impact on him was nonetheless significant. Philip Larkin famously com-
plains that Auden's later poetry was based, not on experience, but on books (125),
and he describes "In Praise of Limestone" as "agreeable and ingenious" but lacking
in "poetic pressure," accusing the author of "indulg[ing] his tastes in reading and
travel" (126–27). Despite Larkin's doubts, it is one of the most moving poems of
Auden's later years. Larkin is right that "In Praise of Limestone" relies heavily on
books—D'Arcy and Wallace Stevens are clearly present, while Dante and Augustine
linger under the surface—but no one could accuse the poem of ignoring personal
experience. "In Praise of Limestone" is one of Auden's most successful attempts
to integrate experience with "bookish" knowledge, and it was likely written with
D'Arcy's analysis of Christian love in mind.

The poem's opening evokes Auden's 1930s love poems with its focus on a limestone landscape that appeals to "we, the inconstant ones" (*CP* 540). The poem
describes a series of allegorical terrains in which the characteristics of each landscape reflect a different type of person. The average, "inconstant ones" appreciate
the limestone landscape which looks like solid rock, even though "it dissolves in

water" so that "beneath, / A secret system of caves and conduits" permeates it (540). Both landscape and lover play at permanence but easily allow for transience and change. Other types of people appreciate other landscapes, so the "saints-to-be" prefer the "granite wastes" because they are solid and constant, and the "Intendant Caesars" prefer "clays and gravels" because of their malleability (541). But there are still others, whom the poet calls "the really reckless," who respond to "an older colder voice, the oceanic whisper" (541). Auden would soon explore what he called the "Romantic iconography of the sea" in *The Enchafèd Flood* (1950), in which the ocean often represents the primal chaos of subconscious desires, and in "In Praise of Limestone" the ocean speaks distinctly in terms of Rougemont's description of eros as an escape into the illusive freedom of nothingness: "I am the solitude that asks and promises nothing / . . . There is no love; / There are only the various envies, all of them sad" (*CP* 542). To indulge completely in the eros of "various envies" isolates the reckless person completely, denying the possibility of any type of love, whether eros or philia or agape.

However, in the second stanza, the speaker takes up the voice of "the inconstant ones," announcing that the limestone landscape "is not the sweet home it looks" (*CP* 542). The locale, the Italian island of Ischia, where Auden rented a summer home between 1948 and 1958, also contains marble statuary that makes a poet uneasy because the statues "so obviously doubt / His antimythological myth" of "calling / The sun the sun, his mind Puzzle. . . ." (542). The poet identified here is, for once, not Auden himself but Wallace Stevens,[26] as Fuller and Mendelson both explain (*Commentary* 408, *Later* 295). Fuller quotes an unpublished lyric that Auden wrote about Stevens and eventually sent to Ursula Niebuhr: "No sooner have we buried in peace / The flightier divinities of Greece, / Than up there pops the barbarian with / An antimythological myth, / Calling the sun, the sun, / His mind 'Puzzle' . . ." (qtd. in *Commentary* 408). The classical statues in Italy disquiet the modern, skeptical poet not only because they give credence to myths, but also because, as Mendelson suggests, the poet "elevates his mind over the glories of the created world . . ." (*Later* 295). Ironically, art that affirms the goodness of physical existence troubles the modern artist, and the poem's speaker shares some of Stevens's anxiety about the physical world he inhabits. Speaking on behalf of all "the inconstant ones," the speaker offers what he calls "our Common Prayer" that wishes "not, please! to resemble / The beasts who repeat themselves, or a thing like water / Or stone whose conduct can be predicted . . ." (*CP* 542). It is not immediately clear what the prayer is actually asking for, but the obscurity is part of the point; it is an attempt to express a wish the nature of which the speaker does not really want to acknowledge.

The prayer expresses an anxious desire to escape the finitude and predictability of physical existence, contingent as it is on the laws of physics. Jonathan Hufstader suggests that it "is the prayer of those who, without a god, must provide their own self-justification" and that it "voices [a] post-Freudian fear of regressing from the standards of civilization and succumbing to instinct" (247, 246). Auden's own categories, however, are somewhat different. The prayer implies a frustration with the entire natural world, which includes not only instinct, but also the very fact of human embodiment. The opposition is not merely between civilization and instinct, but between the historical world of conscious choice and the natural world of cyclical repetition, the realms of the Virgin and the Dynamo, respectively (see *DH* 61–63). The speaker's prayer expresses a wish that Auden ultimately does not endorse, though he acknowledges the tendency of humans to attempt to exist solely in one world or the other. As a prayer, it is an impossible request, not unlike Augustine's prayer, "Grant me chastity and continence, but not yet" (*Confessions* 8.7), since the very act of making the request requires a physical body.

What bothers the modern artist most is his own embodiment, which is the real subject of the poem, as Mendelson argues: "The poem treats the limestone landscape as an allegory of the body and of the body's relation to ultimate questions" (*Later* 293). The "ultimate questions" that the poem engages are theological, particularly the forgiveness of sins and the resurrection of the dead, which the poem suggests are the basis for art: "But if / Sins can be forgiven, if bodies rise from the dead, / These modifications of matter into / Innocent athletes and gesticulating fountains, / Made solely for pleasure, make a further point: / The blessed will not care what angle they are regarded from, / Having nothing to hide" (*CP* 542). The doctrine of the resurrection validates the existence of the physical world because it envisions salvation as a transformation of the body rather than an escape from it. In many previous works, particularly "The Sea and the Mirror," Auden had affirmed the fundamental goodness of human embodiment, including even the sex drive. "In Praise of Limestone" is more elusive, but it too affirms the value of the human body in the complex analogies the poem draws between the human body and the limestone landscape. The transformation of stone into human-like statues at the end of the poem reflects the initial analogy between stone and the human body.

The poem is, above all, a love poem: "Dear, . . . / when I try to imagine a faultless love / Or the life to come, what I hear is the murmur / Of underground streams, what I see is a limestone landscape" (*CP* 542). The limestone that had represented inconstancy and even infidelity at the beginning of the poem also points toward the "faultless love" that may occur in "the life to come," at least "if bodies rise from the dead." What is now inconstant and mutable may yet be transformed, although the last lines imply that "a faultless love," or a complete redemption of eros by agape in charity, is possible only in the resurrection. And the possibility of the resurrection is somewhat undermined in the poem by the hedging "if" and "when I try to imagine" that frame the evocation of "the blessed" who have "nothing to hide" (542). Yet, if the poem reveals ambivalence about the resurrection, its subjunctive mood also invites the reader to consider alternate possibilities: if sins cannot be forgiven, and if bodies do not rise from the dead, the "modifications of matter" into statuary, "made solely for pleasure," are pointless, and the entire analogy between stone and the body is undermined as well. The poem does not deny that possibility, but neither does it deny the reality of "the life to come," though the speaker remains tentative about his own prospects of sharing in "faultless love."

Richard Bozorth rightly argues that the poem "suggests that even in the 1940s, [Auden] was of two minds about the spiritual meaning of the body and sex—that he was quite able to conceive of homosexual eros as sacred" (243). Bozorth indicates that the conflict between the sacred and the sexual in Auden's work might be resolved by an appeal to Catholic natural theology that envisioned eros as a Platonic first-step up the ladder of love (243–44). Although Bozorth is generally correct about the Catholic tradition of natural theology growing out of Thomas Aquinas and ultimately Platonism,[27] he seems unaware of Auden's absorption of a different strain of natural theology through writers such as D'Arcy, Cochrane, and ultimately Augustine, all of whom acknowledge important distinctions between Christianity and Platonism.

Auden's continuing antipathy toward Platonism found much reinforcement in Cochrane, who explains this delicate but important difference between Platonic and Augustinian views of love: "the 'passion' of Plato is a passion for transcendence; behind it lurks the assumption of an hiatus or discontinuity between the sensible and the intelligible worlds which this concept is intended to bridge. . . . In this case the fallacy lies in the original assumption; and from this standpoint, Plato's invention turns out to be entirely gratuitous, since the connection which he labors so industriously to establish already exists. . . . This connexion, however, does not . . . have to be 'established'; it needs only to be recognized. . . . To recognize its existence is to recognize the existence of divine grace" (502). Perhaps Cochrane overstates the difference between Platonism and Christianity on this point—some Christian theologies, including Augustine's, owe a significant debt to Platonism—but Auden accepted Cochrane's critique, and this passage reflects views that Auden had come to hold by the time he wrote "In Praise of Limestone." In Auden's view, Platonism would use the body as only a temporary ladder to transcendence, to be discarded once it had been climbed, but Augustinian theology would pull up the ladder after itself, bringing the body into transcendence by way of the resurrection. In his later essay, "The Protestant Mystics," Auden would identify Dante with the Augustinian view of love: "The Vision of Eros is not, according to Dante, the first rung of a long ladder: there is only one step to take, from the personal creature who can love and be loved to the personal Creator who is Love. And in this final vision, Eros is transfigured but not annihilated" (*FA* 68). Or, as D'Arcy explains in a sympathetic summary of Rougemont's account of eros, "The temporal is not just a shadow, not a ladder to be kicked away; the overflowing life of communion with God begins here and now in the present, as the Word of God was made flesh and dwelt amongst us" (39).

For Augustine, as Cochrane explains, the intrinsic goodness of the physical world makes possible the transformation of eros into agape: "The problem of salvation is thus not to destroy or to suppress the affections; it is rather that they should be reoriented with a view to the supreme good. That good lies in God, the search for whom (secutio) may be thus described as the appetitus beatitudinis, of which love constitutes the dynamic" (Cochrane 342). There is some irony in the description of a "desire" or an "appetite" for beatitude, but Augustine has reasons for using the language of physical desire to describe spiritual aspirations. In a 1972 fragment, Auden announces, "Nothing can be loved too much, / but all things can be loved / in the wrong way" (*CP* 885). Physical desires, which Auden often associates with eros, are not wrong in themselves. If physical desires are often unconscious expressions of ultimately spiritual needs, then the process of transference can be reversed insofar that eros becomes a conscious metaphor for agape. Soon after writing "In Praise of Limestone," Auden argued that a complete rejection of eros is not Christian at all, but fallaciously dualistic: "In some circles recently there has been a tendency to see the notion of love as eros (or desire for getting) and the notion of love as agape (or free-giving) as incompatible opposites and to identify them with Paganism and Christianity respectively. Such a view seems to me a revival of the Manichean heresy which denies the goodness of the natural order. . . . Agape is the fulfillment and correction of eros, not its contradiction" (*Prose III* 198).

Auden is perhaps referring to Nygren's denunciation of eros as inherently anti-Christian, and he suggests that such a view is actually closer to Manichaeism. In contrast, he believed that a perfected love, an agape that includes a redeemed eros, is the basis of all ethical behavior, a concept that Cochrane explains: "love subsumes the four cardinal virtues of Classicism which, at the same time, it irradiates with fresh significance. In this way the self-same principle which, when directed to the pursuit of mundane ends, gives rise to moral confusion and ruin, is conceived by Augustine to yield the motive power necessary to a realization of creative peace, the Kingdom of God" (342). So, when eros is a desire for self-aggrandizement or for exploitation of others, it is destructive and deadly, but when eros is a desire for reconciliation and happiness in God, it is healthy and productive. As Auden said in his review of Rougemont's *Love in the Western World,* eros and agape are not dualistically opposed, but dialectically related (*Prose II* 139).

Ideally, Auden would like to have experienced agape within a mutual relationship between human equals, which is probably why Cicero Bruce argues that, for Auden, agape "always entails a love relation between those who love each other equally, or who share a common object of desire" (53). However, as Auden says in "The More Loving One" (1957), a selfless, admiring agape is not always reciprocated: "Looking up at the stars, I know quite well / That, for all they care, I can go to hell / . . . / If equal affection cannot be, / Let the more loving one be me" (*CP* 584).

The speaker does not "burn with passion" for stars any more than they do for him, since he says, "I cannot, now I see them, say / I missed one terribly all day" (585). Instead, he is a distant admirer, though he also calls his admiration "affection" and even "loving." His love of the stars is disinterested, and as such quite close to agape, which exists even in the absence of reciprocity. As such, Bruce's narrow definition of agape is too limiting for a critic who is attempting to rehabilitate Auden as a Christian poet. After all, if agape exists only between peers who love each other equally, then God could not possibly have agape love toward humans, nor humans for God. Auden believed instead that, in the absence of equal love, he was personally responsible to be the more loving one.

At least, that is what Auden said he believed about love in his most lucid statements on the subject. The fact that he did not always act or write in accordance with these beliefs is obvious and forgivable. He faced strong temptations from what he regarded as a misguided eros, and these temptations were not always sexual in nature. For example, Auden explores the temptation to pride, an intellectual form of eros, in an essay on *Othello* in *The Dyer's Hand,* in which he argues that the character of Iago is especially relevant to the modern world because he is "a parabolic figure for the autonomous pursuit of scientific knowledge through experiment" (270). In Auden's reading of the play, Iago is "trying to find out what Othello is really like," since for Iago, "to-know in the scientific sense means, ultimately, to-have-power-over" (271, 270). Iago becomes for Auden a figure of the modern Baconian scientist who desires empirical knowledge for the sake of technological control.

The lust for knowledge and control is a purely intellectual form of eros, but Auden argues that it is not on that account any less sinful than sexual lust. As a social phenomenon, Auden argues, intellectual eros is far more dangerous: "in our culture, we have all accepted the notion that the right to know is absolute and unlimited. The gossip column is one side of the medal; the cobalt bomb the other. We are quite prepared to admit that, while food and sex are good in themselves, an uncontrolled pursuit of either is not, but it is difficult for us to believe that intellectual curiosity is a desire like any other, and to realize that correct knowledge and truth are not identical. . . . [T]o entertain the possibility that the only knowledge which can be true for us is the knowledge we can live up to—that seems to all of us crazy and almost immoral. But, in that case, who are we to say to Iago—'No, you mustn't'?" (*DH* 271–72). Auden's conviction that "intellectual curiosity" can be a dangerous form of eros has led some critics, particularly A. S. P. Woodhouse, to identify a streak of "anti-intellectualism" in Auden (290), but Auden's choice of the word "curiosity" is telling in its derivation from Augustine. In the *Confessions* Augustine identifies what he calls "curiosity" (*curiositas*) as a sin that arises from "a certain vain and curious desire, veiled under the title of knowledge and learning . . ." (10.35). Earlier in the *Confessions,* Augustine identifies his appetite for theatrical shows as one symptom

of his intellectual "cupidity" (3.2), a passage that is often unjustly cited as a categorical rejection of art. But while Augustine did deplore the erotic and obscene nature
of the shows he attended as a young man, his primary objection was not to their
content but to his own corrupt motivation for attending them. As Auden explains,
the only knowledge that is good for humans to have is "knowledge we can live up to"
(*DH* 272), whether that knowledge be sexual or scientific.

In a 1957 essay Auden provides his account of the development of modern attitudes toward scientific knowledge: "So long as man's thinking and feeling are integrated his search for knowledge is conditioned by the question 'What ought I, what
am I meant to know?' He is aware, like Goethe, that knowledge can only be true as
long as it is not in excess of his feelings or, as Nietzsche put it, that "man ought not
to know more of a thing than he can creatively live up to." In the present epoch man
has almost lost all sense of this categorical imperative and he asks instead 'What
would I like to know?' and truth becomes for him either that which it is amusing to
know or that which increases his power to do as he likes. The Gossip Column and
the Hydrogen Bomb are two sides of one coin" (*Prose IV* 130). Augustine's argument
that curiosity was a lust like any other took on new urgency for Auden, living as he
did in an era of technological propaganda and biological and nuclear weaponry. For
both Auden and Augustine, knowledge could never be separated from ethics.

Several years earlier, in 1944, Auden had explained in his review of Cochrane
that Augustine's ethical sensibilities were rooted in his understanding of humanity
as fallen, even though "his existence was and still is meant to be, capable of loving
God in the same way that God loves him" (*FA* 36). Auden continues, "When a Christian, like Augustine, talks about ethics, therefore, he begins not with the rational
act or the pleasant act, but with the *acte gratuit,* which is neither reasonable nor
physically pleasant, but a pure assertion of absolute self-autonomy" (36–37). Auden
cites Dostoyevsky's protagonist in *Notes from the Underground* as an example, but
in a later lecture on *Othello* he gives Augustine's account of the pear tree from the
Confessions as a quintessential example of the *acte gratuit* (*Lectures* 196–99). In book
2 of the *Confessions,* Augustine recounts a time when, as an adolescent, he and his
friends stole pears from a nearby orchard, "not for our eating, but to fling to the very
hogs, having only tasted them. And this, but to do what we liked only because it was
misliked" (2.4). His desire to sin, his "cupidity" as he calls it, was not motivated by a
rational desire for pleasure, but was instead an irrational and arbitrary decision to
break a just law.[28]

Auden explains, "Man . . . always acts either self-loving, just for the hell of it,
or God-loving, just for the heaven of it; his reasons, his appetites are secondary
motivations. Man chooses either life or death, but he chooses; everything he does,
from going to the toilet to mathematical speculation, is an act of religious worship,
either of God or of himself" (*FA* 37). The *acte gratuit* is a gratuitous assertion of the

will that cannot be traced directly to a conscious desire for pleasure or to rational calculation. There may be an identifiable, subconscious desire that is manifested in a criminal act, but behind the transference itself there is also a basic desire to assert one's autonomy. Most of the examples that Auden gives in his works of the *acte gratuit* are negative, and as such they are examples of unmitigated, subconscious eros. Besides the example of Iago that Auden gives in his lecture on *Othello*, one of Auden's lectures in *The Enchafèd Flood* identifies Claggart, the fiendish accuser in Melville's *Billy Budd, Sailor*, as another example of a literary character whose motivation can be reduced to the *acte gratuit*. Auden sees the motivation of a character like Iago or Claggart as "purely" evil in the sense that his crime can be rationalized but not fully explained in terms of rational motivation; it is a fundamentally gratuitous act. There are, however, good forms of the *acte gratuit*. In earlier poems like "Leap Before You Look" and "In Sickness and in Health," both written in 1940, Auden pictures Christian marriage as a positively gratuitous act, which is an idea that he drew from Rougemont's argument that Christian marriage must ultimately be an "arbitrary decision" in the sense that it is a deliberate act that is not based either on an emotional impulse or on a rational calculation of probable consequences (Rougemont 285–94). Auden seems to have believed, at least in the early 1940s, that eros could be redeemed by agape through the *acte gratuit* of Christian marriage, such that the married partners would both desire to benefit personally from the relationship at the same time that they sacrifice their own self-interests for the good of the other partner.

But because there is always an element of unredeemed eros—purely selfish and destructive motives—in every human love, there will always be a real tension between eros and agape. As Auden says in the last lines of "Thanksgiving for a Habitat," "always, though truth and love / can never really differ, when they seem to, / the subaltern should be truth" (*CP* 716). Even though eros and agape are hypothetically reconcilable, they will always be in conflict for those who prefer "love" to "truth," a juxtaposition that suggests that by "love" Auden means in this poem something closer to eros than to agape. Humans can fool themselves into thinking that their eros is actually an expression of agape, so it is necessary to privilege truth over any impulse that seeks to establish its own supremacy by claiming to be "love." However, in a 1958 review of *The Art of Eating* by M. F. K. Fisher, Auden points out that "the central rite of the Christian religion, its symbol of agape, freely given love untainted by selfish desire or self-projection, [is] the act of eating bread and drinking wine," and he explains how the symbolism of eating differs from the symbolism of sex: "even at its crudest, the sexual act contains an element of giving, while eating is an act of pure taking" (*Prose IV* 167). Auden concludes, "only the absolutely necessary and selfish can stand as a symbol for its opposite, the absolutely voluntary and self-sacrificing" (167–68). So within human relationships, eros is never found in a pure form, but is always mixed, at least symbolically, with the gift-love of agape. But neither can agape's redemption of eros ever be complete in this life, and perhaps that is one reason that Auden wrote so few poems that say anything explicitly about agape.

BY THE 1950S Auden's poetic concerns had shifted away from his earlier explorations of the tension between eros and agape and toward other topics, such as the nature of history and the tension between the poet's public and private roles. Nevertheless, it may seem strange that, given Auden's enthusiasm for Rougemont and his repeated insistence in the 1940s that he was morally obliged to aspire to agape, Auden's later poetry says very little about agape at all. References to eros, however, do continue to appear. In "Dichtung und Wahrheit," an aphoristic essay that Auden subtitled "An Unwritten Poem," he explicitly states that "we are speaking of eros, not of agape" as he explains the impossibility of writing a love poem that will satisfy his own demands on his art (*CP* 655). And in "Glad," one of "Three Posthumous Poems," he addresses a sometime prostitute whom he engaged in Vienna, asking, "How is it now between us? / Love? Love is far too / Tattered a word. . . . / Let me say we fadge . . ." (*CP* 747). They "fadge," or "fit" each other, but only in the very pragmatic sense that they met, Auden says, "At a moment when / You were in need of money / And I wanted sex" (746). Unlike Auden's earlier lyrics that aspire to a fusion of intellectual and physical intimacy, an aspiration that had been inspired in part by Rougemont, his few later love poems make no pretension to an agape that redeems eros and instead remark detachedly on his occasional indulgences in sheer eros.

Perhaps the most important reason that Auden did not write many poems about agape, or "charity" as he sometimes called it, is that he firmly believed that agape is expressed by rightly motivated actions, and not by words, however well intentioned. For Auden, the expression of agape was almost entirely outside the abilities of poetic language. In *The Dyer's Hand,* he claimed, "A direct manifestation of charity in secular terms is . . . impossible. One form of indirect manifestation employed by religious teachers has been through parables in which actions which are ethically immoral are made to stand as a sign for that which transcends ethics" (202). Auden may have had in mind the parable of the unjust steward in the Gospel of Luke, in which the steward's cheating of his master becomes a lesson in serving God with the world's goods (Luke 16:1–9). There are, of course, other parables in the Bible, such as the Good Samaritan (Luke 10:25–37), that do depict acts of agape. But Auden's point is that, outside of an explicitly didactic context, it is very difficult to portray a saint acting on pure agape, and even within a religious context, artistic depictions of pure agape tend not to be aesthetically convincing. Auden's faith did not require him to write about agape at all, though it did require him to personally perform acts of charity.

However, Auden's biographies record few acts that could be considered truly charitable. Auden readily admitted that he frequently acted uncharitably (see *FA*

69–70), and while it is possible that acts of charity are not interesting to biographers or to the people who read them, Auden also acknowledged that real agape always desires to act anonymously. As he remarks in "Dichtung und Wahrheit," "It is as much of the essence of erotic love that it should desire to disclose itself to one other, as it is of the essence of charity that it should desire to conceal itself from all" (*CP* 655). A few of Auden's charitable deeds have been recorded—in 1935 he agreed to marry the German actress Erika Mann in order to provide her with a British passport and help her escape the Nazis (Carpenter 175–77), and in 1956 Auden intervened when Dorothy Day's Catholic Worker organization was fined because its homeless shelter had violated fire code regulations, and Auden paid the fine himself (Mendelson, *Later* 401 and Carpenter 382). These acts happened to become public, but had Auden himself written poems about them, he would have exploited the acts for aesthetic purposes and emptied them of all charity. Auden firmly believed that agape consists of good actions, rightly motivated, and not of merely writing about ethics. Agape was neither theatrical nor thrilling, neither public nor poetic. He was more correct than he knew when he called Rougemont's description of agape within marriage "absurdly straitlaced to the hedonist and shockingly coarse to the romantic" (*Prose II* 140–41), for in his later years he came to recognize that real acts of charity are mundane, unremarkable, and anticlimactic.

4. HUMAN NATURE AND COMMUNITY

As Auden was in the process of returning to Christianity in the early 1940s, he met Reinhold Niebuhr and his wife Ursula, the American protestant theologians who were, like Auden, socialist in their political outlook and currently residing in New York City. Despite the fact that Auden and the Niebuhrs met frequently and exchanged numerous letters, Auden's theological interaction with Reinhold Niebuhr has been overlooked by most Auden critics.[1] Carpenter and Davenport-Hines give the relationship only a brief mention (Carpenter 306–7; Davenport-Hines 203, 214). In *Later Auden*, Mendelson acknowledges the intellectual side of the relationship in more detail but still treats it largely in outline, and Kirsch's *Auden and Christianity* does not elaborate significantly on Mendelson's treatment.

While there are a few shorter accounts of Auden's use of certain aspects of Niebuhr's theology (see Conniff, "Auden, Niebuhr"), Auden's use of Niebuhr's theology, especially Niebuhr's Augustinian view of human psychology, has been largely neglected, despite Niebuhr's status as a major American theologian of the twentieth century. Auden absorbed much of Augustine's anthropology through Niebuhr, who was also a significant source of Auden's later views on the relationship between individual and society, though he also appears to have drawn certain ideas from Augustine himself. Neither theologian was a major source of Auden's views of the poet's role in civic life—in this he was shaped by figures like Alexander Pope and Eugen Rosenstock-Huessy, who are not especially Augustinian. Indeed, Auden appropriated an explicitly Augustinian theory of human nature, and Augustine contributed to Auden's conceptions of the relationships between history, human beings, and time. Mendelson argues that, in the early 1940s, "most of Auden's political and ethical positions were indistinguishable from Niebuhr's" (*Later* 173), and the same is true of Auden's post-conversion view of human nature, which he drew from Niebuhr's recovery of an Augustinian psychology.

In 1941, Niebuhr published the first volume of *The Nature and Destiny of Man*, in which he outlined his Augustinian-Protestant view of human nature, which he contrasts both with the classical-dualist view in which the essentially good soul is corrupted by the essentially evil body, and with the morass of modern views, which agree only in their common belief that some element of human nature is untouched by evil. Niebuhr argues instead that human beings are created in the *imago dei*, the "Image of God," as Genesis claims. He identifies the *imago dei* with the human tendency toward transcendence, including the capacity for self-consciousness, which renders sin possible but not necessary. The individual human being is therefore restless, or "homeless," in the world, being unable to find a proper place within its merely physical surroundings. Following Augustine's assertion of his own heart's restlessness at the beginning of the *Confessions* (1.1), Niebuhr argues that the human heart remains restless until it finds its true home in a right relationship to God. As Auden would state years later, "A Christian is at once commanded to accept his creatureliness, both natural and historical, not to attempt to escape into a fantastic world untrammeled by the realities of space and time, and forbidden to make an idol of nature or history" (*Prose III* 209). Humans typically seek to assuage their restlessness by attempting to establish absolute self-sufficiency, thus rejecting their own contingent finitude, which is Niebuhr's definition of sin. For Niebuhr as for Augustine, freedom of the will is essential to human nature, and while freedom makes sin possible, it does not make it necessary. However, sin biases the will against God, and so humans tend toward pride and sensuality, thus effectively curtailing the will's freedom to do what is good.

Even before he read Niebuhr, Auden had been perplexed by the questions about free will raised by his earlier Marxism. In 1939, *The Prolific and the Devourer* had expressed his reservations about the Marxist view of history as developing along certain predetermined lines, since it seemed to negate individual free will. Yet Auden still thought that history developed arbitrarily, and he wanted to believe that causal necessity operates in history without contradicting his intuition that the individual will was free. After encountering Niebuhr's explication of Augustine's view of human free will as curtailed by its own self-corruption, Auden became able to articulate his own view of the relationship between freedom and necessity within human nature. He came to believe that humans exist as a unity-in-tension, existing simultaneously on two planes, that of physical nature, in which time is cyclical and events occur by causal necessity, and that of history, in which time is linear and events occur by free, conscious choice. While Auden eventually replaced Niebuhr's language with his own, he maintained the Augustinianism, and Augustine made a significant contribution to Auden's later understanding of historical time. As his theological thought matured, Auden also began using the language of Augustine's distinction between the City of God and the City of Man, a distinction that contributed to his understanding of the nature of history and of the place of the individual person within it.

AUGUSTINE AND REINHOLD NIEBUHR

The first volume of Niebuhr's *The Nature and Destiny of Man* aims to recover an explicitly Augustinian view of human nature that answers the dominant concerns of the modern world—there are more references for "Augustine" in the index than for any other proper name. The book's first few chapters lay out various classical and modern views of human nature, each of which Niebuhr considers faulty because they reject either the physical or the spiritual aspect of humanity. In chapter 6, Niebuhr turns to his Augustinian analysis of human uniqueness, which he equates with the *imago dei*, the Image of God in which Genesis states that humans are created (Genesis 1:27). Niebuhr argues that "Augustine is . . . the first Christian theologian to comprehend the full implications of the Christian doctrine of man" (154–55), and explains that Augustine locates the *imago dei* in the human capacity for self-knowledge and introspection, and he offers a long quotation from Augustine's *On the Trinity* to make his point. Niebuhr explains Augustine's observation that it is this very capacity for self-transcendence that makes it possible for humans to know God: "[Augustine] concludes that the power of transcendence places him so much outside of everything else that he can find a home only in God . . ." (156). Niebuhr concludes, "When some of Augustine's earlier lapses into neo-Platonism are discounted, it must be recognized that no Christian theologian has ever arrived at a more convincing statement of the relevance and distance between the human and the divine than he. All subsequent statements of the essential character of the image of God in man are indebted to him . . ." (158).

In the next three chapters, which Auden identifies in his 1941 review of the book as "the most brilliant chapters of Dr Niebuhr's book . . ." (*Prose II* 133), Niebuhr explores the nature of human sin, which he defines as any attempt to transgress the limits of our own being, either in sensuality, which is a rejection of our spiritual nature, or in pride, which is a rejection of our physical finitude (179–81). In language that Auden was already accustomed to using, Niebuhr states, "[man] stands at the juncture of nature and spirit; and is involved in both freedom and necessity" (181). Niebuhr explains the practical consequences of this duality in human nature: because humans are "both free and bound, both limited and limitless," they are by nature "anxious" (182). Anxiety always accompanies the individual's recognition of the tension between one's own freedom and finitude, and this constant anxiety becomes the temptation and opportunity for sin. While Niebuhr insists that anxiety is not the same thing as sin, he argues that anxiety inevitably encourages sin, though he also allows "the ideal possibility that faith" may in some cases "purge anxiety of the tendency toward sinful self-assertion" (182–83).

Niebuhr defines two types of sin, pride and sensuality. Pride is frequently exhibited in what he calls "collective pride," which is most clearly manifest in the modern state. Following Augustine, he goes so far as to argue that "sinful pride and idolatrous pretension are thus an inevitable concomitant of the cohesion of large political groups" (210). Here Niebuhr is fully within the Augustinian tradition which has grown out of the *City of God*, in which Augustine argues at great length that the human political and social entities, variously called the "City of Man," the "earthly city," or the "city of this world" (*civitas terrena* in Latin), are based on pride, avarice, and self-aggrandizement. Augustine contrasts the "City of Man" with the church, which he equates with the "City of God" mentioned in Hebrews 11:8–16, whose history he traces from the Hebrew patriarchs through the kingdom of Israel to the New Testament church. However, Niebuhr critiques Augustine on this point, arguing that Augustine's distinction between the two cities "was partially obscured by his identification, however qualified, of the city of God with the historic church, an identification which was later to be stripped of all its Augustinian reservations to become the instrument of the spiritual pride of a universal church in its conflict with the political pride of an empire" (216). Niebuhr's sentiments on this point concur with Auden's letter to Ursula Niebuhr, admitting that "as organizations, none of the churches look too hot, do they? But what organization ever does?" (qtd. in Spender 106). In a 1950 essay Auden defined "the Church" not as an institutional structure but as "the community of all the souls of the faithful living and dead, past and to come" (*Prose III* 176). Auden refused to identify the church with temporal, social, or political arrangements, which always tend toward collective pride.

The opposite of pride, whether individual or national, is the sin of sensuality, which Niebuhr defines as "the destruction of harmony within the self, by the self's undue identification with and devotion to particular impulses and desires within itself" (228). This definition is virtually identical to Auden's own definition of sin in *The Prolific and the Devourer*, which Auden had written before he met the Niebuhrs: "we rarely act in such a way that even the false self-interests of all our different selves are satisfied. The majority of our actions are in the interest of one of these selves . . . at the expense of the rest. The consciousness that we are acting contrary to the interests of the others is our consciousness of sin, for to sin is consciously to act contrary to self-interest" (*Prose II* 427). Auden and Niebuhr were clearly thinking along very similar lines. Niebuhr also takes pains to clear up a common misconception about Augustine's views of sexuality. Citing *The City of God*, Niebuhr asserts, "Whatever Augustine may say about the passions of the flesh and however morbidly he may use sex as the primary symbol of such passions, his analyses always remain within terms of this general statement. He never regards sensuality as a natural fruit of the man's animal nature" (231). Niebuhr argues that Augustine, for all his prudish attitudes toward sexuality, locates sin ultimately in the soul, not in the body (230–31). Niebuhr concludes: "What sex reveals in regard to sensuality is not unique but typical in regard to the problem of sensuality in general. Whether in drunkenness, gluttony, sexual license, love of luxury, or any inordinate devotion to a mutable good, sensuality is always: (1) an extension of self-love to the point where it defeats its own ends; (2) an effort to escape the prison house of self by finding a god in a process of person outside the self; and (3) finally an effort to escape from the confusion which sin has created into some form of subconscious existence" (239–40). For Auden, steeped as he was in post-Freudian psychoanalysis, such an analysis of the psychology of sensuality must have been compelling.

In his final chapters, Niebuhr takes up the question of Original Sin, especially as Augustine treats it. Niebuhr explains, "Original sin, which is by definition an inherited corruption, or at least an inevitable one, is nevertheless not to be regarded as belonging to his essential nature and therefore is not outside the realm of his responsibility. Sin is natural for man in the sense that it is universal but not in the sense that it is necessary" (242). The idea of an inherited corruption seems, on one hand, to absolve the sinner of responsibility for sin, but on the other hand, it is difficult to otherwise explain the seemingly natural tendency to do evil. Niebuhr approvingly cites the Augustinian theological tradition to resolve the paradox: "The Pauline doctrine, as elaborated by Augustine and the Reformers, insists on the one hand that the will of man is enslaved to sin and is incapable of fulfilling God's law. It may be free, declares Augustine, only it is not free to do good" (243). Niebuhr hastens to add that the literalistic attempt to locate the origin of Original Sin in a historic Fall after a brief "golden age" in paradise is unnecessary to his analysis of Original Sin, and is instead deleterious to his entire project because it views Original Sin as being biologically inherited from historical ancestors, an idea that erroneously locates the origin of sin in the body rather than in the soul (260–64). Niebuhr argues instead that the story of the Fall is emblematic of every individual human fall into sin. The innocence of "Paradise" represents the human consciousness prior to any act, and the Fall occurs in any act, any movement of the will, that arises from the anxiety of one's own finitude (278–80). Salvation, therefore, is gained through an acceptance of one's own finite existence as a created being, which is possible only through faith in God's love of his creatures (289).

In his review of the book, Auden remarks especially on the last chapter, in which Niebuhr distinguishes between the Augustinian-Protestant and Thomist-Catholic views of the Fall. The Thomist view holds that a literal, historical Adam was given a "supernatural gift" of perfection in addition to his naturally good nature, so the Fall entailed a loss of that gift of "original righteousness" but did not corrupt "natural righteousness," thus leaving certain natural inclinations of humans, such as the rational faculty, essentially uncorrupted. On the other hand, some extreme Protestants, such as Martin Luther, assert that the Fall destroyed all essential goodness in human nature, and thus conceive of humans as absolutely evil—an obvious impossibility if the Augustinian theory of evil as privation is accepted, since a creature's corruption is contingent on its continued existence; humans could not exist at all if they lost all goodness. Niebuhr points out that "Augustine is very explicit in his affirmation that the evil of sin cannot completely destroy the goodness of what God has created in man . . ." (267).

Niebuhr proceeds to quote the *Confessions* (7.12) to the effect that, insofar as human faculties continue to exist, they continue to be good in themselves, though they are now corrupted and therefore not as good as they should be: "'whatsoever is, is good,'" a sentiment with which Auden was very familiar (267). In opposition to both extreme Protestants and Thomist Catholics, Niebuhr advances an Augustinian argument that there is a difference between essential human nature and the ability of individual humans to conform to it. Thus while the *imago dei* is not destroyed by sin, the human ability to freely conform to that divine image is hamstrung. That is, humans remain somewhat aware of the law, but as Augustine observes, a defect in the will renders them unable to keep it even if it is fully revealed to them (280, 288). Auden's review sums up Niebuhr's position: "Niebuhr's theology is Augustinian, i.e. he rejects the Catholic version of the Fall in which original justice only is destroyed but natural justice is still uncorrupted, and I agree that modern psychology and sociology confirm the Augustinian position and render the Catholic theory of natural law ultimately untenable . . ." (*Prose II* 134). Auden likely absorbed some of Niebuhr's theories through personal conversation with him, since Auden had known the Niebuhrs for about a year when the book came out, and Carpenter notes that "he and the Niebuhrs discussed many points of theology" (307). Soon after Auden read and reviewed the first volume of *The Nature and Destiny of Man*, ideas and even language from the book began to appear occasionally in "The Sea and the Mirror" and "The Age of Anxiety," though it took him some years to fully appropriate Niebuhr's views on the transmission of Original Sin, which appear in "Horae Canonicae," as well as in later lyrics and several prose pieces. Niebuhr's explicitly Augustinian theology of human nature and of sin provided Auden with a nuanced language in which to express his understanding of human nature, an understanding that was formed quite early by his interest in psychoanalysis but that achieved coherence only under the influence of Augustinian thought.

THE FALL, SELF-CONSCIOUSNESS, AND ANXIETY

In *New Year Letter*, Auden had already begun resorting to the Augustinian concept of evil as privation to describe the Fall, though at that time he conceived of self-consciousness as the product of sin, though he was not entirely consistent on the subject. In *The Prolific and the Devourer*, Auden describes sin as the attempt to satisfy any of one's competing desires at the expense of the whole person, which would seem to place the advent of self-consciousness before the Fall, since the satisfaction of one desire at the expense of another presupposes the existence of a divided self (426–27). In his note to line 1063 of *New Year Letter,* he states that the "Golden Age" was not "a time when Man did not do evil," but that "there was once a time when he did not sin, i.e. when society was relatively so closed that freedom was confined to obedience to causal necessity . . . , when human law was not felt as coercive but regarded as a perfect codification of Natural law . . ." (125). Here he seems to imagine a community of more-or-less conscious human beings who nevertheless exist prior to the advent of sin because they have not yet recognized the full potential of their own freedom. In such a time, some degree of human consciousness exists without a divided or anxious self-consciousness.

Elsewhere he speaks of the divided, conscious self as the direct product of the Fall, as in "For the Time Being," in which the Four Faculties declare that they were "one" prior to "his act of / Rebellion" (*CP* 355). So which comes first, the Fall or self-consciousness? Are they synonymous, or does one cause the other? Even after Auden became friends with Niebuhr, his mind was not altogether settled on the matter, since the idea of the rise of the Four Faculties, which he derived from Jung, was still in competition with the Augustinian ideas about self-consciousness to which he was being introduced. He had always associated the myth of the Fall—in whatever terms he described it—with the rise of individual self-consciousness, but soon after he read the first volume of Niebuhr's *The Nature and Destiny of Man,* he became more consistent in following Niebuhr's Augustinian argument that the advent of self-consciousness precedes the Fall. Consciousness presents the *opportunity* for sin, but it is neither the product of sin nor identical with sin itself.

However, in "For the Time Being," which Auden began writing just a few months after reviewing Niebuhr's book, he is still operating under his earlier assumption that the Fall occurs prior to self-consciousness, and that self-consciousness begins with the recognition of one's own guilt. He had already related the awakening of his own sense of guilt in *New Year Letter,* where he describes the northern English landscape in which he says he first became conscious "Of Self and Not-self, Death and Dread," and of guilt (*CP* 228). The consciousness of guilt comes long after the initial sin, as the "Boys' Semi-Chorus" in "For the Time Being" states, "for even in / The germ-cell's primary division / Innocence is lost and sin, / Already given as a fact, / Once more issues as an act" (366). This is perhaps Auden's most severe description of the Fall. Only a few years earlier, in *The Prolific and the Devourer,* Auden had taken pains to distinguish between "doing evil" and "sinning," explaining that "doing evil" is merely acting contrary to self-interest, which is possible even for unself-conscious animals as well as self-conscious human beings because one cannot always know what is actually in one's own self-interest. However, humans are distinguished by their additional capacity for what Auden calls "sin," which attempts to satisfy the demands of any one of our various selves at the expense of the rest (*Prose II* 426–27). The Boys' Semi-Chorus describes "sin" but not "evil" because growth by division is in the embryo's self-interest. The lines also suggest that even the growth of the embryo in utero, occurring at the expense of the mother, is a selfish act and is therefore implicated in sinfulness and cannot be considered innocent. Augustine makes similar arguments for the sinfulness of infants in book 1 of the *Confessions*, and "For the Time Being" follows Augustine closely on this point. In the poem, the Fall is at least partially a "fortunate Fall," since it gives rise to self-consciousness, which is necessary for the operation of free will, and since the Incarnation can occur only by Mary's free assent, the Fall becomes instrumental in its own correction.

For all of Auden's insistence on the intrinsic goodness of the body, an idea that he endorsed in the late 1930s and maintained throughout his subsequent career, his statements in "For the Time Being" that locate sin in the pre-conscious embryo seem to undercut his insistence that embodiment is itself good, for the Boys' Semi-Chorus sounds very much as if Original Sin is located in the body and transmitted genetically from parents to children. Niebuhr's work is written partly to correct such a theological error, as he argues that the Augustinian literalism that equates Original Sin "with the idea of an inherited corruption" and that "make[s] concupiscence in generation the agent of this inheritance" (261) is untenable in light of Augustine's locating sinfulness in the soul, rather than in the body as the Manichees did. Even though Auden drafted the passages containing the Boys' Semi-Chorus and the Four Faculties after he had read Niebuhr's book, he chose to follow Augustine's more literal conception of Original Sin as physically inherited, in contrast to Niebuhr's typological understanding of it. It seems Auden found interesting poetic possibilities in the idea that sin is inseparable from the fact of embodiment. As his first long poem after his return to Christianity, "For the Time Being" is transitional. It contains many ideas that Auden was entertaining for the first time, as well as many old ideas that had appeared in his previous poems. Some new ideas, such as the centrality of the Incarnation in human history, he maintained for the rest of his life, but others he eventually discarded. For example, Mendelson points out that Auden became dismissive of the "Four Faculties" passage later in life: "In 1965, as he was looking through a copy of 'For the Time Being,' he wrote in the margin of the speeches of the Four Faculties: 'Bosh, straight from Jung'" (*Later* 247). Similarly, Auden was soon to rethink his statement on the locus of Original Sin.

"The Sea and the Mirror" finds Auden edging closer to Niebuhr's rejection of the idea of a historical "golden age" of innocence prior to the Fall, either individually or collectively, despite his taste for personal Edenic or Arcadian myths. By the time he was drafting Caliban's monologue, he had embraced Niebuhr's argument that "every individual is inclined to give a chronological and historical version of the contrast between what he is and what he ought to be; for he regards the innocency of his childhood as a symbol and a reminder of his true nature," even though such attempts to recall an idyllic childhood, either of an individual or of the whole human race, are specious (Niebuhr 268). Caliban is severely critical of those who long to recover just such an innocent childhood prior to the coming of age that seemingly introduced guilt and misery into the consciousness. Caliban concedes that there seems to have been a point at which each child had "no mirror, no magic, for everything that happened was a miracle," so "it was therefore only necessary for you to presuppose one genius, one unrivaled I to wish these wonders in all their endless plentitude" (*CP* 435). There appears to have been, too, a coming of age in which self-consciousness becomes acute and the inevitable conflict between actuality and possibility is recognized. Thus, it seems entirely reasonable to wish to return to that innocent childhood prior to the agony of self-consciousness, and Caliban warns that some in the audience will attempt to recover childhood innocence by immersing themselves entirely in the life of the body, effectively giving Caliban (the body) unbridled control. Caliban imagines such people pleading with him to return them to their private Edens: "Carry me back, Master, to the cathedral town where the canons run through the water meadows with butterfly nets and the old women keep sweet-shops in the cobbled side streets. . . . Give me my passage home, let me see that harbour once again just as it was before I learned the bad words" (437). The images in the rest of the passage—frozen rivers, greenery, steam rollers, farm dogs, a ruined opera house—are a mixture of stock juvenile arcadias and the peculiar, allegorical landscapes that Auden enjoyed describing, yet they are obviously overwrought in their naive earnestness.

Thus Caliban warns against serious attempts to reenter a prelapsarian childhood by giving the body absolute reign: "I shall have no option but to . . . transport you, not indeed to any cathedral town or mill town or harbour or hillside or jungle or other specific Eden *which your memory necessarily but falsely conceives of as the ultimately liberal condition, which in point of fact you have never known yet*, but directly to that downright state itself," which Caliban describes as a state of absolute loneliness and despair (*CP* 438, emphasis added). Like Niebuhr, Caliban insists that the innocent, idyllic world of pure subjectivity has never existed and is instead the construct of already-anxious souls longing to escape their anxiety.[2] The Augustinian idea of a physically inherited Fall is here replaced by Caliban's final assertion that "Our performance . . . which we were obliged, *all of us*, to go on with . . . right to the final dissonant chord, has been so indescribably inexcusably awful" (*CP* 443, emphasis added). The disastrous opera that Caliban describes at the end of his monologue represents the sinful human condition, and there is no explaining how anyone happened to become involved, only the statement that "all of us," including Ariel and Caliban, are always already implicated in the guilt.

Auden's rejection of a literal, pre-Fall Eden is crucial here, for if Original Sin were transmitted through procreation from ancestor to descendent, then Caliban would himself be responsible for the transference of Original Sin, especially insofar as he represents sexuality. It was for just this reason that Auden had suspected *The Tempest* of a Manichean bias, since it appears to absolve the spirit (Ariel) of moral responsibility for evil while holding only the body (Caliban) culpable (*DH* 130). In reality, Auden suggests, both the body and the imagination are at the command, weak though it is, of the anxious, self-conscious soul that is free only to sin, or, as Caliban states, to become "unforgettably conscious of the ungarnished offended gap between what you so questionably are and what you are commanded without any question to become . . ." without presuming that the awareness of that "gap" is the same as crossing it (*CP* 442). Despite all good intentions and efforts, failure is inevitable and must be accepted in order to be redeemed by "that Wholly Other Life" to which Caliban alludes in his conclusion (444). "The Sea and the Mirror" reflects a subtle shift in Auden's Augustinian conception of evil as privation, as a corruption of one's love and hence a crippling of the will to do good. He has replaced a literalistic Augustinian idea drawn directly from the *Confessions*—Original Sin is physically inherited—with a more sophisticated Augustinian idea drawn from Niebuhr— Original Sin is a corruption of the will and arises from our anxious attempts to transcend our own finite contingencies.

Niebuhr's influence is perhaps clearest in Auden's "Age of Anxiety," as the premise of the poem is largely drawn from Niebuhr's explication of the restless heart of Augustine's *Confessions*. The very title, which is usually taken as referring to the historical modern age, also refers to the age of an individual who has emerged into self-consciousness and thus into anxiety, and Auden is indebted to Niebuhr for the use of the term in this sense.[3] Niebuhr defines "anxiety" as "the inevitable concomitant of the paradox of freedom and finiteness in which man is involved. . . . It is the inevitable spiritual state of man, standing in the paradoxical situation of freedom and finiteness" (182). Niebuhr also notes that "anxiety is the internal description of the state of temptation" (182), though he hastens to add that anxiety "must not be identified with sin because there is always the ideal possibility that faith would purge anxiety of the tendency toward sinful self-assertion" (182–83). Auden appropriates Niebuhr's language for his long poem, which is ultimately an interior view of an individual person from the points of view of the four Jungian faculties—intuition, thought, feeling, and sensation—which appear as the rather flat characters of Quant, Malin, Rosetta, and Emble, respectively, representing a fragmented, anxious, self-conscious psyche on an allegorical quest for coherence.

Occasional references to Niebuhr's Augustinian psychology occur throughout the poem. For example, the second part of the poem is titled "The Seven Ages," which is based on Jaques's speech in Shakespeare's *As You Like It*, which reiterates the commonplace Elizabethan division of the human lifespan into the "seven ages of man." Malin begins "The Seven Ages" by describing "the infant, helpless in cradle" who is still "righteous," although his dreams anticipate "the gulf before him with guilt beyond . . ." (*CP* 465). In contrast to the already-fallen embryos in "For the Time Being," Auden here describes a baby boy who is sinless because he has not yet crossed the threshold into anxious awareness of his own freedom, though he is already subconsciously capable of committing a guilty act and therefore anticipates a point at which he will "[join] mankind, / the fallen families freedom lost . . ." (465). Following Augustine's identification of sin in the earliest of a child's willful actions, Auden describes a small boy who is already manipulative and vindictive, who "Accuses with a cough, claims pity / With scratched knees, skillfully avenges / Pains and punishments on puny insects . . ." (465). Malin's speech also alludes to Augustine's description of his robbing of a neighbor's pear tree with a gang of his young friends: "His emptiness finds / Its joy in a gang and is joined to others / By crimes in common" (465). The description of a social unit held together by common crimes echoes Augustine's own description of an episode from his early adolescence: "A pear tree there was near our vineyard, laden with fruit, tempting neither for colour nor taste. To shake and rob this, some lewd young fellows of us went, late one night . . . and took huge loads, not for our eating, but to fling to the very hogs . . ." (2.4). Auden often alludes in his prose to the gratuity of Augustine's theft, but in "The Age of Anxiety" Auden focuses on the communal aspect of the crime. The gang of peers provides the motivation for a crime that would not otherwise have been a temptation, as Augustine opines: "Why then was my delight of such sort, that I did it not alone? . . . I had not done this alone; alone I had never never done it" (2.9). Just as the state of anxiety becomes the opportunity and motive for sin, but not the sin itself, so the company of others becomes the opportunity and motive for sin in both the *Confessions* and Malin's speech.

Later in "The Seven Ages," Auden reiterates Niebuhr's insistence that childhood Edens are specious. In his description of the sixth age, that of the deteriorating body, Malin observes that a man wishes for "some / Nameless Eden where he never was" (*CP* 477). The other three characters add their own descriptions of the lost paradise (478–80), though only Malin, who represents thought, seems fully aware that such a place has never existed as a historical reality. Given that the emergence of self-consciousness and the Fall into sin are relatively simultaneous—and the poem is never quite clear about which comes first—any "memory" of an idyllic, innocent childhood must be an illusion. This fact makes the seventh age, the regression into a second infancy, all the more poignant, since the re-entry into a childlike state does not entail a return to innocence, but a total disillusionment, until he joins the silent majority, the "mildewed mob and is modest at last" (481). The description of death as a joining of a mob parallels the earlier description of communal crime in childhood, in which the immersion of the self in a crowd entails an abdication of free moral choice.

Near the end of the poem, the four characters are disappointed by the futility of their quest and express their mutual longing for a messianic figure who will rescue both Nature and Man, "for a brief bright instant, from their egregious destructive blunders," since "it seemed impossible to them that either could have survived so long had not some semi-divine stranger with super-human powers, some

Gilgamesh or Napoleon, some Solon or Sherlock Holmes, appeared . . ." (*CP* 515). The four then repair to Rosetta's apartment, where she and Emble fall in love and exchange lovers' vows, but as she is showing Malin and Quant out, Emble passes out on her bed. Malin and Quant quickly part ways, and the four are isolated once again, each still wishing in his or her own way for a messiah who does not appear as the four reenter the mundane, workaday world. Though temporarily united in their mutual quest, they have failed to achieve a lasting unity, and they end much the same as they began. They have been able to articulate their sad wish for salvation, a desire that was only implicit in the beginning but that becomes more explicit as the poem closes. If the poem begins as a quest for the reintegration of the faculties into a unified personality, which is the Augustinian conception of salvation,[4] the mutual cooperation of the faculties has clearly not produced the kind of lasting integration the characters had initially hoped for, and the end of the poem makes it clear that the faculties are not, on their own, capable of reuniting permanently and must therefore receive divine aid in doing so—it is an Augustinian, not a Pelagian, view of salvation—and while the poem expresses the wish for salvation, it declines to portray the event of salvation itself.

HISTORY AND TIME

A perusal of the titles of Auden's poems and books, from *Another Time* to "The Age of Anxiety" and "Horae Canonicae," will immediately reveal his keen and sustained interest in the nature of time, especially as it is experienced by individual humans and recorded in history. Mendelson observes that Auden's interest in time intensified in 1939, when "he abandoned place names [in poem titles] in favor of time-conscious titles" (*Later* 82). Although Auden's beliefs about time changed over the course of his career, the language in which he described time remained remarkably consistent throughout his life. There were two aspects of time to which Auden repeatedly returned in his poetry: first, the effect of time on human relationships, in which "time" becomes a kind of euphemism for infidelity and transient affection; second, the passage of time in the unfolding of human history, both individually and collectively. Specifically, the early Auden had accepted the idea that history, like nature, was a force, and that events in both natural and historical realms occur by necessity, though the kinds of events that take place in each realm are qualitatively different. Revolutions, like geological formations, have necessary causes that compel them to occur.[5] In "Spain 1937," for example, Auden envisions the forces of history moving Spain toward the establishment of social justice. But in 1939, Auden questioned his Marxist view of history and began to suspect that individual freedom and causal necessity might coexist in other ways. His interest in these two aspects of time, personal and historical, were closely linked because each had important moral implications for the individual.

While Auden's obsession with time predates any serious contact he had with Augustinian theology, Augustine did eventually provide a key component of Auden's later views of the nature of time. In *The Dyer's Hand*, Auden identifies Augustine as the first representative of what he calls "The Punctual Man," a character type that Auden suggests did not exist in the classical world, at least before the advent of Christianity. While the ancient Greeks had developed methods of accurate time keeping, Auden remarks that "it was never said in praise of any Caesar, for instance, that he made whatever was the Roman equivalent for trains run on time" (*DH* 140). That is, punctuality was possible in the classical world, but was not culturally significant. Auden claims, "It is certain at least that the first serious analysis of the human experience of time was undertaken by St. Augustine . . ." in the last books of the *Confessions*, and Auden goes on to claim that "the notion of punctuality, of action at an exact moment, depends on drawing a distinction between natural and historical time which Christianity encouraged if it did not invent" (140). Auden saw Augustine as the Christian fountainhead of Western notions of time.

Elsewhere in the volume, as well as in his later prose generally, Auden explains more fully his distinctions between natural and historical time (e.g. *DH* 61–62). As Mendelson explains, "History, as [Auden] described it, was the realm of unique, voluntary, irreversible events that occur in linear time. Nature, in contrast, was the realm of recurring, involuntary, reversible events that occur in cyclical time. Human experience occurs in both these realms" (*Prose III*, xv). So as a physical being, each person inhabits the world of natural time where he or she is subject to the laws of physics and chemistry, but as a conscious and therefore spiritual being, each person also inhabits the world of historical time in which he or she makes free choices. Auden had been attempting to make such distinctions since his early career, but he did not always draw precisely the same distinctions, nor did he always make consistent moral inferences, but once he settled on the Augustinian view of human nature that he appropriated through Niebuhr, he was able to make the distinctions clearly and consistently. Thus, while Augustine did not introduce Auden to the distinction, he did help Auden comprehend why the Western understanding of time had developed as it did, and how this dual nature of time affected him as an individual and as a poet.

Auden's explorations of time are numerous in his early works, but a few examples will suffice to establish his conception of time just prior to his conversion. In his 1939 poem "Another Time," which was eventually titled after the volume in which it appeared, he portrays those who wish to live in the past as denying their dual existence in both nature and history. The poem compares all people to flowers and animals in that they naturally live a merely cyclical existence instead of living in the historical moment (*CP* 276). Here Auden is relying on an implicit distinction between historical and natural time well before he could have gleaned it from

Cochrane, though Fuller suggests that Rosenstock-Huessy provided the poem's view of the human tendency to retreat from history into mere nature (*Commentary* 247). While Auden had yet to recognize Augustine's place at the head of his ideas about time, the poem demonstrates his attempt to explain human problems in terms of faulty relationships with time. In another, better known poem from the same volume, "As I Walked Out One Evening," "Time" appears as a synonym for infidelity. While an idealistic lover makes grandiose vows to his beloved, the voices of the clocks warn that "you cannot conquer Time" because of the anxiety and boredom that attends monogamy (*CP* 134). Sterility and death appear in everyday objects like teacups, cupboards, basins, and beds in the clocks' attempt to bring the lover to an acceptance of his responsibility for the eventual failure of his love. Near the end, the poem resorts to explicitly theological language as it modifies the biblical command: "You shall love your crooked neighbor / With your crooked heart" (135). Not only does the poem show Auden's vocabulary approaching the theological language of his later poems well before his formal return to the church, but it also encapsulates the anxiety of impermanence that pervades much of Auden's love poetry.

The theological language intensified in his unfinished 1939 prose work, *The Prolific and Devourer*, which Mendelson explains was written with Augustine in mind: "One of the models he chose for his book, in addition to Pascal's *Pensées* was Augustine's *Confessions*, and Auden set to work renouncing his political errors in the same way Augustine renounced his philosophical and erotic ones" (*Later* 62). Despite Augustine's attention to the nature of time in books 10 through 13 of the *Confessions*, and Auden's own attention to time in his contemporaneous poems, the subject seldom comes up by name in *The Prolific and the Devourer*. Time is discussed almost exclusively in terms of history, and Auden does include a significant qualification of the fashionable Marxist view of history as the inevitable movement of social forces. He asserts that, while history has a general and inevitable trajectory toward socialism, individuals are free to either advance or retard that progress (*Prose II*, 447), so while individuals act freely within their own limited contexts, necessity operates on the grand scale in history, and Auden believed this view of history to be consistent with Marxism, which "teaches that historical development is asymptotic to perfection. Its line isn't straight: it wiggles and makes spirals, but its general direction is perfectly clear" (453). Auden warns that his fellow socialists, "in accepting the use of violence and hatred now," are unintentionally "doing the opposite of what they imagine: they are ranging themselves on the side of the retarders" (447). The movement of history, therefore, does require the moral action of individuals, although some who believe they are advancing with history may actually be working against it.

While Auden's qualification of his earlier, simplistic view of Marxist history helps to explain why fascism and not socialism was, at the moment, sweeping across Europe, as well as explaining how freedom and necessity could both compete and cooperate in history, it did little to resolve the actual contradiction between freedom and necessity within history. If individual choices really are free, how can history have a clear direction, even in general? Why should the sum of free, individual choices inevitably move the world toward a more just society and not, say, toward fascism or anarchy? Auden's attempt at a compromise between freedom and necessity was tenuous and would not last long. Mendelson points to Auden's traumatic experience with Nazi sympathizers in a New York theater as the point at which he was forced to reevaluate his early beliefs about history: "Everything in *The Prolific and the Devourer* about the inevitability of progress now seemed false" (*Prose II* xviii), and as Auden himself later remarked, "confronted by such a phenomenon, it was impossible any longer to believe that the values of liberal humanism were self-evident" (*Prose III* 578). It was no longer possible for him to believe that justice would ever be the necessary outcome of history.

Nevertheless, Auden continued to feel that history had to have a shape and even possibly a direction. *New Year Letter* and other poems of the early 1940s are intensely interested in tracing the movements of history in order to explain the present. Part 3 of *New Year Letter* attempts to trace many modern problems to historical events (the Protestant Reformation, the American Revolution) and persons (Plato, Rousseau, Burke), but the poem represents the central philosophical question of Western culture as the relationship between freedom and necessity, between free will and predestination (*CP* 237). In the poem, Auden wishes to avoid the twin "heresies" that reject either necessity ("Pelagian") or freedom ("Jansenist") by maintaining a paradoxical tension between the two (237), and the poem proceeds to envision the "Just City" that most people would like to live in: "how grandly would our virtues bloom / In a more conscionable dust / Where Freedom dwells because it must / Necessity because it can / And men confederate in Man" (240). Auden's note on these lines is not at first enlightening, saying merely, "For this quotation and for the source of many ideas in the poem v. Charles Williams, *The Descent of the Dove*" (*New Year Letter* 154). The borrowed passage describes the Augustinian agreement between Luther and Calvin on the roles of free will and predestination in salvation, after which Williams states, "Freedom existed then because it must; necessity because it could" (175). Auden's use of the statement extends the possibility of co-inherence of freedom and necessity into the secular realm. Neither Williams nor Auden explains exactly how freedom and necessity can co-inhere, remaining for the moment content to assert that they do.

Elsewhere in his contemporaneous verse and prose, Auden entertains the idea that freedom and necessity might co-inhere within the individual human as well as in history at large. In a December 1939 essay called "Jacob and the Angel," Auden identifies the "Unconscious" and "Instinctive" element of personality with "the Determined" (*Prose II* 37) and argues that contemporary Westerners, "having discovered that we cannot live exactly as we will, deny the possibility of willing anything and are content masochistically *to be lived*" (38, emphasis in original). Following Freud, Auden suggests that the unconscious and instinctive powers against which the individual ego struggles are located in both the *id*, within the individual, and in the *superego* shaped by the collective will, outside the individual. Auden concludes, "in the last analysis we *are* lived . . . the unconscious It fashions the conscious forebrain; the historical epoch grows the idea; the subject matter creates the technique—but it does so precisely in order that it may itself escape the bonds of the determined and the natural" (39).

A few months after writing "Jacob and the Angel," Auden read Williams, who encouraged Auden in his intuition that freedom and necessity must somehow be able to coexist. Freud and Marx had given their answers, but Auden finally found them unsatisfactory in their ability to explain his present experiences. About this time, he was also reading Paul Tillich, who introduced Auden to a nuanced view of *kairos*, and whose influence appears both in *New Year Letter* (e.g., *CP* 134) and in "Kairos and Logos," which Mendelson dates "Early 1941." The poem experiments with several themes that Auden would treat in greater depth in "For the Time Being," particularly the boredom and self-centeredness of the late classical world that made esoteric mystery cults so attractive. Into the Roman Empire, which has stagnated under totalitarian politics and mystery cults, the Incarnation "fell . . . into time, / The condescension of eternal order" (*CP* 306). "Time" in the poem is associated with death and suggests an impermanence similar to that with which Auden had associated the word "time" in earlier poems. In the "Advent" section of "For the Time Being," Auden emphasizes the cyclical conception of time that dominated classical thinking before the spread of Christianity, pointing up the contrast between the repetitiveness of Rome and the utter uniqueness of the Incarnation.

To describe this interruption of normal history, Auden uses the Greek word *kairos*, which he later defined in *The Dyer's Hand* as "the propitious moment for doing something," a concept which he notes "contained the seed of the notion of punctuality, but the seed did not flower" in pre-Christian Greece (140n). In Auden's language, then, one of the wonders of the Incarnation was its punctuality. The very title of "For the Time Being" indicates an emphasis on the nature of time, especially regarding the relationship between freedom and necessity, which Simeon provides with a tidy gloss: "in Him we become fully conscious of Necessity as our freedom to be tempted, and of Freedom as our necessity to have faith" (*CP* 388). Thus it is "necessary" that humans exercise their freedom in the sense that it is impossible to abdicate one's own moral freedom; as Pascal famously declares, one cannot not choose—to live is to choose. Simeon then asserts "our necessity to have faith," which sounds false on its surface. But if "faith" is taken to mean not "faith in God" but "assent to presuppositions which cannot be immediately proved true or false," as Auden defined it in a 1940 essay (*Prose II* 94), then Simeon's statement does provide a comprehensible account of precisely how freedom and necessity can co-inhere in human experience, an explanation that was noticeably lacking in *New Year Letter*. The individual is free to assent to one of any number of unprovable presuppositions, but one cannot avoid accepting *some* presupposition as true *a priori*.

Simeon also states that "the course of History is predictable in the degree to which all men love themselves, and spontaneous in the degree to which each man loves God and through Him his neighbor" (*CP* 388), which suggests that Auden was still thinking of history as involving a degree of determination, and if history is no longer the domain of the "necessary," it is nevertheless largely "predictable" insofar as individuals act selfishly rather than altruistically. A few years later, however, Auden complicated Simeon's view of history. In "The Age of Anxiety," Rosetta and Quant debate the nature of time. Rosetta, representing the faculty of feeling, describes history as largely a series of cycles, in which the images of a juke box and an escalator evoke the repetitiveness of modern, technological life (475–76). Quant, representing intuition, disagrees with Rosetta, arguing, "Time returns, a continuous Now / As the clock counts" (476), that history is a determined sequence of distinguishable events, so his description of history is filled with proper names. Hence, for Quant as for the early Auden, "We move on / As the wheel wills; one revolution / Registers all things . . ." (476). The two views of history are clearly more similar than either character would like to admit, since both ultimately envision history as deterministic, yet Rosetta's preference for mechanism and Quant's preference for proper names are irreconcilable, so the faculties are united only in their restless anxiety.

In placing these similar but distinct views of history in the mouths of Rosetta and Quant, Auden offers a critique of both, since neither can quite do justice to the whole experience of the individual, whose feeling suggests one view and whose intuition suggests another. The more he came to accept Augustine's view of human nature as an anxious fusion of body and spirit, the less he thought of history as formally determined, and while he sustained his interest in grand schemas of history throughout his life, he stopped characterizing historical eras as determined, and his prose began describing history as the realm of free human choice, either to do good (which was difficult) or to do evil (which was likely). In his essay "The Virgin and the Dynamo" in *The Dyer's Hand*, he distinguishes between "natural time" and "historical time." Natural time, which Rosetta perceives, is the realm of natural cycles which can be described mathematically. Auden implies that the physical body exists and operates primarily in natural time, and that, in the realm of natural time, "Freedom is the consciousness of Necessity," where events are effects produced by efficient causes (61). Historical time, on the other hand, is the realm of unique events which can be described in human language only by analogy. It is the realm in which human consciousness operates, perceiving time as a linear sequence of discrete moments. In historical time, Auden reverses the maxim applied to natural time, saying that in historical time "Necessity is the consciousness of Freedom" (61). In historical time, real freedom exists in a way that it does not in natural time. But

Auden insists that both kinds of time are real and that the individual human simultaneously inhabits both realms, being subject to causal necessity in natural time but exercising free will in historical time (65).

While "The Virgin and the Dynamo" was not written until later, Auden's poems from the late 1940s and 1950s make much of the distinction between historical and natural time, and of the inevitable tension between the two. The "Horae Canonicae" sequence portrays the conflict between nature and history, and the first poem, "Prime," depicts the psychological process by which the human consciousness emerges in sleep from the world of purely natural time into the tension of historical time in which free choices inevitably precipitate the Fall. Later in the sequence, the poem "Compline" records the opposite process of falling asleep, in which the individual is reimmersed in purely natural time in which the body works to restore "the order we try to destroy" (*CP* 636). Auden distinguishes between natural and historical time, not in order to vilify one and exonerate the other, but in order to avoid either a Manichean suspicion of the body or a romantic suspicion of the intellect in maintaining the continual tension between body and soul. In "Lauds," Auden depicts a morning in which the natural time of crowing cocks and the shining sun peacefully coexists with the historical time of dripping mill-wheels and mass bells.

In a 1950 article in the *Partisan Review*, written in response to the editors' request for statements by religious intellectuals, Auden explains the importance of his conception of time to his faith: "Christianity, of all religions, attaches a unique importance to history; e.g. the clause in the creed 'He suffered under Pontius Pilate' expresses the belief that, for God, a particular moment in history when the Jews had reached a certain point in their development, religious, intellectual, political, and the gentiles in theirs, was 'the fullness of time,' the right moment for the eternal vow to be made Flesh and the Divine Sacrifice to take place" (*Prose III* 170). Auden describes the idea of *kairos* without using the word, but also points out that Christianity rejects the classical notion of merely cyclical time, insisting instead that natural time coexists with historical time, and that Christianity must therefore see the development of history as meaningful, if not necessarily determined. Later in the essay, Auden cites Augustine as an example of an early Christian thinker to whom the Christian conception of time was important.

The very idea of an autobiography, Auden contends, would be impossible without a clear sense of historical time: "in *The Confessions* St Augustine gives a detailed account of his personal historical situation, his parents, his friends, his intellectual development, his character," not in order to demonstrate that his conversion occurred by causal necessity, "but as evidences that the God of love must permit his creations free will which can refuse grace at the same time that they are seeking it" (*Prose III* 170). In Augustine's case, both freedom and necessity cooperate in his conversion, since the place of his birth and his physical desires are necessary facts for him, as is God's love, and the *Confessions* is the story of the turning of Augustine's will toward God. While some read the *Confessions* as heavily deterministic, seeing in the story a divine coercion by circumstance, Auden reads the book as an account of free will encouraged by anxiety to accept grace. As the very form of the *Confessions* demonstrates, the Christian affirmation of both natural and historical time makes possible the art of the particular, especially as it depicts unique names and events. Critics have often wondered at Auden's penchant for writing occasional verse in his later years, and for dedicating many of his poems to personal friends. Auden knew himself to be, like Augustine, a punctual man for whom the idea of *kairos*—the propitious moment for action—was all-important. For both Auden and Augustine, specific names and dates reveal the operation of providence in hindsight, which is how both kinds of time can be redeemed.

As seriously as Auden took his distinction between natural and historical time, it sometimes appears in humorous poems. "On the Circuit," for example, portrays his publishing company as existing in the realm of natural time in which causal necessity is the rule, such that he is an "instrument" that is "Predestined nightly to fulfill / Columbia-Giesen-Management's / Unfathomable will" (*CP* 729). While the use of Calvinist theological language to describe a modern corporation is intentionally outrageous, the poem points out the way in which a bureaucracy operates solely within the realm of natural time in which market cycles and mathematical calculations obscure the particular names and faces that exist in historical time, which the corporation cannot treat as real. As an agent of the corporation, Auden describes his own "circuit" as an extension of the publishing company's privileging of natural, cyclical time. The immersion in natural time disorients the poet, such that "I cannot now say where I was / The evening before last . . ." (729). However, the occurrence of "some singular event" which "intervene[s] to save the place" brings him back to a consciousness of historical time in which events are unique and therefore memorable. They must necessarily be "unscheduled on the Giesen Plan," for it is the surprising interruption of natural, corporate time that gives historical shape to an otherwise utterly repetitive journey.

Many of Auden's later poems reassert the distinction between natural and historical time. "Lines to Dr Walter" (*CP* 769–70), "Ode to Terminus" (809–11), "A Reminder" (823–24), and "The Art of Healing" (835–36) are among the poems that draw directly on the tension between natural and historical time, and most of these are also occasional poems, the nature of which encouraged Auden's continuing interest in time. Auden's personal insistence on punctuality became notorious in his middle age, and in his aphoristic poem "Profile," compiled between 1965 and 1966, he quipped about himself, "Without a watch / he would never know when / to feel hungry or horny" (775). Such an obsession with historical time naturally led Auden to produce "punctual" poems for specific events, such as a birthday, a marriage, a retirement, or a death, and with a few exceptions, such as "Moon Landing" (843) and "Elegy for J.F.K." (754), the bulk of his occasional verses commemorate not

"Historic" events but events of some personal importance, very much as Augustine had memorialized his own personal history in the *Confessions*. In his later years, Auden abandoned his earlier idea that history had a visible direction, or at least that he had any insight into it, preferring instead to observe history as it unfolded in surprising ways. He sometimes chides those who think they can perceive the direction of history well enough to predict it, as in the 1959 poem "Secondary Epic," in which he berates Virgil for supposing that Aeneas "can learn / His Roman history in the future tense . . ." (598). Virgil's attempt to treat "hindsight as foresight" is nonsensical (598), though it is an ancient and noble error, perpetuated by Aeneas' conversation with his father in book 6 of the *Aeneid*. As Niebuhr argues in *The Nature and Destiny of Man*, "History . . . does not conform to the systems of rational coherence which men construct periodically to comprehend its meaning. . . . History can be meaningful, therefore, only in terms of a faith which comprehends its seeming irrationalities and views them as the expression of a divine wisdom, which transcends human understanding" (289). Auden came to believe that he could not fulfill his own vocation as a poet unless he accepted the limitations of his own historical horizons.

CROWD, SOCIETY, COMMUNITY, AND PUBLIC

Auden's poetry and prose of the 1940s, and especially "The Age of Anxiety," clearly presuppose that individuals, whether individual humans or individual faculties or even individual events or objects, tend to congregate into various types of groups. In his prose from this era, he repeatedly distinguishes three kinds of groups, the most important of which he draws directly from Augustine. First, a "crowd" is a group of individuals related only by their happening to be in the same locale at the same time, and "a crowd loves neither itself nor anything other than itself" (*DH* 63). Secondly, a "society" is a particular number of individuals, all "present and properly related"; it is "a system which loves itself" and seeks its own preservation (63–64). These two kinds of groups are distinguished from the third, a "community," a concept that Auden draws directly from Augustine: "A community is comprised of *n* members united, to use a definition of Saint Augustine's, by a common love of something other than themselves" (64). Auden uses this definition numerous times in his prose, though he does not always acknowledge Augustine as its source.[6] The definition is derived from Augustine's *City of God*, especially 1.15 and 14.28. In the context of Augustine's argument, the ideal community is the church, which Augustine argues at great length has existed throughout history, from the beginning of time to the present day. But within history, it is impossible for the whole community to congregate physically, so as Auden observes, "to achieve an actual existence, [a community] has to embody itself in a society or societies which can express the love which is its *raison d'être*.

A community of music lovers, for example, cannot just sit around loving music like anything, but must form itself into societies like choirs, orchestras, string quartets, etc., and make music" (*DH* 64). So the church must organize itself into individual churches in order to express the members' common love for God. However, Auden also adds that, "of a community, it may be said that its love is more or less good" (64).Thus, Augustine's gang of adolescent friends could participate in the community of those who love crime for its own sake, being united into a society in which the wills of the individual members are subordinated to the will of the whole. Even though the young Augustine was probably not the only boy in the gang who would have hesitated to rob the pear tree on his own, as a part of an efficiently operating society, he allowed the will of the group to govern his individual will.

As important as these distinctions clearly were to Auden, they do not often appear explicitly in his poetry. Instead, they form the basis of his understanding of how a good poem is constructed. Auden believed that the poet's task was to take a crowd of words and organize them into a society in which each word stands in proper relation to the others, all in the service of embodying a community of words (*DH* 67–69). But these definitions also helped him explain his own relationships to diverse groups of people, or even a group of selves contained within an individual psyche, which is one of the premises of "The Age of Anxiety." The poem follows a number of discrete faculties as they emerge from a crowd at a bar and form themselves into a society that embarks upon a quest for coherence in community. The poems of the late 1940s and early 1950s, roughly from "The Age of Anxiety" to "Horae Canonicae," represent Auden's Augustinian psychology of anxiety and sin at their full maturity. Although the pre-conversion Auden had always been concerned with human anxiety and guilt, and with the wish for integration and community, he had had no stable language in which to express these concerns. From the secret agent and the explorer to the helmeted airman and the hermit, Auden had run through a long series of figures and images, many of them lovers, in his attempt to depict the anxious, homeless self in search of coherence and community, but it was Augustine, mediated largely through Reinhold Niebuhr, who finally afforded Auden a compelling and nuanced language in which to describe feelings about which he had always written. Auden's psychological language had never been fully his own, but after his conversion he went to less trouble to conceal his sources.

"Horae Canonicae" articulates an Augustinian psychology with renewed vigor, but it also develops a compelling account of how the fallen individual becomes integrated into equally fallen crowds, societies, and communities, and thus implicated in both personal and communal guilt. Additionally, the poems were written as Auden was beginning to contemplate his own civic role as a poet and, consequently, was exploring the nature of public life in relation to history. Of all Auden's major, post-conversion works, "Horae Canonicae" presents the strongest and most disturbing picture of how the individual fits into what Augustine described as "the City of Man." The series begins not with the community but with the individual. "Prime" depicts the process of waking up in the morning in language drawn directly from Niebuhr's Augustinian psychology of the Fall. The speaker describes the moment of initial consciousness prior to any act of the will, a moment in which Niebuhr locates the initial state of moral innocence, remarking "without a name or history I wake / Between my body and the day" (*CP* 627). The self is conscious, but without memory of its identity, and without any consciousness of its previous acts, it has momentarily reentered a state of perfection. Niebuhr argues that "the original righteousness of man stands, as it were, outside of history" (280); hence the poem's description of a moment "without . . . history" (*CP* 627). The poem proceeds to describe the awakening self as the sinless "Adam still previous to any act" (627). The language is again drawn directly from Niebuhr, who argues that "perfection before the Fall is . . . perfection before the act" (278). Such a moment cannot last, for any act whose motive is a resolution of anxiety entails a Fall.

The deed that Auden describes as reenacting the Fall is the seemingly innocent act of breathing: "I draw breath; that is of course to wish / No matter what, to be wise, / To be different, to die and the cost, / No matter how, is Paradise / Lost of course . . ." (*CP* 628). For the speaker, even to will to draw a breath reveals a will to be something other than what one is, and thus proceeds from the anxiety of the speaker's situation as a restless, discontented being. Niebuhr's definition of "act" helps to explain Auden's identification of conscious breathing with the Fall: "it is important not to give too narrow a connotation to the concept of 'act.' The self may act even when the action is not overt. It acts whenever, as anxious self, it thinks or moves for its own protection in the welter of perils and passions which constitutes its world. Every thought, mood, or action which proceeds from the self as anxious, finite, and insecure has some taint of sin upon it" (278). Niebuhr is clearly the source for Auden's identification of Milton's lost Paradise with the moment of consciousness prior to an act, but the locus of such an event in the moment of waking up is Auden's own, as is his use of conscious breathing as an example of such an act. Conscious breathing—as opposed to unconscious breathing—is an attempt to take control of an automatic action that does not actually need conscious interference to go on functioning.

In "Prime," Auden has finally resolved the longstanding ambiguity with which he had described the advent of Original Sin. The speaker has emerged into consciousness "previous to any act" (*CP* 627) but also remains dissociated from his own body since "the will has still to claim / This adjacent arm as my own" (627). The Fall will occur only with the first actual motion of the will, so consciousness must precede the Fall, if only by a moment. With this first conscious act, the speaker reenters the realm of human history, recovering the memory of his previous existence and anticipating his future actions. Much later, in a 1964 essay, Auden would reiterate his position on the locus of the Fall, especially as it relates to the advent of consciousness, arguing that, while the sin is not physically present in the body, "our every bodily movement, touch, gesture, tone of voice is that of a sinner. From the moment consciousness first wakes in a baby, (and this may be before birth) it finds itself in the company of sinners, and its consciousness is affected by a contagion against which there is no prophylaxis" (*FA* 54). While maintaining his rejection of a genetic theory of Original Sin, Auden explains that the social context into which one is conceived may be the agent most responsible for the transmission of sin, and that a child's conscious existence in a social world even before birth could explain why babies seem to be born already fallen. Here, as in "Prime," consciousness precedes the Fall, but only by a moment. Every move and gesture, Auden argues, is tainted by sin, hence his use of breathing as an example of the Fall.

As the speaker reenters his fallen world, he finds that he has also regained his name along with his history, both of which have been suppressed in sleep, and his name signifies his role within "a lying self-made city" (*CP* 628), that is, the historical world of human relationships after the Fall. Auden's choice of language evokes Augustine's long and complicated distinction between the "City of God" and the "City of Man" in his *City of God*. It is not clear whether Auden ever actually read the whole *City of God*,[7] but it is clear from his language in "Prime" and many other poems from the late 1940s and 1950s that he was familiar with the general argument of the book, which he could easily have deduced from a number of sources, including Williams, Cochrane, and Niebuhr. It is clear, however, that Auden had *The City of God* in mind when he drafted the poem. In a 1950 lecture, "Nature, History and Poetry," he recounts the composition of "Prime": "The chief difficulty was the end," and after several rewrites, "I began to believe that the idea I wanted was to go from this personal thing, of calling myself Adam, to the idea of the two cities, the *civitas dei* and the *civitas terrene*; and then [I gave up that idea] but kept the idea of the city. And that seemed to be right, and so that was finally what came out" (*Prose III* 650). The terms "*civitas dei*" and the "*civitas terrene*" come from Augustine's *City of God*, and while Auden eventually omitted most of the explicit references to Augustine from the poem, traces of Augustine's ideas remain in the final version.

Throughout *The City of God*, Augustine makes his pivotal distinction between the two "cities" on the basis of the love that motivates each of the two communities. The City of God is a community united by its love for God and is realized in the society of the church, whereas the City of Man is a community united by pride, greed, and self-aggrandizement and is realized in all secular societies, from the Tower of Babel to imperial Rome, the term "city" or "seculum" being emblematic of any society in which either community is realized. The psychological basis for defining a community according to its love is articulated in the *Confessions*, where Augustine identifies love with the faculty of the will, such that what one loves exerts a kind of gravitational pull on the self, directing the self toward that which it most loves (13.8). So the City of God is comprised of all those who love God—that is, who will to know him and to imitate his goodness, insofar as it is possible for finite beings to do so. But the City of Man is comprised of all those who love themselves— that is, who will to accrue power and wealth in order to satisfy their own lusts and conceal their own insecurities. It is into this "City of Man" that the Fall introduces each human being.

One of the recurring themes of "Horae Canonicae" is the foundation of the City of Man. The third poem in the series, "Sext," describes the differences between an individual and a crowd. Individual human beings see discrete objects and events, but insofar as they are united into a crowd, they see only the crowd itself doing "whatever is done" (*CP* 633). As they gather into a crowd, individuals lose their distinguishing characteristics, but paradoxically, the crowd is the ultimately demo-cratic condition, for "joining the crowd / is the only thing all men can do" (633). Implicitly, it is the crowd that is responsible for "Good Friday," the execution that ends the previous poem, "Terce," since "Sext" concludes by describing the way in which the crowd "worship[s] / The Prince of this world . . . / at this noon, on this hill, / in the occasion of this dying . . ." (633). As members of the crowd, the individu-als share moral responsibility for their execution of the innocent man, but because their wills and identities are collapsed into the crowd, they are only vaguely aware of their own personal guilt.

The next poem, "Nones," reflects on the awakening sense of individual guilt for a communal act. The poem quotes a representative individual, who insists: "'It was . . . / A crowd that saw him die, not I,'" but the attempt to transfer responsibility to the crowd does not assuage the feelings of guilt that gather now that "we have lost our public" (*CP* 634). The word "public" had a very specific meaning for Auden, which he explains in an essay several years earlier: "A public is a disintegrated community. A community is a society of rational beings united by a common tie in virtue of the things that they all love; a public is a crowd of lost beings united only negatively in virtue of the things that they severally fear, among which one of the greatest is the fear of being responsible as a rational being for one's individual self-development" (*Prose II* 154). Although Auden does not attribute the definition of "community" to Augustine here, he is well aware that his definition of a "public" hinges on his understanding of Augustine. In both a community and a public, there is no tension between the individual will and the communal will, but the difference is that in a community all members consciously accept responsibility for their love, while the members of a public attempt to evade moral responsibility for their own actions by merging into a group, which is the central theme of "Nones." The dispersed mem-bers of the public would like to forget the ways in which "some chance rhyme / Like *will* and *kill*" (*CP* 634), as well as seemingly innocent children's games, remind them of their blood guilt, which each would like "to misrepresent, excuse, deny, / Mythify . . ." (635). The only means of escaping guilt seems to be an escape from consciousness entirely, if only in sleep. Although "our dreaming wills may seem to escape" while "our own wronged flesh / May work undisturbed, restoring / The order we try to destroy" (636), anxious guilt also surfaces in dreams, and the respite is only temporary.

In the next poem, "Vespers," Auden returns more explicitly to the nature of the City of Man. The poem is about an imagined meeting of two representatives of contrasting types, the Arcadian and the Utopian. Despite their extreme differences in taste—the Arcadian enjoys picturesque landscapes, elaborate rituals, and aesthetic pleasure, while the Utopian enjoys rational organization, hard work, and political equality—they also dimly recognize that their meeting is "a rendezvous between two accomplices who, in spite of themselves, cannot resist meeting . . ." in order to remind each other that both visions of the ideal society can be achieved only by killing innocent people (*CP* 639). The poet lists Abel and Remus as examples of sacrificial victims "on whose immolation . . . arcadias, utopias, our dear old bag of a democracy are alike founded" (639). The poem concludes with the assertion that all societies, no matter how superficially just, are founded on one profound injustice: "For without a cement of blood (it must be human, it must be innocent) no secular wall will safely stand" (639). The word "secular" is telling, for it connotes its Latin root, "seculum," which can variously mean "cosmos" or "world," but also the present, temporal affairs of the world. Auden knew (or could easily have guessed) that the word is used throughout the *City of God*, in which Augustine argues that the City of Man is essentially founded on injustice, despite its many pretensions to the defense of a just order. For all its modern language, "Vespers" replicates a crucial argument within the *City of God*: no secular order can legitimately claim to embody absolute justice.

The last poem in the sequence, "Lauds," offers some solace after the long, difficult exploration of individual and communal guilt that pervades "Horae Canonicae." The poem evokes something like a good community, without attempting an actual description. The repeated lines "Men of their neighbors become sensible" and "*In solitude, for company*" imply the formation of a community based on the love of one's neighbors (*CP* 641–43). In his prose, Auden occasionally remarked that the essence of Christianity is the command to "love your neighbor as yourself" (e.g. *Prose II* 342, and *Prose III* 589), which Auden believed was the earthly expression of one's love for God. Auden had said that, of any given community, "it may be said that its love is more or less good" (*DH* 64). "Lauds" suggests the possibility of a community whose love is good, or at least better than the self-love of the secular community depicted in the rest of the sequence. The poem is one of Auden's very few attempts to talk about the City of God in his poetry, even though the subtle treatment is indirect.

The presence of the "mass-bell" in the poem draws attention to some important features of the City of God, which Augustine identified with the institutional church, but which Auden as a Protestant following Niebuhr preferred to regard as a more informal arrangement. First, the sacrifice of the innocent victim, with which the rest of the sequence is concerned, is also present in "Lauds," since the mass is ultimately a memorial and a reenactment of the sacrificial death of Christ. Auden also saw participation in the mass, or in any religious ritual, as the only real means of achieving emotional catharsis. In his 1947 essay "Squares and Oblongs," Auden remarked, "if I understand what Aristotle means when he speaks of catharsis, I can only say he is wrong. It is an effect produced, not by works of art, but by bull-fights, professional football matches, bad movies and, in those who can stand that sort of thing, monster rallies at which ten thousand girl guides form themselves into the national flag" (*Prose II* 346). Auden detects a religious fervor in all the events he lists, and he implies that Aristotle is in error because he treats tragedy apart from its role as an element of religious ritual. Auden's point is that it was the whole festival culminating in ritual sacrifice, not the performance of the tragic play alone, that had a cathartic effect on the ancient Greek audience. By extension, the common feelings of fear and guilt may be purged by any religious ritual, perhaps especially when the ritual is not fully recognized as being religious. In "Lauds," the ritual must be consistent with the explicitly Christian context of Good Friday within which the sequence operates. In the mass, the innocent victim is neither denied or excused, as the Utopian or the Arcadian would have it. Only in the ritual remembrance of the death can the perpetrators receive forgiveness.

Auden had planned to write the series of poems on the canonical hours since 1947 (see Mendelson, *Later* 311–13), though the sequence was not finished until 1954. Meanwhile, Auden's poetic concerns centered largely on the nature of human history and on the individual's role within the secular city. Despite Auden's awareness of Augustine's arguments in the *City of God*, he seldom alludes to Augustine in his poems on civic life. One exception is his 1949 poem "Memorial for the City," a poem that both anticipates several themes that he would flesh out in "Horae Canonicae" and elaborates on several Augustinian themes in which he had a longstanding interest. The poem is in part a lament for the destruction of cities during the two world wars, but it considers the subject broadly and attempts to place the twentieth century in the larger context of Western civilization's repeated, futile attempts to build the Just City. The poem's view of history is drawn from many sources, including Cochrane's *Christianity and Classical Culture* and Williams's *The Descent of the Dove*, but especially Eugen Rosenstock-Huessy's 1939 book *Out of Revolution: Autobiography of Western Man*, whose eccentric history of revolutions in the Western world came to dominate Auden's ideas about history for several years, and while Rosenstock-Huessy is not particularly Augustinian in his thought, Mendelson suggests that it was Reinhold Niebuhr who first gave the book to Auden (*Later* 260).

Additionally, "Memorial for the City" begins with an epigraph from Julian of Norwich that makes direct reference to Augustine: "In the self-same point that our soul is made sensual, in the self-same point is the City of God ordained to him from without beginning" (*CP* 591). Fuller points out that Auden would have found the quotation in Williams, to whom the poem is dedicated,[8] and he explains that Auden's use of Julian is an expression of his continued suspicion of Manichaeism (*Commentary* 417), though Fuller makes no further attempt to examine the poem in light of Augustine's thought. Augustine's presence in the poem is neither overt nor obvious, but the poem's rejection of an ancient Greek attitude of resignation to fate relies heavily on Cochrane's Augustinian analysis of the late classical world. Cochrane argues that the late Roman Empire, which Auden refers to in "Memorial for the City" as "the Post-Vergilian City" (*CP* 592), became philosophically paralyzed by its failed attempt to correlate natural law and civic law, to locate in the world of nature the principles on which civic justice could be based. Cochrane argues that it was only Christianity, and particularly the theology of Augustine, that was able to break the philosophical stalemate between the idealists, who rejected the material world as intrinsically evil, and the materialists, who denied the existence of transcendentals.

"Memorial for the City" opens with the dual perspectives of the crow and the camera, which suggest the viewpoints of detached nature and of impersonal technology respectively, but which have essentially the same disinterested viewpoint, seeing "a space where time has no place" (*CP* 592). Both the camera and the crow "See as honestly as they know how, but they lie," not only because their perspectives are severely limited, but also because they portray historical events as natural events, which take place by necessity and are therefore exempt from moral judgment. For the crow and the camera, "That is the way things happen" and "there is no one to blame" (592). In opposition to the lying eyes of crow and camera, the speaker insists that "our grief is not Greek" (592). While the grief at historical atrocities is real, the difference is that, while the "Greek" or Homeric grief involves a resignation to blind fate, the contemporary world knows that historical events have reasons and causes, so its grief can avoid despair.

The two middle sections of the poem are a condensed history of Western culture, from the early Middle Ages to the present day, and each stanza describes a different historical attempt to locate the basis of the Just City in some principle, but each attempt has distinct problems and is overthrown by subsequent attempts. The history itself is drawn largely from Rosenstock-Huessy, but the underlying problem of turning the City of Man into the Just City is indebted to Augustine, who insists over and over in the *City of God* that the City of Man is founded on pride and injustice, despite the best efforts of a few noble figures in classical history. The problem in the West is compounded by the strong cultural presence of the church, which ought to represent the City of God, but which Auden thought was generally complicit in the City of Man. So, for example, when Pope Gregory claimed political independence for the Roman church from secular rulers, and also claimed power to enthrone and depose emperors, the practical results were both the cultural unity of medieval Christendom, which Auden calls "the Sane City" (*CP* 593), and a facile civic religion against which Luther protested, calling it "the Sinful City" (593). In the fourth century, Augustine had claimed that the two cities were distinct and contrary in both principle and purpose, but Auden's poem focuses on the practical problems that occurred in the wake of Christendom's first attempts to establish a coherent relationship between the two cities. In the poem's view, no practical arrangement is able to achieve a permanently just state, leaving the modern West with the "abolished City" (594) of post-world-war Europe that is defined not by an attempt to reestablish justice but by the arbitrary borders established by barbed wire.

At this point, Auden shifts the poem away from its survey of recent history and looks in hope toward what he calls "our Image" (*CP* 595), which he locates both "behind the wire" and "behind the mirror" (595). It is the physical body, which is "behind the mirror" in the sense that it does not participate directly in the reflection of self-consciousness, and it is "behind the wire" because the barbed wire of the Abolished City is a real, physical presence, not just a mental or symbolic border. The body has "no age" and "no sex" because the concepts of age and sex are largely mental constructs that impart to the body meanings that are not intrinsic to it. The body inhabits a world of natural time, in which natural cycles are the mode of existence, whereas age, sex, memory, creed, and name (595) are all contingent on a recognition of historical time, in which unique events are the mode of existence. The final stanza is spoken by the body itself in an enigmatic monologue reminiscent of Celtic and Anglo-Saxon "Who am I?" riddles. The body dissociates itself from the historical events with which the rest of the poem has been engaged, turning instead to mythic events to describe its own limited but redemptive role in human life.

While "Memorial for the City" is largely concerned with historical events such as wars and revolutions, which are unique in time, the body's monologue is concerned almost solely with mythic events, such as the theft of fire by Prometheus and Galahad's quest for the Grail. Auden explains the difference between history and myth in a literary sense in *The Dyer's Hand* (407–8, 69–70): a mythic character is one for whom a reader can imagine any number of further adventures for the character that the author, as it were, neglected to record—examples are Sherlock Holmes and Don Quixote. The mythic character is, in a way, perpetually repeatable, just like a mythic event such as the Fall and the Incarnation is perpetually repeatable, as Niebuhr argued in volume 1 of *The Nature and Destiny of Man*. A historical character, on the other hand, is a character who is inseparable from his or her linear narrative as recorded by the author—examples are Anna Karenina and Prince Hal. A historical event is a unique event, such as the Protestant Reformation or the Battle of Waterloo; it happens only once. Mendelson remarks that, in the list of events to which the body alludes in "Memorial for the City," the only historical event is the crucifixion of Christ (*Later* 327n), though as "Horae Canonicae" indicates, that event is also mythic because it is repeated in every human life.

Given the initial focus on historical events, the shift to the mythic is jarring. The poem's final lines resemble the end of "The Sea and the Mirror," in which one of Shakespeare's few mythic characters, Caliban, speaks on behalf of the body in a borrowed voice about his relationship to another mythic character, Ariel. In both speeches, the body speaks in a borrowed voice since it has no voice of its own.[9] Just as Caliban borrows the language of Henry James, so the body in "Memorial for the City" borrows mythic language, and neither speaker deals with the historical world as such, but with mythic metaphors that provide analogues to any number of historical events to which the audience cares to relate them. As presented in both poems, the body is itself a mythic entity, and in "Memorial for the City," the body is "our Image" that "is the same / Awake or dreaming," is unconscious of itself, and "can be counted, multiplied, employed / [and] destroyed" (*CP* 595). Auden had described the body's physical operations in "Compline" as valves opening and closing, glands secreting, and vessels contracting and expanding (636); the body's processes are perpetually repeatable throughout time and thus not responsible for the unique, ethical choices that the conscious ego makes in linear history.

Mendelson explicitly links this section of the poem to a passage from *Christianity and Classical Culture* in which Cochrane states, "To Augustine . . . body is neither absolute reality nor absolute appearance; it is the organ by which mankind establishes contact with the objective world" (Cochrane 437; qtd. in Mendelson, *Later* 322). The body is an instrument of the soul and is therefore not to be blamed for the poor choices of the ego: "I was not taken in by the sheep's eyes of Narcissus," the body says (*CP* 595), since Narcissus' pride and self-absorption was a purely intellectual sin, as Auden further explains in *The Dyer's Hand* (94–95). The body's voice continues, "I was innocent of the sin of the Ancient Mariner" who shot the albatross out of pure spite and not out of any corporeal need (*CP* 596). At the end of its speech, the body announces, "As for Metropolis, that too-great city; her delusions are not mine, / Her speeches impress me little, her statistics less . . ." (596). The body has no interest in building what Augustine called the City of Man.

Augustine argues that the City of Man operates on the basis of pride and the achievement of personal glory (see *CG* 5.15, 14.28), and following Niebuhr's Augustinian psychology, Auden attributes such hubris to the conscious ego, not to the body. In contrast to the City of Man, Augustine indicates that the City of God is characterized by love and harmony and is always already existing among God and his followers, including the angels, the martyrs, the church, and the dead and living saints (*City of God* 14:28, 19.13). While Auden was critical of Augustine's identification of the City of God with the historical, organized church, he did not see the City of God as a purely eschatological entity, but as a worldwide community of all people who really love their neighbors (see *Prose III* 176). Historical expressions of such a community in earthly societies are rare and short-lived, but they are nonetheless real. It is therefore puzzling that Fuller should suggest that in this poem, "The human clay is seen finally, despite Dame Julian, as still awaiting the City of God" (*Commentary* 420). Augustine maintains throughout *The City of God* that the divine city does not exist in the same way that the earthly city does. For Augustine, it is true (and perhaps this is what Fuller means) that a society that Auden elsewhere calls "the Just City" is not finally achievable through the present modes of civic and political life, since the earthly city is based on unjust self-aggrandizement. As a community, the City of God is always already present in human history whenever humans truly love each other.

In *The Enchafèd Flood*, a work based on lectures given in 1949, the same year he wrote "Memorial for the City," Auden reiterates Augustine's clear distinction between these two cities. The ships in Melville's fiction, he says, can represent "the *civitas terrena*, created by self-love, inherited and repeated, into which all men since Adam are born, yet where they have never totally lost their knowledge of and longing for the Civitas Dei and the Law of Love" (66). This places the various characters into "absurd contradictions, like the chaplain on a man-of-war who is paid a share of the reward for sinking a ship and cannot condemn war or flogging, or the devout Baptist [a pacifist] who earns his bread as captain of a gun," and while a saint like Billy Budd can obey the "Law of Love" even in the face of execution, "the rest of us cannot avoid disingenuous compliances" (66–67). Auden's assertion that no human is able to establish or maintain the City of God on earth suggests that a reader of "Memorial for the City" should not be surprised that utopian liberal humanism does not triumph at the end of the poem. For Auden as for Augustine, the concept of the political Just City is an idealized form of the City of Man; it is not to be confused with the City of God. Auden makes a similar point in his review of Cochrane's *Christianity and Classical Culture*, where he remarks on the dubious project of conflating the two cities: "Our period is not so unlike the age of Augustine: the planned society, caesarism of thugs or bureaucracies, paideia, scientia, religious persecution, are all with us. Nor is there even lacking the possibility of a new Constantinism; . . . Cochrane's terrifying description of the 'Christian' empire under Theodosius should discourage such hopes of using Christianity as a spiritual benzedrine for the earthly city . . ." (*FA* 39). While Auden was not about to give up trying to encourage the present Earthly City to become more just and humane whenever he could, by the time he wrote "Memorial for the City" he was under no illusions that any human society could bring the New Jerusalem to earth.

That fact does not, therefore, absolve the individual of moral responsibility for what happens in the secular realm, and Auden's late poetry occasionally reflects on such personal responsibility. "Aubade," for example, which is dedicated to Rosenstock-Huessy, returns to the subject matter of "Prime," tracing the process of waking up and reentering the historical world. As the speaker awakes, he emerges into his conscious identity as described by Augustine: "again, as wrote Augustine, / I know that I am and will, / I am willing and knowing, / I will to be and to know . . ." (*CP* 881). Auden quotes from the *Confessions* 13.11, where Augustine explains how the psychological trinity of being, knowing, and willing reflects the divine Trinity of Father, Son, and Spirit in the sense that the three are distinguishable but insepa-rable, and as such, the human soul is the ultimate locus of the *imago dei*. For Auden, such self-consciousness of one's willful existence in time is "the domain of Deeds" in which "We are free to choose our paths / but choose We must . . ." (882). At the end, Auden equates the realm of historical time with the secular city "where each inhab-itant has / a political duty / nobody else can perform . . ." (882). The poem does not indicate what these "political duties" might be. Because each person's duty is unique to his or her time and place, the poem cannot endorse this or that specific action and must instead speak at the level of generality. The poem is typical of the mod-est social aspirations that appear in Auden's later poetry and prose, which prefer to focus on the difficulty of tasks that attend everyday life, rather than on grand social or political schemes.

However, Auden's continued "existential" focus on living out one's faith by lov-ing one's neighbor can sometimes appear to fall into the Pelagian heresy, the idea that divine grace is, strictly speaking, unnecessary, and that Christian virtue can be achieved and maintained through sheer will power. Niebuhr had been clear in his assertion that, as Augustine perceived, the very will of every person is itself cor-rupted in that it is free to do evil but not good, and that divine grace is neces-sary to make the will again capable of choosing the good (243). While Auden was intentionally reticent on the subject of salvation, he did eventually accept Niebuhr's Augustinian description of salvation by grace as valid, and it is reasonably clear that he came to accept the Pauline formula of salvation "by grace through faith" (Ephesians 4:8). However, when on rare occasions Auden used the word "faith," he did always have a specific definition in mind. In a 1940 essay, he defines "faith" as an "assent to presuppositions which cannot be immediately proved true or false, as, or example, science presupposes that the world of nature exists" (*Prose II* 94). In this sense, everyone acts on faith of some kind, since "faith" is not limited to an assent to the transcendent or the supernatural but could also describe the acceptance of physical phenomena as real.

By implication, the Christian has faith that God exists and that he intervened in history by way of the Incarnation, which are propositions that Auden came to accept. By defining "faith" as assent to unprovable presuppositions, Auden estab-lishes faith as the basis of action, and he seems to have been especially impressed by the Christian life described in the book of James, in which "faith without works is dead" (2:17–26). Auden recognized that the practical demand of Christianity was to love one's neighbor, which he freely admitted that he and all other Christians found very hard to do with any consistency. As Auden famously states in his 1966 Westminster sermon, "it is almost the definition of a Christian that he is somebody who *knows* he isn't one, either in faith or in morals" (qtd. in Carpenter 298n). That is, the first thing a Christian is aware of is his or her failure to live up to the ideals of Christ's life and teachings, though Auden also warns that "we shall not improve . . . by a morbid and essentially narcissistic moaning over our deficiencies" (298n). Rather, it is important to continue to act charitably whenever possible without succumbing either to spiritual pride in a pretended perfection or to spiritual despair in the face of one's continued moral failures.

For Auden, it was only the grace offered through the sacraments that made this tension bearable. Auden had always had a taste for rite and ritual, and in his return to Christianity he found his taste advantageous, since the high-church tradition to which he was drawn emphasized the impartation of God's grace through the physical enactments of rituals, particularly that of baptism and the Eucharist. His taste for ritual also directed the formation of his theology. Auden explains in his essay in *Modern Canterbury Pilgrims* that ritual, even when it disintegrates into mere routine, has spiritual value: "A man may go to confession in a frivolous state of mind, rattle off some sins without feeling any real contrition, and go away to commit them again, but as long as he keeps up the habit he cannot forget that there are certain actions which the Church calls sinful, and that he has committed them . . ." (*Prose III* 579–80). To thus psychologize the sacramental rituals is not necessarily to deny their spiritual power, especially in light of Niebuhr's insistence that the "spiritual" element in human nature is the capacity to know God. Grace need not entail a blinding light on the road to Damascus, but more often appears in a religious habit that one cannot quite shake off.

The liturgy of the Eucharist always includes the confession of sins and the offer of forgiveness. Auden did not frequently allude to forgiveness in either his poetry or his prose, and when it does appear it is fraught with difficulty. A familiar example is the ending of "In Praise of Limestone," in which Auden makes the significance of artistic works, and especially marble statuary, contingent on the possibility of forgiveness and resurrection: "but if / Sins can be forgiven, if bodies rise from the dead, / These modifications of matter into / Innocent athletes and gesticulating fountains, / Made solely for pleasure, make a further point: / The blessed will not care what angle they are regarded from, / Having nothing to hide" (*CP* 542). The poem is about the nature of embodiment and the relation of the body to love and to art, and it holds out hope, however qualified, that sins can be forgiven.

5. POETRY AND TRUTH

As a professional writer, Auden knew of Augustine's important place in Western literary culture, and although he held Augustine's theological insights in high regard and frequently drew historical comparisons between the late Roman Empire and his own twentieth-century milieu, he was also aware of the wide cultural gap between Augustine and himself. In a 1954 review, Auden notes that while "by the Hellenistic period there were large libraries and a kind of literary scholarship which seems very similar to our own, it was not till the final days of the Roman empire, as proved [by] St Augustine's surprise when he saw St Ambrose doing it, that reading in our sense, silently by eye, was thought of. The lack of subjectivity which this implies, is something we can hardly imagine" (*Prose III* 418). It was this very absence of subjectivity that provided Augustine a cultural space to explore the interior life as no thinker before him had done, and in Auden's mind, the practical results of his records of human psychological phenomena include the rise of a poetic tradition that privileges the interior life over public deeds.

Auden's post-conversion view of poetry, which he reiterated throughout his later prose, is grounded in his Augustinian theology and psychology. He argues that all art, including poetry, "is a mirror in which the spectator sees reflected himself and the world, and becomes conscious of his feelings good and bad, and of what their relations to each other are in fact" (*Prose III* 102).

In the same essay, he lists the presuppositions that necessarily underpin such a view of art:

(a) All created existence is a good.
(b) Evil is a negative perversion of created good.
(c) Man has free will to choose between good and evil.
(d) But all men are sinners with a perverted will.
An art which did not accurately reflect evil would not be good art. (102)

Again, each of these presuppositions is derived directly or indirectly from the works and thought of Augustine. Auden's encounter with Augustinian theology confirmed his pre-conversion intuition that evil consists of privation and that all existence is fundamentally good, and Augustine gave him hope that it might be possible to transform eros into agape love. Augustine's description of the *imago dei*, the image of God in each human, as the human tendency toward self-transcendence provided Auden with a compelling psychological account of human free will and its relation both to sin and to causal necessity. Each of these Augustinian ideas had major implications for Auden's concept of art, and of his view of himself as a professional poet. In particular, Auden derived three important aesthetic ideas from Augustine, and these serve to frame the poet's aesthetics.

First, Auden believed that art is gratuitous. The creation of a work of art, he thought, was an *acte gratuit*,[1] "an act which is quite unnecessary, unmotivated by any given requiredness, [which is] an absolutely freely self-chosen individual act" (*Prose II* 311), and he found the idea most clearly exemplified in Augustine's *Confessions*. Auden began using the term in about 1947, but even before that time, the idea was an important component of his thinking about both poetry and ethics.

Second, Auden frequently noted the human tendency to regard certain emotional pains as pleasures, especially those pains evoked by works of art. Following Augustine, who described such indulgence in intense grief as a type of eros, Auden acknowledged the temptation in readers of poetry, no less than in poets themselves, to become self-absorbed by way of vicarious emotional experience.

Third, Auden attempted to articulate the ethical responsibilities of poems as analogous to, but not identical with, the ethical responsibilities of individual human beings. On one hand, Auden argued, it was wrong to regard art as "magic," as a means of manipulating other humans by repressing the operation of their free will. On the other hand, Auden also deplored the attempt to isolate art within an autonomous realm of amoral self-referentiality, and he used Augustine's phrase *fantastica fornicatio*, the fornication of the mind with its own images, to describe such self-referentiality. Rather, a work of art is the artist's attempt to become conscious of his or her own feelings by naming them, serving as a mirror in which the reader's own feelings may be identified.

Stan Smith argues that Auden's prose continually deals with "the doubleness of the text, which is both a historical product, subject to all the pressures on language of its originating moment, and yet a discourse that floats free of its origins, finding as many moments of meaning as it has readers, in a perpetually open-ended play of history and signification" (4). For Smith, the impetus of art toward self-referentiality is an advantage; for Auden, it was a problem. As a form of play, poetry operates according to certain rules that, while arbitrarily imposed, are nevertheless binding on those who choose to play the game, and that make the game intelligible to observers and players alike. The "doubleness" of a poem is not the tension between the poem's historical origin and its interpretation as an artifact, but the tension between demands that the poet makes on him or herself as a poet and the demands that a reader may legitimately make on a poem.

ACTE GRATUIT: THE GRATUITOUS ACT

Auden's 1947 essay "Squares and Oblongs" is a series of aphorisms and notes in which he comments on the nature of poetry as an art form, and in one of the longer notes, Auden explicitly links Augustine's idea of the *acte gratuit* with the craft of writing poetry: "St. Augustine was the first real psychologist for he was the first to see the basic fact about human nature, namely that the Natural Man hates nature, and that the only act which can really satisfy him is the *acte gratuit*" (*Prose II* 341). That is, Augustine perceived that the ego, which inhabits primarily the realm of historical time, "resents every desire of his natural self for food, sex, pleasure, logical coherence, because desires are given not chosen, and his ego seeks constantly to assert its autonomy by doing something of which the requiredness is not given, that is to say, something which is completely arbitrary, a pure act of choice" (341). Thus the ego takes pleasure in actions that are "arbitrary," or "gratuitous," in the sense that they do not satisfy a biological need, or even a basic intellectual need for intelligibility or coherence, and he gives as an example Augustine's robbing of the pear tree in book 2 of the *Confessions.* Auden observes that the act can be explained as a symbolic transference of libido, but that the transference itself must also have an unconscious motive which he identifies as the desire to commit an act of arbitrary choice (341). The *acte gratuit* often has an ostensible rationale, but the decision to act is never compelled by actual necessity.

In the same essay, Auden also explains "why so many *actes gratuits* are, like that of St Augustine, criminal acts" (*Prose II* 341). Individuals wish to feel both free and important, but relatively innocent *actes gratuits* are seldom regarded as important, so in a gratuitous, criminal act, "The freedom is asserted by disobeying a law of God or man which gives the importance. Nearly all crime is magic, an attempt to make free with necessities" (341). It is this "magical" quality of many criminal acts that so confuses the psychologist who wishes to identify a logical motive for destructive actions. In his 1947 review of Max Wertheimer's *Productive Thinking,* Auden critiques the author's optimism about human nature, suggesting that "Professor Wertheimer was so obviously a man of good-will that I doubt if he could conceive of the existence of real malice; he would always have tried to explain it away as ignorance or stupidity" (317). Conventional psychology, Auden suggests, cannot account for the *acte gratuit*, which he calls "the malicious act" in this review and defines as "the occasion on which the subject is perfectly clear as to the structure of the situation and its vectors and nevertheless deliberately defies it," and he concludes that, "if such pure malice without any blindness ever occurs, however rarely, then much of our psychology must be revised" (317). Auden implies that a return to Augustine, the first psychologist, would do much to enrich modern psychology.

Auden's own awareness of the *acte gratuit* came partly through literature, and in *The Dyer's Hand*, he identifies Shakespeare's Iago as a character who commits the quintessentially gratuitous act when he deceives Othello. Auden classes Iago with other Shakespearean villains like Don John in *Much Ado about Nothing* and Iachimo in *Cymbeline* whose great crimes seem out of proportion to their rather petty motives, as opposed to other characters like Claudius in *Hamlet* and Antonio in *The Tempest*, who are clearly motivated by the desire for personal gain (247). Auden goes to great lengths to show that, despite Iago's tenuous claims to a personal grudge against Othello, he actually acts from what Coleridge calls "motiveless malignancy" (248), since "a man does not always require a serious motive for deceiving another" (254). Although Auden does not use the term *acte gratuit* to describe Iago's actions, the idea of the arbitrary or gratuitous choice is clearly his topic, and he concludes that *Othello* continues to fascinate modern audiences "because none of us can honestly say that he does not understand how such a wicked person can exist" (270), and because modern individuals can all identify personally with Iago's desire to commit gratuitously malicious acts, to destroy merely for the sake of destruction.

Although the phrase *acte gratuit* does not appear in Auden's poems, several significant poems from the 1950s do describe the concept. In "The Shield of Achilles," the modern world pictured on the shield Hephaestus forges for Achilles is grounded in the arbitrary. In the first scene, the poem describes "an artificial wilderness" that is "without a feature" and defined only by its "blankness" (*CP* 596). The erasure of all distinguishing marks intensifies the arbitrary nature of the place and of the "unintelligible" and faceless army standing in it. The second scene explicitly refers to the prison camp's location as "arbitrary" (597), and when Thetis looks for scenes of positive gratuitous behavior, such as games and music, she sees only a ragged boy arbitrarily throwing stones at birds. In his cruel, anarchic world, the boy can assert his freedom only by attempting to kill weaker animals, though according to Auden's assessment in "Squares and Oblongs," his motiveless malignity does not result in self-importance because his actions do not defy the human laws of his world but are rather in full accord with his society's moral conventions. For him, there are no ethical laws left to defy.

The *acte gratuit* appears in a more positive light in "Sext," the third poem of the "Horae Canonicae" sequence, in which the poet describes the absorption in one's vocation as a species of the gratuitous act. He imagines "nameless heroes" such as "the first flaker of flints / who forgot his dinner, / the first collector of sea-shells to remain celibate" (*CP* 630). In defiance of natural demands on their bodies for food or sex, these nameless heroes take up an artistic vocation through which they assert the freedom of their wills, and in doing so, they make possible the progress of humanity toward civilization. The gratuity of a vocation like shell collecting or stone craft, or poetry by extension of the principle, does not negate the psychological compulsion that a given individual might feel to pursue his or her vocation, for the nameless heroes Auden describes do clearly feel an obsession with their vocations that make their pursuit a felt need, if not a biological necessity. Nor does the gratuity of such vocations imply that they are unimportant in the course of human history. On the contrary, in a nod to Adam Smith's argument that civilization arises with the division of labor, the poem asserts that civilization would not have been possible without individuals who freely chose to pursue a specific vocation.

However, as "Vespers" states explicitly, the establishment of civilization requires a "cement of blood" (*CP* 639), and without the "nameless heroes" at the dawn of civilization, "at this noon, for this death, / there would be no agents" (630). The choice of one's vocation is gratuitous, and as an individual choice it may be harmless enough, but the availability of free choice always includes the freedom to do evil. And since, in the modern world, so many *actes gratuits* are criminal acts, even seemingly innocent games betray the inevitable evil concomitant with freedom. As Auden points out in "Squares and Oblongs," "there is a game called Cops and Robbers, but none called Saints and Sinners" (*Prose II* 343). That is, "cops" and "robbers" both obey the same rule of freedom through self-assertion, the cops asserting their freedom by playing at pursuing a vocation and the robbers by playing at violations of the law. But "saints" and "sinners" are qualitatively different in that "saintly" behavior is not arbitrary but required and therefore serious, as opposed to the malicious act, which is arbitrary and therefore, in a sense, frivolous.

In the same essay, Auden points out that "the alternative to criminal magic is the innocent game," which is an *acte gratuit* because "necessity here consists of rules chosen by the players," so while it is less important than the criminal version, it is also more free because the rules themselves are gratuitous and not required (*Prose II* 341). For example, a game of golf is less important than an act of vandalism because the rules obeyed by the golfer are arbitrary, while the rules broken by the vandal are universal, moral laws. But the golfer is more free than the vandal because he might have decided to play tennis instead, whereas the vandal is always subject to the law he breaks in the act of vandalism. Yet there is a dark side even to games. Like the gratuitous vocations in "Sext," a game that is innocent in itself nevertheless evokes the freedom to do evil. As the next poem in the sequence, "Nones," indicates, "This mutilated flesh, our victim, / Explains too nakedly, too well," the fact that all hobbies and games, as gratuitous acts, necessarily point to the gratuitous act of the crucifixion:

We shall always now be aware
Of the deed into which they [games] lead, under
The mock chase and mock capture,
The racing and tussling and splashing,
The panting and the laughter,
Be listening for the cry and stillness
To follow after: wherever
The sun shines, brooks run, books are written
There will also be this death. (*CP* 635)

The passage implicates even the literary arts in the universal guilt, since it includes the writing of books along with other frivolous and gratuitous games that implicate the participants in the death of the innocent victim.

Auden makes the same point in "Squares and Oblongs," in which he likens Augustine's gratuitous robbing of the pear tree to the writing of poetry: "Similarly, there are no doubt natural causes, perhaps very simple ones, behind the wish to write verses, but the chief satisfaction in the creative act is the feeling that it is quite gratuitous" (*Prose II* 341). As such, all art is a type of the *acte gratuit*. Like any game, a poem proceeds according to certain rules, and while Auden typically preferred formal verse to free verse, he intuited that even free verse is constructed according to tacit rules, and even the term "free verse" implies a certain gratuity of formlessness. As Auden remarked elsewhere about the poetry of the American Transcendentalists, "The prose of Emerson and Thoreau is superior to their verse, because verse in its formal nature protests against protesting; it demands that to some degree we accept things as they are, not for any rational or moral reason, but simply because they happen to be that way; it implies an element of frivolity in the creation" (*Prose III* 146). Especially in *The Dyer's Hand*, Auden repeatedly refers to poetry as "frivolous," a term that predictably raises the ire of some readers, such as Philip Larkin, who warns that the belief that poetry is "frivolous" is bound to result in banal poems (128). Insofar as philosophical aesthetics are concerned, "gratuitous" is the more precise term, since it denotes an arbitrary act of free will that might be either good or evil, without commenting on the relative importance of the act. Auden preferred the more provocative term "frivolous," perhaps partly because it annoyed so many of his critics, but also because he could use it in opposition to the word "serious."

Casual readers of Auden's prose tend not to realize that, in using the apparently simple vocabulary of "serious" and "frivolous," Auden has specific and sophisticated definitions of each term in mind. The distinction he makes is not the same as the general differences that readers might make between, for instance, "popular" and "classical" music, or between "light verse" and "Poetry." For Auden, the idea of "frivolity" has nothing whatsoever to do with artistic merit. By "frivolous," he means an activity that one is not externally obliged to take on, and while some "frivolous" acts such as games are relatively unimportant in themselves, others, such as criminal acts, may be extremely important without violating their basic frivolity, or gratuitous nature. On the other hand, by "serious" Auden means a moral obligation, and specifically the obligation to love God and one's neighbor. One can therefore commit a frivolous act—a criminal *acte gratuit*—in violation of a serious moral imperative, but Auden indicates that a good frivolous act, such as a game, should not therefore be imagined to fulfill a serious moral command.

The choice of one's vocation, for example, is a gratuitous choice, and Auden explains in *The Dyer's Hand* that, of most occupations, "one must say that, in themselves, they are frivolous. They are only serious in so far that they are the means by which those who practice them earn their bread and are not parasites on the labor of others, and to the degree that they permit or encourage the love of God and neighbor" (432). For example, a man is not ethically obliged to make shoes instead of poems, or to grow wheat instead of building houses. He is morally free to choose his vocation, and in that sense, the choice of his vocation is frivolous; he is not morally obliged to choose one particular vocation rather than another, though he may well be limited in his choice by mental or physical capabilities. (There are, of course, vocations from which he is ethically barred, such as being a torturer or a hired assassin.) But once he chooses a particular vocation—a frivolous decision in itself—the way in which he goes about pursuing that vocation becomes serious because it is subject to the moral law. He must earn an honest wage so as not to be a parasite, and his vocation must enable the love of God and of his neighbor. An action is serious to the degree that it is subject to the judgment of moral laws, and it is frivolous to the degree that it is amoral, and the distinction has important moral and social implications for Auden beyond the writing of poetry. In "Squares and Oblongs," he defines "serious" as "what . . . all possess equally, independent of fortune, namely their will, in other words their love, and the only serious matter is what they love, themselves, or God and their neighbor" (*Prose II* 342). Auden resorts to a fully Augustinian equation of one's will with one's love, which Augustine most famously explains near the end of the *Confessions.*[2] According to Auden's Augustinian vocabulary, the orientation of the will, that is, of one's love, is a serious matter because all humans are under equal obligation to love. In making practical distinctions between the serious and the frivolous, Auden applies the principle that whatever individuals possess unequally is frivolous, and whatever they possess equally—free will and moral responsibility—is serious.

The relegation of poetry to the realm of the "frivolous" has certain ethical implications. Auden argues in an essay on Henry James that, because "writing a book, like playing baseball, is a totally unnecessary act, it could not be undertaken by a man who was lacking in free will," and so a novelist who "describes man as the absolute victim of circumstance and incapable of choice, contradicts his assertion by the mere fact that he has written a novel," and Auden praises James as an antidote to such a misconception (*Prose II* 297–98). A poem or a novel may be frivolous, but it is also proof of human free will in the face of a mechanistic, modern society that Auden believed was increasingly denying the freedom of the will. He adds that artists should "under no circumstances . . . have any truck with magic, whether in its politer forms like diplomatic cultural missions, or in its more virulent varieties . . ." (301–2). Poets and other artists are always tempted to use their arts "as a magical means for inducing desirable emotions and repelling undesirable emotions in oneself and others," a view of art[3] that Auden insists is wrong despite being held by the ancient Greeks, Agit-Prop, and MGM (345). Poetry is instead "a game of knowledge, a bringing to consciousness, by naming them, of emotions and their hidden relationships" (345), and while he seldom remarked on the fact, the heightening of self-awareness through a game can make moral choices clearer, if not easier to make.

Auden also suggests that, while most innocent *actes gratuits* are amoral, some have serious moral implications, so while the *acte gratuit* is frequently frivolous, it is not necessarily so. It is always serious when it touches on moral matters, for as Auden argues, "one thing, and one thing only, is serious: loving one's neighbor as one's self" (*Prose II* 302), and a given act may be seriously evil or seriously good. For example, the view of marriage that Auden briefly but enthusiastically appropriated from Denis de Rougemont's *Love in the Western World* fits his description of the *acte gratuit*, though he would not begin using the phrase until some years later. Auden's "In Sickness and in Health" speaks of the "arbitrary circle of a vow" (*CP* 319), which follows Rougemont's statement that the decision to marry "must always be arbitrary" (287) in the sense that it should not be based on rational calculation of future happiness or on a perceived physical need for companionship, affection, or sex. In Rougemont's estimation, the decision to marry is "arbitrary"—that is, gratuitous—in the sense that no one is morally obliged to get married. However, Rougemont also maintains that "the pledge exchanged in marriage is the very type of a *serious* act, because it is a pledge given once and for all. The irrevocable alone is serious!" (291). Auden may have thought of his own decision to "marry" Chester Kallman as gratuitous though not required, but he certainly did not think it unserious or unimportant. Nor did he think that, once his marriage was established, it was exempt from the ethical demands of fidelity.[4] For Auden, all forms of gratuity, whether serious or frivolous, are deeply important elements of human existence.

In Auden's estimation, the *acte gratuit* is a crucial feature of human nature because it expresses the freedom of the will as nothing else can. Free will is something all human beings hold in common, so the fact of free choice is always serious, though individual choices may in themselves be frivolous. Nevertheless, human societies are responsible to guard the freedom of humans to make frivolous choices. Auden states in *The Dyer's Hand* that "the peasant may play cards in the evening while the poet writes verses, but there is one political principle to which they both subscribe, namely, that among the half dozen or so things for which a man of honor should be prepared, if necessary, to die, the right to play, the right to frivolity, is not the least" (88–89). To deny the right to play is to place all aspects of human existence within the strict confines of moral or legal obligations, and to collapse the distinction between freely chosen acts and legal obligations is the definition of tyranny.

"I HAD RATHER BEEN DEPRIVED OF MY FRIEND THAN MY GRIEF"

One of Auden's best-known verses is his "Stop All the Clocks," which is now generally known as "Funeral Blues." An earlier version was composed as part of Auden and Christopher Isherwood's collaborative play *The Ascent of F6*, and a heavily revised edition appeared in the 1940 volume *Another Time* under the title "Funeral Blues." Though the poem is often read as a serious lament, it was not inspired by a real death and is a piece of theatrical pastiche, as Fuller points out (*Commentary* 280). Following the elegiac tradition, the poem says precious little about the character of the departed and focuses instead on the parade of mourners, which in the modern world includes traffic policemen and skywriting airplanes. Even the third stanza, which claims "He was . . . / My noon, my midnight, my talk, my song" (*English Auden* 163), reveals nothing in particular about the nature of the dead man himself. The real subject of the poem is not the deceased friend, but rather the grief of the living lover.

The poem exemplifies an attitude in poets that Auden would come to associate with both laments and love poetry, and that he saw exemplified by Augustine's description in the *Confessions* of his own grief at the death of a close friend. In an introduction to a volume of selected poems of Tennyson, Auden discusses the psychology surrounding the composition of *In Memoriam*, explaining that the death of Tennyson's friend Hallam gave the poet an occasion to collect and express all of his fears, many of which had nothing directly to do with the death of his friend. Auden then states that "St Augustine gives an illuminating account of a similar experience" (*Prose II* 209) and offers a long quotation from book 4 of the *Confessions* in which Augustine describes the feeling that he and his friend had been one soul in two bodies, and that even though his friend has died, Augustine has no wish to die too, being rather repulsed by death and shocked at life going on without his friend. However, Augustine also states, "Gladly as I would have changed it, I would rather have been deprived of my friend than my grief" (*Confessions* 4.6; *Prose II* 209), a statement that Auden would repeat in his prose when he wished to exemplify an artist who becomes more interested in his or her own emotions than in the external subject of the art.

In "Squares and Oblongs," he uses the same quotation from Augustine to characterize the tendency of self-absorption in the poet: "the girl whose boy-friend starts writing her love poems should be on her guard. Perhaps he really does love her, but one thing is certain: while he was writing his poems he was not thinking of her but of his own feelings about her, and that is suspicious. Let her remember

St Augustine's confession of his feelings after the death of someone he loved very much: 'I would rather have been deprived of my friend than of my grief'" (*Prose II* 346). Augustine recognizes his own emotional perversity in that he begins to take more pleasure in his own grief than he took in the presence of his friend, and in the larger context of the *Confessions*, the statement is but one more example of the young Augustine's disordered love. For Auden, Augustine's statement can apply equally to feelings of either grief or eros, and Freud was not the first to notice the close connection between the emotions surrounding eros and death. In light of Augustine, Auden detects a certain duplicity on the part of the poet who writes love songs, since the writing of poems requires attention not only to the details of composition, but also (and primarily) to the poet's own emotional state, rather than to the qualities and character of the beloved. Auden grew increasingly suspicious of his own art form after Rougemont's book introduced him to the theory that the courtly love tradition of lyric poetry had grown out of twelfth-century Manichean mysticism, and his subsequent poems on love—"Pleasure Island" and "The Love Feast," for example—display an uneasiness both with the human body and with the lyric tradition they evoke. While Rougemont, following Augustine, persuaded Auden for a time that eros could be transformed and thereby redeemed by agape love, Auden avoided writing anything like conventional love poetry for the rest of his life, and even wrote poems like "'The Truest Poetry is the Most Feigning'" and "Dichtung und Wahrheit: An Unwritten Poem" that emphasize the emotional duplicity of the poet who writes erotic lyrics. The poetic idealization of the beloved always conceals the particular, historical nature of the individual about whom the poem is written, and so inevitably falsifies the actual character of the beloved even when the poet attempts to accurately portray the erotic emotions aroused by the relationship.

After the 1940s, there is a peculiar coincidence between Auden's suspicion of his own craft and Augustine's infamous denunciations of Virgil and other classical authors in the *Confessions* (1.12–17, 3.2–4). Augustine deplores his own adolescent fascination with the *Aeneid*, largely because as an adult he now sees the futility of the emotions aroused by reading about Dido's grief over her abandonment by Aeneas (1.13). Like Plato, Augustine denounces Homer's descriptions of the gods, accusing the Greek poet of endorsing immorality and injustice in the gods' behavior (1.16). His mistrust of classical poetry grows out of his observation that it did nothing to advance his own moral or spiritual development. He stops short of accusing the poetry itself of causing him to delay his conversion, and while he opines that it brought him no closer to conversion and distracted him from his own sinfulness, he is always careful to lay the final blame on himself rather than on the poems or the poets. Nevertheless, Augustine expresses significant concern for the moral effects of the poetry on the reader, and like Auden, he senses a certain dishonesty in artistic fictions that can all too easily be taken for fact. The difference is that, while Augustine is primarily concerned with the moral state of the reader, Auden is more concerned with the moral state of the author, for whom the writing of a poem may be symptomatic of a narcissistic self-absorption that, in theological parlance, is called pride.

However, Auden does express reservations about the effects of drama on its audience, and in a 1952 essay, he remarks that "the old prejudices against the theatre are not totally unjustified, for the representation of characters by flesh and blood individuals gives rise to dangerous ambiguities, even more severe in the audience than among the actors" (*Prose III* 332). Augustine is certainly a major figure among those who hold such "old prejudices against the theatre," though his critique is more sophisticated than others'. He was not the first to remark on the strange human phenomenon of being fascinated by the sufferings of others and of being moved to apparently real emotions at the sight of imitated suffering onstage, but in the *Confessions* he also observes the masochistic tendencies in a viewer who finds that "this very sorrow is his pleasure" and "applauds the actor for these fictions the more, the more he grieves" (3.2). Again, Augustine finds the most fault with himself as a member of the audience when he recalls that in his youth he "loved to grieve, and sought out what to grieve at, . . . [and] that acting best pleased me, and attracted me the most vehemently, which drew tears from me" (3.2). Augustine thinks his pleasure in pain absurd because, as all the philosophers taught, humans desire to gain happiness and avoid pain, yet the young Augustine clearly found a certain perverse happiness in the very emotional pain that it would be rational to avoid. Augustine also points out that drama, as he experienced it, was not emotionally cathartic, and although Aristotle's *Poetics* was unknown to him and his contemporaries, he disputes the Aristotelian theory when he states that "a man is the more affected with these actions, the less free he is from such affections" (3.2). So rather than purging the emotions, Augustine contends that drama encourages mere sentimentality: an ongoing indulgence in emotion for its own sake. He proceeds to distinguish between what Aristotle might call "pity" and the quality of real mercy: when the viewer "suffers in his own person, it uses [*sic*] to be styled misery: when he compassionates others, then it is mercy. But what sort of compassion is this for feigned and scenical passions? for the auditor is not called on to relieve, but only to grieve . . ." (3.2). Thus, in Augustine's mind, there is no cathartic function to drama because the imitation excites pitiful emotions without also motivating merciful actions.

Auden, too, disputed Aristotle's theory that drama produces catharsis, and on similar grounds. In the same 1952 essay, he asserts, "catharsis is properly effected, not by works of art, but by religious rites" (*Prose III* 332), although such "rites" may not be overtly religious in nature, since Auden gives examples of sporting events and patriotic rallies as rituals that effect catharsis in the observers. Following Augustine, Auden recognizes the inability of drama to depict reality directly, suggesting that "in order to grasp the truth the theatre claims to illustrate, I must, on my own initiative, make a correction which the theatre is impotent to impose upon me" (332).

The audience must "correct" its own misperceptions of suffering and happiness, for the truth at which drama aims is to show that the unreal, depicted sufferings and triumphs show "that suffering and happiness are not what I choose to believe them to be" (332–33). That is, the members of the audience really desire the tragic hero's status without his fall and the comic hero's final happiness without his suffering. Drama's function is to depict our own impossible desires for us, to help us recognize and name our own fantasies, and thereby provide us with the opportunity to correct them. Drama does offer truth in a way, but it is powerless to prevent the audience from mere indulgence in emotional titillation, as Augustine found in his own case.

For Auden, Augustine's observation of his taking pleasure in his own pain provided a clue to the psychology of poetry. In a 1955 BBC lecture, he argues that "essentially poetry is an affirmation of Being, and the main negative motive for writing it a dread of non-being. The Poet feels like St Augustine: 'I would rather have been deprived of my friend than of my grief'" (*Prose III* 541). He turns Augustine on his head, stating that, "even when he says 'Since never to have been born is beyond all comparison the best', he is rejoicing that he is alive to make that statement" (541). Thus there is a tension in even the darkest of poems between grief and joy. For the poet, the difficulty lies not in describing a state of being, but in describing a process: "for him, therefore, anything which has a history, which changes, contains an element of non-being, which resists poetic expression. His very medium, language, is ill-fitted to describe becoming" (541). A hundred poems could be mustered to show that a poem can successfully portray change, but Auden appears to have had his own personal limitations in mind, for he claims that, "when I come to describe even the non-human organic world which does not even have a real history but only a cycle of growth, I run into difficulties. I may possess names for certain stages, e.g. acorn, sapling, oak, but the exact point at which I abandon one term to use the next is arbitrary" (541). So a poem that appears to depict the process of "becoming" is actually a series of snapshots, run together as in a film reel, such that it creates the illusion of movement, but in Auden's mind the poem still privileges the static over the dynamic, being over non-being.

FANTASTICA FORNICATIO: "THE PROSTITUTION OF MIND TO ITS OWN FANCIES"

Augustine was also concerned, as was Auden, that poetic language not be used as mere propaganda for unethical ends. In several places in the *Confessions* (e.g. 4.2), Augustine deplores the use of his professional craft, rhetoric, to advance an ideology by deceiving or manipulating people. Nor should lies be used to bolster truths, Augustine believed, a temptation common to orators making arguments in courts of law. Cochrane explains that Augustine's Christianity condemns the use of language as sheer propaganda, arguing that patristic theology was not a mere propagandistic ideology formed in order to prop up Constantinian Rome: "For an ideology, in this sense, is simply a rationalization invented by the discursive reason in order to bridge a chasm which its own activity creates; its value for this purpose being in no sense dependent upon its inherent truth but wholly upon its capacity to stimulate 'action'. . . . For such perversions of intellectual activity Augustine has a name and it is a strong one; he calls them *fantastica fornicatio*, the prostitution of mind to its own fancies" (418). Auden makes direct reference to *fantastica fornicatio* in Simeon's speech in "For the Time Being," where it is used in a slightly different way. In that poem, the phrase refers not to the intellect in general, but to the artistic impulse specifically, which tends toward mere self-referentiality (*CP* 388). For Auden, art is never an entirely closed system, though the aesthetic principles on which it operates are different from the physical and ethical principles upon which the real world operates. Rainer Emig rightly suggests that "For the Time Being" anticipates the emergence of deconstruction and other poststructural theories of signification (139–44), but he seems unaware that Simeon's speech also includes a pointed critique of self-referential tendencies in art that the heirs of poststructuralism would later celebrate; Auden bases his critique on Augustine's critique of the tendency of the human mind toward *fantastica fornicatio*.

Simeon indicates that the fact that the Word has become flesh makes real signification possible—meaning is no longer infinitely deferred (*CP* 388). The central theme of Simeon's meditation is the Incarnation's resolution of the philosophical problem of the One and the Many, a problem that on its surface seems abstract and arcane to casual readers but that Auden's commitment to socialism continually raised: to what extent do human beings have independent identities, and to what extent is their identity a function of their social group? The Incarnation, as the historical realization in an individual human being of the eternal and unconditional God, provides a stable reference point according to which "the true significance of all other events is defined" (388). From such a reference point, Simeon asserts, "Reason is redeemed from incestuous fixation on her own Logic, for the One and the Many are simultaneously revealed as real" (389). The phrase "incestuous fixation" echoes the "promiscuous fornication" of which Simeon accuses the imagination. Both reason and art assert false claims of absolute authority, but their tendency toward self-referentiality undercuts their claims. As Auden states in *The Dyer's Hand*, "The Incarnation, the coming of Christ in the form of a servant who cannot be recognized by the eye of flesh and blood, but only by the eye of faith, puts an end to all claims of the imagination to be the faculty which decides what is truly sacred and what is profane" (457). Imagination is not wrong in itself, any more than eros as a survival instinct is wrong in itself, but once sublimated, it seeks only to perpetuate itself at the expense of all other aspects of the human person. In a 1950 essay, Auden likens the would-be poet to parents who beget children, not in order to bring unique individuals into existence, but merely to live vicariously through them and thereby achieve a kind of extended longevity. Similarly, the would-be poet's "desire is not for creation but for self-perpetuation," and is ultimately a refusal to accept one's mortality (*Prose III* 232). The identification of self with image is a permutation of Augustine's *fantastica fornicatio*, and Auden notes that "the sterility of this substitution of identity for analogy is expressed in the myth of Narcissus" (232). Auden's use of sexual language and analogies to describe self-centeredness recalls Augustine's own language to describe the tendency of the imagination toward self-referentiality.

Auden's attempt in middle age to critique the tendencies of his own craft lead many critics to regard his statements on the subject as excessively strict, especially as he treats it in "Dichtung und Wahrheit," a series of pensées subtitled "An Unwritten Poem," written in 1959. McDiarmid argues that "Dichtung und Wahrheit" plays out its argument "with philosophical fastidiousness," and Mendelson calls the work's aphoristic arguments "elaborations on the emotional grammar set out in the essays on language Auden had been writing for several years" (McDiarmid 44, *Later* 432). Indeed, the work is skeptical of the ability of language to genuinely represent personal love almost from the start: "Expecting your arrival tomorrow, I find myself thinking *I love You*: then comes the thought:—*I should like to write a poem which would express exactly what I mean when I think these words*" (*CP* 649).[5] For this proposed poem, Auden sets himself very high standards: the poem must be good, it must be genuine, and it must be true (649).

He does not doubt his ability to write an aesthetically good poem, nor does he anticipate difficulty making it "genuine," by which he means "recognizable, like my handwriting, as having been written, for better or worse, by me" (*CP* 649). The main difficulty for the poet is to write "I love You" in such a way that it is true, that is, that it accurately represents the inner disposition of one real, historical person for another, and not merely a typical or universal feeling of one generic, fictional character for another. Auden is quick to point out, however, that the concern for truth in the poem exists only for the poet, not for the reader: "I read a poem by someone else in which he bids a tearful farewell to his beloved: the poem is good (it moves me as other good poems do) and genuine (I recognize the poet's 'handwriting'). Then I learn from a biography that, at the time he wrote it, the poet was sick to death of the girl but pretended to weep in order to avoid hurt feelings and a scene. Does this information affect my appreciation of his poem? Not in the least: I never knew him personally and his private life is no business of mine. Would it affect my appreciation if I had written the poem myself? I hope so" (649). Auden speaks strictly from the point of view of the author of the poem, and as such, the poet makes demands on his work which readers, on the whole, should not. As a reader, Auden indicates that he does not care whether somebody else's poem is dishonest in the sense in which he uses the term in *The Dyer's Hand*. A poem's aesthetic quality does not depend on its correspondence to any biographical reality that it purports to represent.[6] However, as an author, Auden is concerned with more than his poem's aesthetic quality; he is also concerned that his proposed poem transmit an honest message to a specific person.

The primary difficulty, Auden argues, is that a poem cannot identify "I," the speaker of the poem, and "You," the addressee and object of the poem, as specific, historical people without also making "I" and "You" fictional characters: "this poem I should like to write is not concerned with the proposition 'He loves Her' (where He and She could be fictitious persons whose characters and history the poet is free to idealize as much as he may choose), but with my proposition *I love You* (where *I* and *You* are persons whose existence and histories could be verified by a private detective)" (*CP* 656). Auden admits that, if the verb in the phrase "I love You" were changed to something different, and if it were in the third person, the difficulty would disappear: the validity of statements like "She marries Him" or "He fights with Him" can be independently verified, which is why the epithalamion and the heroic epic are comparatively easy to write (652–54). "But," Auden asks, even given the phrase "He loves Her," "how is [the poet] to speak truthfully of lovers? Love has no deed of its own: it has to borrow the act of kind which, in itself, is not a deed but a form of behavior . . ." (652). Auden uses the word "kind" in its archaic sense of "nature," such that, he argues, the poet must borrow the language of sex to talk about feelings of attraction and love. Even though Auden says explicitly that the "unwritten poem" is "speaking of *eros* not of *agape*," the difficulty remains that no act is in itself an unquestionable proof of love, even as mere eros (655). For the same reason, it is even more difficult to write a poem about agape, because "it is as much the essence of erotic love that it should desire to disclose itself to one other, as it is of the essence of charity that it should desire to conceal itself from all" (655). According to Auden's argument, eros wishes, if only subconsciously, to disclose itself, but it has no language proper to itself and therefore must fall back on slippery sexual metaphors, whereas agape, or charity, wishes to conceal itself entirely, so writing a poem about one's own agape is impossible because a desire for self-disclosure is entirely foreign to agape. Auden concludes, "this poem will remain unwritten" (663).

"Dichtung und Wahrheit" is a direct, philosophical restatement of an idea Auden had already written a poem about in 1953. "'The Truest Poetry Is the Most Feigning,'" whose title is one of Touchstone's lines in Shakespeare's *As You Like It*, mocks poetic hyperbole while offering a tongue-in-cheek exposé of the poet's ingenuous tricks. The poem begins with the premise that Christian charity is no subject for poetry, not because charity is unwilling to disclose itself, but because it is not exciting enough for poetic diction. The "Christian answer" to the question "How much do you love me?" is "*così-così*" (*CP* 619). Christian charity, being a moral obligation, is in a sense too serious a subject for poetry, but eros can be a moving poetic subject, provided it is exaggerated. So, the speaker advises, when writing about the feeling that "You're so in love that one hour seems like two," a young poet should inflate the emotional drama until "Each second longer darker seemed than all / . . . / Those raining centuries it took to fill / That quarry whence Endymion's Love was torn" (619–20). Readers of poetry, the speaker argues, are not interested in strict realism, but in the ability of poetic exaggeration to heighten emotional tension. Although Auden does admit there are some critics "whose crude provincial gullets" want only "Plain cooking made still plainer by plain cooks" (619), he suggests that most readers prefer a vicarious experience of aestheticized emotion. In fact, the poem argues, realism in poetry is impossible, so if the beloved becomes inaccessible because of death or infidelity, the speaker explains that "No metaphor, remember, can express / A real historical unhappiness" (620). Grief is always stylized, and in lines that recall Augustine's pleasure in grief, the speaker states, "*O Happy Grief!* is all sad verse can say" (620). The speaker—as opposed to the author—of the sad love poem evidentially takes as much pleasure in his own grief as the readers do.

To reinforce the nature of poetry as hyperbolized fiction, Auden gives the example of political propaganda. The speaker explains how easy it is to begin with a conventional love poem, change the pronouns and selected details, and produce "a panegyric ode which hails / ... / The new pot-bellied Generalissimo" (*CP* 620). While some "honest Iagos" will object to using the conventions of propaganda to write a covert love poem, "True hearts, clear heads," the speaker insists "will hear the note of glory / And put inverted commas round the story" (621).[7] Good readers come to poems expecting fiction and overstatement because they understand something of the nature of a human being: "What but tall tales, the luck of verbal playing / Can trick his lying nature into saying / That love, or truth in any serious sense, / Like orthodoxy, is a reticence?" (621). There is, then, an ironically moral value in poetic exaggeration, for the more obvious a poet's fictionalization becomes, the more he or she reveals the duplicity which the Fall introduces into human nature. To recognize the possibility of lying is to presuppose that it is also possible to tell the truth. As Auden put it in *New Year Letter,* "hidden in [the Devil's] hocus-pocus, / There lies the gift of double focus" (*CP* 220). Humans, the poem indicates, can be tricked by "tall tales" into acknowledging that serious love and truth do exist, even while they elude poetry's grasp, and as Alan Jacobs observes, "Auden uses poetry to remind us of what poetry can never give us. But, in the end, this assigns poetry a genuine and important role, as it points always beyond itself in a strangely mute witness to that of which it is unable definitively to speak" ("Auden" 32).

That is not to say that poetry is devoid of truth. Rather, the truth to which poetry speaks is often the true nature of emotional tension or inner conflict. As Auden put it in one of his notes to *New Year Letter,* "poetry might be defined as the clear expression of mixed feelings" (119). If a poem cannot accurately depict transcendent theological truths or unique historical persons, it can at least speak accurately of universal human experience. Anne Fremantle relates her dialogue with Auden on the subject of mystical experiences, at the end of which Auden quoted Augustine's maxim (which Augustine derived from Cicero—see *City of God* 3.4), "'that the truth is neither mine nor his nor another's, but belongs to us all, and that we must never account it private to ourselves, lest we be deprived of it'" (qtd. in Spender 91). The quotation is taken inexactly from the *Confessions* (12.25), and Auden uses the same passage in the last entry of his 1970 commonplace book, *A Certain World* (425), in which he invokes Augustine to explain the universality of a poem's subject matter: "What the poet has to convey is not 'self-expression,' but a view of reality common to all, seen from a unique perspective, which it is his duty as well as his pleasure to share with others. To small truths as well as great, St. Augustine's words apply: 'The truth is neither mine nor his nor another's; but belongs to us all whom Thou callest to partake of it, warning us terribly, not to account it private to ourselves, lest we be deprived of it'" (425). Poetry as mere "self-expression" is the essence of *fantastica fornicatio*, and as emotionally exciting as such poetry can be, Auden distrusted it and preferred to think that a poem is aesthetically good to the extent that it describes common experience from a unique point of view, which accords with Augustine's principle that all truth is held in common. Augustine is cited several other times in the commonplace book,[8] but this statement is used at the end to justify the entire project of the book, a collection of truths that come to be held in common.

However, Auden's insistence that a poem genuinely express the author's beliefs seems to be at odds with ideas he had advanced earlier in his career. That is, he states in *A Certain World* (1970) that "one must be convinced that the poet really believes what he says" (425), but in "Dichtung und Wahrheit" (1959) he says explicitly that, as a reader, he does not care whether a poem is "true" in the sense that it accurately represents the poet's real feelings at the time. It is possible that Auden's taste in poetry changed during the decade between which he wrote the two statements, but the two statements are not, upon close examination, wholly irreconcilable. In the passage from *A Certain World*, Auden does not say that the poem must say what the poet really believes, but only that the reader "must be convinced" that the poet believes what he or she says (425). That is, the poem itself should appear to be wholly sincere, even if external evidence might indicate that it is not. Auden appears to be talking about reading the poem by itself, rather than about reading the poem alongside biography, history, and literary criticism. Later in the same passage from *A Certain World*, he refers to the poet's "duty as well as his pleasure to share with others" the truth on which he has a unique perspective (425). But Auden had argued earlier in *The Dyer's Hand* that the act of writing poetry is an *acte gratuit*, not a moral or civic duty at all, but a gratuitous activity undertaken by the will of the poet merely for its own sake. However, the parallel Auden sets up between "pleasure" and "duty" suggests that the two are interlinked. Once the poet makes the gratuitous decision to write a poem, the activity of writing is governed by the rules of the chosen poetic form, as well as by certain moral laws, among which is not to represent "tall tales" as honest fact. That is, once the poet decides to play the game, the rules of the game are binding, while they are not binding on non-participants.

Auden also argues in *The Dyer's Hand* and elsewhere that poetry does fall under certain quasi-ethical obligations, but that those obligations are not exactly the same as those that govern the rest of the poet's life. For Auden, poetry was neither its own private realm to which ethics did not apply, nor a wholly public activity subject to all the moral obligations that govern human relationships. Rather, Auden's fondness for poetical allegorization should be kept firmly in mind: the realm of poetry is an analogy to real life, and the rules that govern it are like, but only like, the rules that govern life.

Such an exemption of poetry and other forms of play from ethical demands may seem an unfair extrapolation from Augustine's idea of the *acte gratuit*. Augustine's views on poetry seem puritanically dour, but that is partly a caricature that distorts his complex views on poetry and art. Augustine does object to obscenity and heresy in art, but he also sees art as largely gratuitous. He would never say that a knowledge of poetry, or an education in the liberal arts, is necessary for salvation or a virtuous life, but he does argue that a knowledge of the liberal arts is a necessary aid to a rigorous study of Scripture (see *On Christian Doctrine* 2.16, 28, 32). Augustine also notes that a broad knowledge of the liberal arts is a vocation appropriate to a few Christians who wish to teach the meanings of the Scriptures to others, but not for all, "so that," Augustine says, "it is not necessary for [all] Christians to engage in much labor for a few things" (2.39). At the same time, Augustine also judges the value of art—visual, theatrical, poetic—primarily on its content. Augustine believed that works of art, and especially poems, should tell the truth. For example, in the first few books of *The City of God*, Augustine approvingly quotes from several poets while disputing with others: he accuses Virgil of lying (1.2); he notes that Lucan is close to the truth in certain matters (1.12); he approvingly quotes Persius at length (2.6); he criticizes Varro for espousing the Noble Lie of Plato (3.4); he cites Lucan as an example of just opposition to criminal acts (3.12); he agrees with Virgil's grim assessment of political murder (3.16); he quotes Horace and Claudian with approval (5.14, 26); and he asserts that his own knowledge of secular history must necessarily rely on pagan sources, including the poets (3.17). Unlike Plato,[9] Augustine would not banish poets either from the earthly city or from the City of God, but he would instead have them speak truth in praise of God.[10]

Augustine's attitude toward poetry is similar to but not identical with Auden's own assessment in his 1961 essay on C. P. Cavafy, in which he states that "poems made by human beings are no more exempt from moral judgment than acts done by human beings, but the moral criterion is not the same" (*FA* 336). One important moral criterion Auden gives for a poem is whether it tells the truth, and whether it therefore puts the reader "in a better position to judge the case justly" (336). A poem is a "witness" to the truth, so a poem should not tell "half-truths or downright lies," but it is also "not a witness's business to pass verdict" (336). A good poem is, by this standard, always in the indicative mood rather than the imperative. Auden adds, however, that there are diverse ways in which a poem can fictionalize without being dishonest: "In the arts, one must distinguish, of course, between the lie and the tall story that the audience is not expected to believe. The tall-story teller gives himself away, either by a wink or by an exaggerated poker face: the born liar always looks absolutely natural" (336). As in "'The Truest Poetry Is the Most Feigning,'" the very exaggerations of the conventional poem point out the artificiality of the "tall tale" being told, such that a poet can describe emotions truly by fictionalizing the historical details of an experience.

Auden agrees with Augustine that it is immoral for a poem to misrepresent its real topic, whether events or feelings or principles. But, it will be objected, Auden also claims in *The Dyer's Hand* that a poem cannot lie. Auden appears to directly contradict himself, arguing in one place that poems frequently lie but should not, and in another place that a poem cannot lie. But the statement that a poem cannot lie must be taken in its full context: "It has been said that a poem should not mean but be. This is not quite accurate. In a poem, as distinct from many other kinds of verbal societies, meaning and being are identical. A poem might be called a pseudo-person. Like a person, it is unique and addresses the reader personally. On the other hand, like a natural being and unlike a historical person, it cannot lie. We may be and frequently are mistaken as to the meaning or the value of a poem, but the cause of our mistake lies in our own ignorance or self-deception, not in the poem itself" (68). Auden's quibble with Archibald MacLeish's "Ars Poetica" has to do with the relationship of words to intentions, not the relationship between words and their referents. That is, Auden argues that a poem cannot lie in the sense that it cannot be hypocritical. It cannot, by itself, mean or intend something other than what it says. Auden uses the word "lie" to denote a statement that is at variance with an inner disposition, not a statement that is at variance with the true nature of the outside world. So from the author's point of view, a poem can tell a lie in the sense that it can misrepresent what the author actually felt or thought about the subject matter, but from the reader's point of view, a poem cannot lie in the sense that it cannot believe or feel something other than what it actually says or implies.

Auden was not only concerned that poetic fiction not be taken as fact, but also that he personally not present dishonest poetry as honest poetry. He obviously has some of his own poems like "Spain 1937" and "September 1st 1939" in mind—both of which he repudiated soon after publishing—when he states in *The Dyer's Hand*, "The most painful of all experiences to a poet is to find that a poem of his which he knows to be a forgery has pleased the public and got into the anthologies. For all he knows or cares, the poem may be quite good, but that is not the point; *he should not have written it*" (18). Presumably, a poem is a "forgery" if it misrepresents a feeling or experience that it purports to be representing accurately, and both poems evidently express feelings (whatever they are) that Auden knew full well he never actually felt. Auden believed that a poet should accurately represent both the real world and the poet's own feelings and beliefs about it. In a 1958 essay, Auden observes, "Almost every aspect of modern life tends to alienate us, poets and nonpoets alike, from a common world and shut us up with our subjective selves, a tendency which is aggravated, not cured, by the writer who likes to think of himself as *engagé*. The only proper resistance is the cultivation of a dispassionate passion to see things as they are and to remember what really happened" (*Prose IV* 181). As such, when Auden says that a poem is a lie, he means that it misrepresents what it purports to portray accurately: the poet's true feelings. Apparently, the temptation to lie is especially strong for poets who are, as Auden once liked to think of himself, "*engagé.*" However, when he says that a poem cannot lie, he means that the poem itself, apart from its author, cannot intend anything other than what it actually says. All too many readers overlook the distinction and either seize on one of Auden's statements while ignoring the other or assume that Auden is simply contradicting himself. Auden's dual use of the word "lie"—a word which he was fond of punning in his poems—may not be clear, but it is not self-contradictory.

However, Auden was well aware that poetry, like all other forms of language, could be used in wrong ways, and he was aware of Cochrane's use of Augustine's term *fantastica fornicatio* to describe the human tendency to construct ideologies in order to rationalize whatever action it wishes to stimulate (Cochrane 418). In a 1940 essay, written the same year in which he first read Cochrane, Auden argues that "when we say that art is beyond good and evil, what we really mean is that "good" and "evil" are terms which can only be applied to our own conscious choices. . . . We do not mean that art has no moral effect, but only that the latter depends upon our individual responses" (*Prose II* 85). He does not often address the moral effects of art on the reader, and while as an artist he denounces the attempts of the state to manipulate art and artists for political ends, he is also leery enough of his own craft to allow for some moral constraints on its content.

A surprising case in point is Auden's response to the question of Ezra Pound's *Pisan Cantos*, which was nominated for Bollingen Prize for Poetry in the same year that Pound was indicted for treason. The possible censoring of the *Pisan Cantos* had been discussed, and Pound's English publisher expunged a few potentially libelous passages in the British edition. Auden was on the award committee that eventually gave the prize to Pound, and the announcement touched off a heated debate between right- and left-wing periodicals. In his written response to the controversial award, Auden took up the question of censorship, which he might have been expected to condemn altogether. However, he asserts that, "whatever its intention, a work of art cannot compel the reader to look at it with detachment, and prevent him from using it as stimulus to and excuse for feelings which he should condemn," and in such a case, the reader "was not capable of exercising free will, and was therefore not reading it as a work of art" (*Prose III* 102). He proceeds to argue that, if it were likely that the *Pisan Cantos* would be read by rabid anti-Semites, "I would be in favor of censoring it (as in the case of the movie, *Oliver Twist*). That would not however prevent me from awarding the *Pisan Cantos* a prize before withholding it from the public. But I do not believe that the likelihood exists in this case" (102). Like the case of Joyce's *Ulysses* before it, the *Pisan Cantos* is a Modernist work of art, difficult to read at all, much less to read as propaganda or as a mere emotional stimulant. Nevertheless, Auden's statement does seem to allow for censorship in at least some cases, and polemical exaggeration aside, his view of human nature eventually compels him to allow some room for censorship, at least in theory. If a reader becomes incapable of exercising his or her free will in regard to a specific book, then he or she should not read it, and in extreme cases it may be appropriate to prevent access to such a book altogether.

Auden's proffered views on censorship may seem superficially similar to other endorsements of censorship, though his reasoning is markedly different from seemingly similar views. The popular justification of censorship is that a bad book not only encourages but actually causes bad behavior, that works of art themselves are the source of certain social problems. Auden insists that it is not the works of art that are to blame, but rather that it is the character of the reader that renders the work benign or malignant. In a 1950 lecture, which he gave at several institutions in the wake of the Pound controversy, he explains that "a poet can no more change the facts of what has been felt than, in the natural order, parents can change the inherited physical characteristics which they pass on to their children. Censorship or eugenics stand or fall together, the judgment good-or-evil applies only to the intentional movement of the will" (*Prose III* 652). It seems that, in principle, there are no dangerous books, only dangerous readers, and whatever the effects of a work like the *Pisan Cantos*, neither the work nor its author can be held morally responsible for any given reader's use of it.

Furthermore, in an anonymous essay for *Commonweal* in 1942, Auden had rejected Tolstoy's argument in *What Is Art?* that works of art should be judged solely by their function, calling the argument "pagan, not Christian" (*Prose II* 167). Offering an analogy to human love, he explains that, "just as love is redeemed by being redefined as agape instead of eros, so art is redeemed when its function is redefined as, not the expression or communication of emotion, but the becoming conscious of emotion" (167). In writing a poem, the poet "is not trying to feel something that he would like or thinks he ought to feel, but to find out what his feelings really are, and, of course, most of these will be neither pleasant nor good. He sings alone before God, but he may be overheard by other men and what they hear may cause them, one by one, to undergo a similar process of discovery" (167).

Thus, poetry-as-naming has a real moral function for the reader, albeit a severely limited one: "Art cannot make a man want to become good, but it can prevent him from imagining that he already is; it cannot give him faith in God, but it can show him his despair" (167). And for someone who does already wish to become good, a work of art can at least warn him or her away from various dead ends.

It will be remembered that, in *New Year Letter,* Auden claims, "Art is not and cannot be / A midwife to society" (*CP* 201), and he was fond of claiming that "the political and social history of Europe would be what it has been if Dante, Shakespeare, Goethe, Titian, Mozart, Beethoven, *et al.,* had never existed" (*Secondary Worlds* 141). The latter statement is rhetorical hyperbole, but it reemphasizes Auden's disdain both for propagandistic verse and for "serious" poetry that thinks too much of itself. As Auden claims in his essay on Cavafy, poetry is a witness to truth, and in "The Cave of Making," he tells the ghost of Louis MacNiece, "Speech can at best, a shadow echoing / the silent light bear witness / to the Truth it is not" (*CP* 693). Language is not, then, the locus of truth. The difficult distinction between language and truth, between signifier and signified, is original neither to Auden nor to Augustine, but it is worth pointing out that in his *On Christian Doctrine,* Augustine writes at length about distinguishing between what he calls "signs" and "things" (2.1–3, 12–25; and 3.1–5). To take the sign for the thing itself—to locate truth in a text that is only a witness to truth—is, Augustine indicates, "a miserable servitude of the spirit" (3.5). In the debate between the "lamp" and the "mirror" schools of aesthetics, both Augustine and Auden were decidedly on the side of the mirror.

Auden denounces the use of art either as propaganda or as escapism while acknowledging that it can indeed be so misused. But his later view of art is not just a product of his liberal upbringing or his socialist politics, but is grounded in his theological commitments. He states in *The Dyer's Hand* that there is no such thing as "Christian art" (458), but he is equally adamant that there is a Christian *view* of art, and that an artist can work in a "Christian spirit" (458) even if the artist does not personally espouse Christian beliefs. While there are many works of art that portray Christians at work or worship, that portray virtuous and charitable acts, or that articulate explicitly religious themes—Dante's *Paradiso,* Herbert's *The Temple,* Melville's *Billy Budd,* Eliot's *Four Quartets*—there are no identifiable aesthetic categories or formal genres that may be called "Christian" or "pagan." For Auden, the question of poetic subject matter was a minor one that could be answered only in reference to the nature of his medium. There were certain aspects of human life, like emotional experience, that poetry could portray with vivid accuracy, but there were other aspects, like the process of intellectual maturation, that it could hardly portray at all. Once he acknowledged the proper limits of his medium, the question became not "What subjects should a Christian poet write about?" but "How should I, as a poet who also happens to hold Christian beliefs, approach the writing of this poem?" Although he began to adjust the limits of his subject matter at about the same time that he became a Christian, it was not because his religion was suddenly imposing moralistic standards on poetic expression. Indirectly, Auden's Christianity did alter some of the things he personally cared about, so Freudian psychology was largely supplanted by Augustinian psychology, and the immanence of a great social revolution was replaced by reflection on past revolutions. In that way, religion affected his subject matter, not because it demanded different kinds of poems, but because it had begun to change his interests, feelings, and motives. For Auden, the choice of subject matter was still, like the choice to write a poem at all, a matter of gratuitous choice rather than of moral necessity.

Auden had come to believe that a Christian artist's religion need not have a direct effect on his or her subject matter, but that it should have an effect on the artist's personal motives for creating a work of art. This Christian artistic spirit, in Auden's view, begins with an affirmation of the whole of existence—both spiritual and physical—as intrinsically good, and with equal clarity it acknowledges and portrays its fallenness: "The effect of beauty is good, therefore, to the degree to which, through its analogies, the goodness of existence, the possibility of paradise, and the historical duty of repentance are recognized. Its effect is evil to the degree that beauty is taken for an imitation, that is to say, as identical with good, so that the artist regards himself as God, and the pleasure of beauty as the joy of Paradise and the conclusion drawn that since all is well in the work of art all is well in history. But all is not well there" (*Prose III* 653). The Christian spirit in art accepts the limits of finitude and refuses the temptation to manipulate the real world through artistic machinations. Its purpose is praise, not propaganda. As such, a poem that honestly describes feelings of doubt about Christian dogma is still operating in a Christian spirit, whereas a propagandistic jingle that attempts to persuade people to accept Christian dogma against their rational judgment is a gross violation of the Christian artistic spirit. The Christian spirit working in art puts a premium on truthfulness, not as a vehicle for communicating abstract ideals or moral commands, which Auden thought subverted the nature of art, but as a fidelity to the artist's true experience of his or her own feelings. Poetry operates most truly in the indicative and subjunctive moods, not in the imperative.

Above all, the Christian spirit operates in art when it praises its subject for its very existence, and Augustine would surely agree: "If bodies [i.e. physical objects] please thee," Augustine says in the *Confessions*, "praise God on occasion of them, and turn back thy love upon their Maker; lest in these things which please thee, thou displease" (4.12). The necessity of praise appears repeatedly in Auden's poems from both before and after his conversion—see for example "A Bride in the 30's" (*CP* 139), "In Memory of W. B. Yeats" (249), "Canzone" (331), "For the Time Being" (365), "Precious Five" (590), and "In Praise of Limestone" (540)—though it was only

Christianity that could explain, defend, and sustain his intuition that the primarily motive and function of poetry is praise. As Auden states in *The Dyer's Hand*, "Poetry can do a hundred and one things, delight, sadden, disturb, amuse, instruct—it may express every possible shade of emotion, and describe every conceivable kind of event, but there is only one thing that all poetry must do; it must praise all it can for being and for happening" (60).

NOTES

INTRODUCTION

1. See Conniff's "Auden, Niebuhr, and the Vocation of Poetry" in *Religion and Literature* (1993), and his "What Really Became of Wystan? Auden, Niebuhr and *For the Time Being*" in *Christianity and Literature* (1995), as well as his later article on Auden and contemporary theology, "Answering Herod: W. H. Auden, Paul Tillich, Ernst Toller, and the Demonic" in *W. H. Auden: A Legacy,* ed. David Garrett Izzo (2002).

2. Despite the efforts of thinkers like Augustine and Kierkegaard to emphasize the "existential" nature of Christian faith, Emig is hardly alone in assuming that religion is antithetical to polyvalence. For an account of the positive relationship between Christianity and polyvalence, see David Lyle Jeffrey's *People of the Book*.

1. EVIL AS PRIVATION

1. Augustine gives the example of contrary explanations of solar and lunar eclipses: while the science of his day showed that eclipses were caused by the alignment of planetary bodies and could predict eclipses with precision, the Manichees thought eclipses were evidence of cosmic battles between good and evil divinities (*City of God* 5.3). Augustine's hope for a reasonable resolution of such contradictions was dashed when he met the Manichean leader Faustus and "found him first utterly ignorant of liberal sciences, save grammar, and that but in an ordinary way" (5.6).

2. For example, Augustine says early in the work, "If bodies [i.e., physical objects] please thee, praise God on occasion of them, and turn back thy love upon their maker; lest in these things which please thee, thou displease." (4.12). Likewise, in book 10, Augustine notes that the pains of hunger and thirst "are removed by pleasure. For hunger and thirst are in a manner pains; they burn and kill like a fever, unless the medicine of nourishments come to our aid. Which since it is at hand through the consolations of Thy gifts, with which land, and water, and air serve our weakness, our calamity is termed gratification" (10.31). For Augustine, it is not wrong to take pleasure in providing for physical necessity; it is wrong, however, to indulge in excess of need (10.31).

3. Auden would later recognize the ways in which the Catholic liturgy's use of sensible objects such as vestments, candles, and incense affirms the goodness of physical existence (see *Prose III* 579), but he was certainly not a Christian while he was writing *The Prolific and the Devourer*, since that work denies several basic tenets of Christianity, including the belief in God as creator (*Prose II* 448). However, before the publication of the full text of *The Prolific and*

the Devourer in the magazine *Antaeus* in 1981, critics were less sure about when exactly Auden embraced theism. In 1978 James Bertram had expressed doubt that Auden was ever a real atheist at all: "I don't suppose Auden was ever less than a Voltairean deist at the height of his Freudian/ Marxist phase" (222). But in part three of *The Prolific and the Devourer*, Auden asks himself, "Do you believe in God and the supernatural?" and then answers, "If by God you mean a creator who is distinct from and independent of the creation, an omnipotent free-willing immaterial agent, no" (*Prose II* 448).

4. Augustine makes just this distinction in his *Nature and Grace*, when he distinguishes between "nature" as the goodness and innocence of human beings as they were originally created by God and "nature" as the weakness and corruption of human beings as they exist after the Fall (81). Auden accepted both definitions of nature. In the first sense, humans are "naturally" good, and in the second sense, they are "naturally" evil. Like Augustine, he eventually rejected the idea that the now-corrupted human being could be made good again by applying social engineering, political pressures, psychoanalysis, or any other external devices. However, Auden never abandoned the idea that humans are "naturally good" in the sense that the human person, including the human body, was originally created to be good, despite its current corruption.

5. The trope of an "overheard" prayer is a very old one, and the *Confessions* are modeled partly on Hebrew poetry, which sometimes uses the same trope. Psalm 51, which recounts the speaker's sins and prays for forgiveness, is a particularly poignant model for the *Confessions.*

6. Auden's engagement of the Satanic literary tradition is complex, drawing on Blake's Satan to the extent that the Devil represents cynicism and despair, and on Goethe to the extent that the Mephistopheles's temptation paradoxically opens the way to salvation for Faust. The Devil figure in *New Year Letter* is certainly not the heroic Satan that Blake perceived in Milton, but Auden generally agrees with Blake that evil is the obstruction of reintegration.

7. Jarrell refers to A. A. Milne's children's poem "Lines and Squares" (Milne 364–65).

8. Murphy goes on to argue that *New Year Letter* anticipates the neo-Marxism of Habermas, who concluded, "If the Just City is to be achieved it will be through communication rather than domination, a conclusion which we might regard as implicit in the very form of a letter" (118). But Auden repeatedly expressed doubts about the ability of language, and especially poetry, to make any significant contribution to social improvement, as *New Year Letter* itself asserts: "Art is not life and cannot be / A midwife to society" (*CP* 201).

9. Auden would elaborate on this idea at length many years later in "'The Truest Poetry is the Most Feigning'" and "Dichtung und Wahrheit." See chapter 5.

10. Auden's use of "absolute" in a negative sense is similar to Conniff's description of Paul Tillich's sense of the "daemonic," which influenced Auden at this stage in his career. Auden cites Tillich in the notes to *New Year Letter*, and Conniff explains that Tillich "consistently characterizes the demonic as the inflation of a finite quality, perhaps an individual personality trait that is presumed to be more than merely human, or an aspect of social organization that is treated as more than a historical product" ("Answering Herod," 312). Both Tillich and Auden clearly have totalitarian regimes in mind.

11. Auden used the term occasionally. For example, in a 1947 review, Auden refers to Blake's prolific and devourer as "mutually co-inherent contraries" (*Prose II* 338), and he uses the term in the title to his 1959 review of Williams's posthumous collection of essays, *The Image of the City* (*Prose IV* 197). Kirsch quotes Auden's 1956 letter to a priest, Brother Rigney: "it does seem to me that the Doctrine of the Incarnation implies the coinherence of spirit and flesh in all creatures, and that materialism and manicheeism are mirror images of each other" (qtd. in Kirsch,

Auden 28). Kirsch points out the connection between the idea of co-inherence and Augustine's thought, saying, "The stigmatization of matter and the body as evil by the Manicheans preoccupied Auden throughout his life and was a major reason for his attraction to Saint Augustine. . . ." (28).

12. Auden placed Goethe within the "existential" tradition begun by Augustine, though he may or may not have associated the intellectual restlessness of Goethe's Faust directly with Augustine's spiritual restlessness. However, the comparison has recently been made by David P. Goldman, who argues that Goethe's portrayal of Faust's restlessness as ultimately virtuous accords with Augustine's restless heart that can find rest only in God (31–34).

13. Auden's description of this early tendency toward sin is a recognizable version of Augustine's, who apparently coined the term "original sin" in the *Confessions* (5.9). See chapter 4 for a fuller account of the development of Auden's understanding of human nature and original sin, which he absorbed largely through Niebuhr. Auden later softened the dour view of early childhood development expressed in "For the Time Being." In a 1962 essay, Auden implicitly rejects Augustine's pessimistic view of anger in babies, arguing that "in the case of young creatures that are not yet capable of looking after themselves, anger is a necessary emotion when their needs are neglected: a hungry baby does right to scream. Natural anger is a reflex reaction, not a voluntary one; it is a response to a real situation of threat and danger, and as soon as the threat is removed, the anger subsides" (*Prose IV* 386). It may be, however, that Auden and Augustine are not describing the same kind of situation, since Augustine's argument emphasizes the jealousy of one sibling for another, whereas Auden's argument in this essay portrays a child acting alone.

14. When Auden was writing "For the Time Being," Aldous Huxley's *Brave New World* had already been published, though Orwell's *1984* would appear in 1948 and Bradbury's *Fahrenheit 451* in 1953. Fuller observes that Herod is effective "not as Hitler, but as a representative of those attitudes which have no ultimate sanction against a Hitler" (*Commentary* 353).

15. Anthony Hecht observes that the phrase "was the title of Robert Lowell's first and privately published book," and Hecht supposes that it was in turn taken "from St. Bernard's *regio dissimilitudinis*, about which Etienne Gilson wrote, in *The Mystical Theology of St. Bernard . . .*" (293). However, Fuller provides a more likely explanation, that Auden got the quotation from Augustine via Chester Kallman (*Commentary* 355).

16. Mendelson notes that there were more references to Augustine in early drafts of "For the Time Being" (*Later* 214). One of these references, to Augustine's statement that he would rather have been deprived of his friend than of his grief (*Confessions* 4.6), was eventually used as part of Prospero's speech in "The Sea and the Mirror."

17. According to the dates given for the poems in the *Collected Poems*, "For the Time Being" was begun in October 1941 and completed in July 1942. Auden then quickly started on "The Sea and the Mirror" in August 1942 and completed it in February 1944. Their order in the *Collected Poems* reflects the order of composition.

18. As Spears states, the poem is "a definition and exploration of the relations between the Mirror of Art and the Sea of Life, or Reality" (*Poetry* 218).

19. Auden's contact with mysticism predates his conversion, as Christopher Isherwood had already joined a community of Eastern monks in California when Auden and Kallman visited him in the summer of 1939. Auden defended Isherwood's conversion in a letter to their mutual friend Stephen Spender, writing that "of all the vocations it is the highest, highest because the most difficult, exhausting, and dangerous," but he privately suspected that Isherwood might be acting out of presumption rather than a sense of true vocation (qtd. in Mendelson, *Later* 161).

20. The theological tradition of mysticism is long and complex, but the term "mystic" might be briefly defined as one who seeks and experiences an ecstatic, personal vision of the Divine, but is thereafter unable to describe it verbally. Anne Freemantle, with whom Auden compiled *The Protestant Mystics* in the 1960s, reports that Ursula Niebuhr told her, "To be absolutely honest, I am rather allergic to what is usually called 'mystical'" (qtd. in *Tribute* 90). Although Auden flatly told Freemantle, "I am not mystical" (90), he did not denigrate mysticism, and his comment to Ursula Niebuhr gently defending the *via negativa* suggests that soon after he wrote *New Year Letter* he considered mysticism to be a beneficial and even necessary component of the Christian tradition, if not of every Christian's individual experience. In his essay "The Protestant Mystics," written as an introduction to the book of the same name on which he collaborated with Anne Freemantle, Auden writes that many who have achieved the vision of God are "those who have chosen the *via negativa*" (74). But Auden, confessing that he had never himself had a vision of God, could find very little to say about it specifically.

21. In his introduction to *The Protestant Mystics,* he identifies Augustine as a model of the co-inherence of medieval academic versions of the Affirmative and Negative Ways: "There seems no *rational* reason why a return to St. Paul and St. Augustine could not have rescued theology from its sterile debate between Realism and Nominalism without leading to Calvinism and, as a defense reaction, to the adoption by Rome, understandably but still, to my mind, mistakenly, of Thomism as the official Catholic philosophy. But history, of course, is not rational or repeatable" (*FA* 76).

22. Spears hints that Alonso's address to Ferdinand suggests the medieval and Renaissance "mirror for princes" genre, which involves letters of advice and caution given to young rulers by elder subordinates (*Poetry* 222). While Alonso is not a subordinate, his warnings about the difficulty of achieving and maintaining a just state strongly suggest the features of the genre. If, in the poem, the "mirror" represents art, then Alonso's speech is a "mirror" in two senses: as a genre and as an artistic contrivance. However, the speech breaks with the genre because it remains in the indicative mood without advancing into the imperative. It gives no real advice, which is to be expected given Auden's doubtfulness about art's ability to command action.

23. Auden would later explicitly identify the image of the sea with romanticism in his 1950 book *The Enchafèd Flood: or The Romantic Iconography of the Sea,* reprinted in *Prose III.*

24. Auden was not only responding to an atheistic existential tradition reaching back to Nietzsche, but anticipating the growth of agnostic/atheistic existential philosophy in the wake of WWII. Sartre's *Being and Nothingness* appeared in 1943, while Auden was writing "The Sea and the Mirror."

25. Auden's poem does not mention that in Shakespeare's play Miranda also teaches Caliban to speak. It is a convenient omission for Auden's allegorical reading of the play because it sets up the opposition between the poet (Prospero) and the body (Caliban) without having to deal with the role of another, female influence on Caliban, which could complicate the allegory significantly. The poem would have developed differently if Auden had chosen to acknowledge or even prioritize Miranda's involvement in teaching Caliban to speak.

26. In *The Dyer's Hand,* Auden imagines a similar situation: "In any village twenty people could get together and give a performance of *Hamlet* which, however imperfect, would convey enough of the play's greatness to be worth attending, but if they were to attempt a similar performance of *Don Giovanni,* they would soon discover that there was no question of a good or a bad performance because they could not sing the notes at all" (468). The provincial players in Caliban's speech, on the other hand, have either deluded themselves into thinking they

can sing the opera, or they have just enough talent to be able to go on with a very bad performance. Given Caliban's description, the latter is the more likely, and the more fitting. Humans have just enough talent for artistic order to make a perfect political mess of the world they inhabit.

27. Following Reinhold Niebuhr's Augustinian psychology, Auden came to identify the human capacity for transcendence and self-consciousness with the "image of God" in which humans are created. See chapter 4.

2. PHYSICAL EXISTENCE AS GOOD

1. Augustine attacks the Neoplatonic view of cyclical history in *The City of God* 12.14–21.

2. Augustine regularly reiterates these arguments in other works. See *The City of God* 11.17–23 and 12.2 for similar statements.

3. It is possible that Auden did not read *Christianity and Classical Culture* in 1940 when it was first published, but "For the Time Being" relies so heavily on Cochrane that Auden must have read the book by late 1941 when the poem was begun (see Mendelson, *Later* 184–86). Auden's phrasing in the review does imply that he first read it sometime in 1940.

4. Auden also claimed to have read Charles Williams's *The Descent of the Dove* several times over (*Prose IV* 30).

5. *New Year Letter* contains no references to Cochrane, which suggests that he read the book only after he finished the poem in April 1940, and he may not have read it until 1941. In any case, Auden's suspicion of dualism was already appearing in his works from the late 1930s, and Cochrane's work confirmed and elaborated on ideas that Auden had been entertaining for some time.

6. Later in *The Dyer's Hand* Auden would distinguish between the subjective, conscious "ego" and the objective, sensory "self" and use the terms quite consistently in his prose thereafter (e.g. 104, 111–12). In this poem, however, the categories are only vaguely distinct.

7. By the twentieth century, the various Protestant traditions had long defined their positions on iconography, and while a few medieval and Renaissance icons were still considered high art by serious critics, contemporary iconography was, often justifiably, considered banal and ignored as a serious art form. In England, religious questions about iconography had temporarily resurfaced in the Anglican Church during the nineteenth-century Oxford movement headed by John Henry Newman and Henry Edward Manning, but by the time Auden rejoined the Anglican communion in the autumn of 1940, the church had largely moved on to other questions, such as liturgical reform. Against this background of disregard for icons as a serious form of expression, religious or artistic, Auden deliberately shaped his poem "For the Time Being" as a kind of iconography.

8. Auden is right that medieval and Renaissance iconography always pictured religious events in contemporary settings, no matter what the historical context of the original event might have been. This habit of dressing biblical and religious characters in contemporary clothes has been a boon to historians and archeologists, who can, for example, derive clues about medieval arms and armor from medieval paintings of the crucifixion and find information about Renaissance carpentry from Renaissance pictures of Noah building the ark.

9. Auden also found this idea explained and reinforced in Cochrane (437–39).

10. "Word" is the usual English translation of the Greek word *logos* in John 1:1, where it describes Christ. The same word had been used earlier by Plato to describe his concept of the Ideal.

11. John Fuller's generally fair assessment of the poem is one example (*Commentary* 345). He admits that he is looking at the subject matter from the outside, so the implications of the Incarnation "must remain a theological mystery to the non-Christian" (346).

12. Auden's charts follow the traditional order fairly closely, though he conflates the first two. Lauds and Matins (midnight and 3:00 a.m.) correspond to the prayer in the garden and the arrest; Prime (6:00 a.m.) corresponds to the mocking; Tierce (9:00 a.m.) to the trial and sentence; Sext (noon) to the crucifixion; Nones (3:00 p.m.) to the piercing; Vespers (6:00 p.m.) to the removal from the cross; and Compline (9:00 p.m.) to the burial (see Mendelson, *Later* 311–13, 333–34; and Fuller, *Commentary* 456–57).

13. Mendelson remarks that this distinction is especially tricky for those who, naturally, use the terms interchangeably (*Later* 339n). Auden defined the *I* as that self-consciousness that is aware that there is another part of itself, the *me*, that projects into the outside world and includes the body. Hence, it is possible to say "my tooth hurts," as if the tooth that feels pain were distinct from the *I* who says it. This is not a strict mind/body distinction, since the self-consciousness is aware of mental processes as well as of bodily sensations. It is a distinction between the *knowing* ego and the *known* self. Auden relies on this distinction in "Precious Five," in which the conscious, knowing *I* addresses the sensory, corporeal *self*. Auden explains the distinction in various prose pieces. See especially *Enchaféd Flood* 117 and *DH* 104.

14. Auden had always associated the Fall with the emergence of self-consciousness, but his views of the precise relationship between the two events was ambiguous, though it clearly altered somewhat over his career, especially after he began to appropriate an Augustinian understanding of consciousness in the 1940s via Reinhold Niebuhr. See chapter 4.

15. Mendelson compares the forms of the two poems: "The stanza form of both poems is the same, but in "Compline" the rhythms are slower, the diction more relaxed, and the internal rhymes less frequent and agitated" (*Later* 355).

16. Auden knew Edgar Alan Poe's fiction well, though he does not mention this particular tale in the introduction to his book of Poe's selected writings, reprinted in *Forewords and Afterwords* (209–20), nor did Auden include "The Tell-Tale Heart" among his selections for the anthology.

17. It is just this tendency toward non-being that urged Augustine and his contemporaries to regard the eternal soul as superior to the mortal body in every way, and for Augustine's Neoplatonic contemporaries, the mutability of the body allowed and even required the denigration of physicality. The body's privation of existence in death was universally considered a grave evil, hence the importance of the doctrine of the general resurrection for Augustine. If bodies rise from the dead in an incorruptible state, then the difference in value between soul and body is significantly lessened.

18. Fuller also gives essentially this definition (*Commentary* 461), but Mendelson states that the term refers to "the mutual 'co-inherence' of the human and divine in Christ" (*Later* 357). Technically, "perichoresis" is a more specific type of co-inherence. The co-inherence of the Trinity and the co-inherence of the two natures of Christ are analogous in some important ways, but they are not exactly the same thing. For example, in the two natures of Christ there is a clear subordination of the human nature to the divine nature, whereas in the Trinity there is perfect equality between the members. The distinction may seem to be pedantic hair-splitting, but the term "perichoresis" is the precise term required for Auden's image, in which individuals enter a community of perfect equality in their common relationship to the "abiding tree," which represents the cross. If the individuals only co-inhered, essential inequalities might remain between

them. The use of "perichoresis" emphasizes the essential equality of the individuals, while also providing the image of a dance.

19. At some level Auden seems to recognize the fact, widely ignored by Dante critics, that Dante's *Comedia*, including the *Purgatorio*, is composed almost entirely of educational situations in which a teacher (Virgil) guides a student (Dante) toward ever-greater knowledge by means of exposition, direct observation, and guest lecturers, so the two metaphors Auden uses here are not totally distinct. I am grateful to Grace E. Schuler for pointing this out to me.

20. Mendelson explains that the title is a British euphemism for the bathroom, in the sense in which a host might ask his guests, "May I show you the geography of the house?" (*Later* 453).

CHAPTER 3: EROS AND AGAPE

1. Portions of this chapter originally appeared as "'Turn her desperate longing to love': W. H. Auden, Denis de Rougemont, and Lyric Love Poetry," *Christianity and Literature* 59 (2010): 619–44.

2. While Auden never claimed that the "natural" human love for God was irresistible, as Augustine suggested, he experienced at least once a love for his neighbors that he described as an "irresistible" agape (see *FA* 69–70). He wrote a poem, which he later titled "Summer Night," about the experience. Later he would describe this experience as a "vision of *agape*" in which he found himself loving his neighbors as himself (69).

3. It was Reinhold Niebuhr who showed Auden the importance of these passages for a properly Christian understanding of human psychology.

4. In 1956 Rougemont would publish a second, heavily revised edition in English, which is still in print.

5. Despite his engaging analysis of the Tristan myth, Rougemont's theory about the connection between the Troubadours and the Cathars is based largely on conjecture and has been discredited by subsequent scholarship. Scholarly critiques of Rougemont began to appear in the 1960s and 1970s, long after Auden had absorbed the ideas into his thinking. In a 1967 lecture, the text of which is printed in *Secondary Worlds*, Auden unreservedly quotes Rougemont's account of the development of "the cult of courtly love" and also quotes a passage from *Love in the Western World* that summarizes the book's general argument that eros can exist only in the presence of barriers to consummation (*Secondary Worlds* 75). Clearly Auden was unaware that, as he was giving his lectures in the late 1960s, the tide of critical and historical opinion was turning against Rougemont's theory.

6. This is not to say that either Rougemont or Auden rejected all forms of mysticism. Auden exhibits a thorough and nuanced knowledge of mysticism in later works such as his essay on "The Protestant Mystics" (*Forewords* 49–78), in which he distinguishes four types of mystical vision—the Vision of Dame Kind, or Nature; the Vision of Eros; the Vision of Agape; and the Vision of God—all of which are consistent with orthodox Christianity. In a 1962 review of a book called *The Drug Experience*, Auden wryly observes, "Some have claimed that their experiences under drugs were mystical visions of religious significance. Well, a tree must be judged by its fruits. In the case of the famous mystics, the effect of their visions, whether true or an illusion, was to increase their desire to do good works and make them capable of heroic deeds of charity. Has this effect been noted in any taker of mescaline or LSD?" (*Prose IV* 385).

7. The history of modern ideas about medieval "courtly love" is long and complicated, and the matter has yet to be settled absolutely. For a trenchant critique of the idea that "courtly love"

was a real historical phenomenon in the Middle Ages, see D. W. Robertson's 1967 essay in *The Meaning of Courtly Love* (1–18), and more recently, David Lyle Jeffrey's 2010 article "Courtly Love and Christian Marriage" (515–30). An example of a more measured critique is Henry Ansgar Kelly's *Love and Marriage in the Age of Chaucer* (see especially 19–28). Despite these and other attempts to demonstrate that "courtly love" was not a medieval phenomenon at all but a romanticized, Victorian misreading of several medieval texts, use of the term persists. For example, see Sarah Kay's essay "Courts, Clerks, and Courtly Love" in *The Cambridge Companion to Medieval Romance* (81–96).

8. See also Schuler, "'Turn Her Desperate Longing to Love.'"

9. See Alasdair MacIntyre's *God, Philosophy, and the University* for a particularly lucid account of the way in which Augustinian and Freudian psychology are mirror images of each other (28–29).

10. Augustine defines the term *cupiditas* in *On Christian Doctrine*, where he juxtaposes it with what he calls *caritas*, or "charity": "I call 'charity' [*caritas*] the motion of the soul toward the enjoyment of God for His own sake, and the enjoyment of one's self and of one's neighbor for the sake of God; but 'cupidity' [*cupiditas*] is a motion of the soul toward the enjoyment of one's self, one's neighbor, or any corporal thing for the sake of something other than God" (3.10). For Augustine, "cupidity" may be directed at a thing, a person, or even a figment of the imagination. Rougemont, on the other hand, argues that "the passion of love is at bottom narcissism, the lover's self-magnification, far more than it is a relation with the beloved. . . . Passion requires that the *self* shall become greater than all things, as solitary and powerful as God" (267). So while Rougemont does sometimes rely on Augustine's language, the meanings of his terms are not always identical with Augustine's.

11. Avery Dulles states that "De Rougemont, like Nygren, confronts us with a stark choice between eros and agape" and criticizes both Rougemont and Nygren for "set[ting] up an unbridgeable gulf between eros, as a passion arising from below, and agape, as a totally altruistic gift from on high" (21). While that is a fair assessment of Nygren, Dulles's criticism is less applicable to the argument in favor of Christian marriage that Rougemont sets out at the end of *Love in the Western World*.

12. "Sin, it has been remarked, is not Eros, but the sublimation of Eros" (Rougemont's note).

13. Auden quotes from Dante's *Purgatorio* (17.104–5). In Allen Mandelbaum's translation, the passage reads, "love is the seed in you of every virtue / and of all acts deserving punishment" (17.104–5).

14. In this passage and in those that follow, Augustine is refuting the Stoics, who, Augustine notes, believed that the passions of desire, joy, fear, and grief were always inappropriate for the wise man (14.8). Augustine argues that, on the contrary, Christians can demonstrate such passions appropriately, since Scripture relates that the apostles and saints often demonstrate rightly ordered desire, joy, fear, and grief (14.9). In Augustine's mind, passions may be good or bad depending on motivation and circumstance.

15. The mythological relationship between the two words should not be overlooked. The Greek god Eros was generally equivalent to the Roman god Cupid; their names connote desire in general, and usually sexual desire in particular.

16. The original, longer version of the poem is preserved in *The English Auden* (136–38), where it is untitled. By the time it was reprinted in the 1945 *Collected Poems*, Auden had given it a title,

dropped four stanzas, and changed the wording of a few remaining lines. The revisions retain the initial tension between the expected *eros* and surprising *agape* but minimize the role of *eros* in the rest of the poem.

17. The account is given in Auden's 1964 essay "The Protestant Mystics," where he represents it as "an unpublished account for the authenticity of which I can vouch" (*FA* 69). No one has ever questioned that that the story is Auden's own. His language at the beginning of the account, "One fine summer night in June 1933 . . . ," makes it clear that the 1933 poem, which Auden later titled "Summer Night," records the same experience.

18. Auden would quote this passage again in a 1967 lecture, the text of which was later printed in *Secondary Worlds* (119).

19. The third and fourth lines sound less than innocent: "Where children play at seven earnest sins, / And dogs believe their tall conditions dead" (*CP* 295). But Fuller's illuminating gloss on these lines points out that the seven sins are "earnest" but not deadly and that they are objects of mere play, such that the scene "is a state of authenticity of being that is achieved largely through love" (*Commentary* 343). Fuller also explains that "the body ('dogs') is free of the interfering super-ego ('their tall conditions,' i.e. their masters)" (*Commentary* 343).

20. Auden would later modify his views on free will and necessity, which were in almost constant flux throughout the late 1930s and 1940s.

21. See chapter 4.

22. Caliban's image is, of course, drawn from the story of the patriarch Jacob wrestling with an angel (or God; the text is ambiguous) until dawn (Genesis 32:24–32). A typical post-Freudian reading of the story would interpret it as an analogue of the internal struggle between the id and the ego, though in "The Sea and the Mirror" Auden uses it to picture the struggle between the subjective *I* and the objective body.

23. See Nicolas Poussin's two paintings titled *Et in Arcadia Ego*, as well as Guercino's painting of the same name.

24. Auden wrote two late poems with this title. This "Aubade" (*CP* 747) was written in 1964 and is part of "Three Posthumous Poems." The other "Aubade" was written in 1972 and quotes Augustine on being, knowing, and willing (881).

25. A few of Auden's statements suggest that he was quite sympathetic to Catholicism, and false rumors that Auden actually became a Catholic continue to circulate. In his essay in *Modern Canterbury Pilgrims*, Auden refuses to say why he had become an Anglican and not a Roman Catholic (43), but in *The Dyer's Hand* he says that the religion of his personal Eden would be "Roman Catholic in an easygoing Mediterranean sort of way [with] lots of local saints" (7). After he moved to Kirchstetten, Austria, he regularly attended mass at the village parish church, though he was not a communicant there. Certain aspects of Catholicism, particularly its Latin mass and its rich artistic tradition, greatly appealed to Auden, though he objected to what he saw as Rome's mistaken theological preference for the systematizations of Thomism over Augustine's existential theology (see *FA* 76).

26. Some critics, writing before Fuller and Mendelson, have taken the poet in the poem to be Auden himself. Lucy McDiarmid, for example, makes much of this supposed identification, and given Auden's penchant for self-referentiality, it is not an unreasonable mistake to make. While the poem's speaker, presumably Auden himself, clearly uses his "Common Prayer" to draw parallels between himself and the figure of Stevens in the poem, certain details of Auden's description of this poet should have suggested that the poet was not Auden, who was never known for

"calling / The sun the sun," nor even particularly interested in demythologization (*CP* 524). On the contrary, Auden's had always been fascinated by allegory and myth.

27. Mendelson suggests that, while Auden was suspicious of natural theology during the 1940s, he became more sympathetic to it later in life (*Later* 484n).

28. See chapter 5 for a fuller analysis of the *acte gratuit* as Auden understood it, and especially how he associated the *acte gratuit* with art.

4. HUMAN NATURE AND COMMUNITY

1. Theological treatment of the Niebuhrs has hardly fared better. Most brief biographies of Reinhold Niebuhr, such as Schlesinger's 2005 *New York Times* piece, make no mention of his friendship with Auden.

2. The argument seems reasonable enough: it would be difficult to consciously remember events that occurred prior to the emergence of one's consciousness.

3. Gottlieb has explored the many similarities between Auden's "Age of Anxiety" and Hannah Arendt's numerous works analyzing twentieth-century social and psychological anxiety. Arendt was herself shaped by Augustine, and her first book, published in 1929, was *Love and Saint Augustine*. However, as Gottlieb acknowledges, Auden did not become aware of Arendt's work until the 1950s, after "The Age of Anxiety" was published. The parallels between Auden and Arendt are compelling as complementary accounts of modern anxiety, and Auden praised Arendt's 1958 book *The Human Condition*, saying that it "answer[s] precisely those questions which I have been putting to myself" (*Prose IV* 184), but Gottlieb does not say how the relationship between Arendt and Auden might have shaped either one's later work.

4. See Cochrane 454–55.

5. Auden was never a thoroughgoing Marxist, but this was one of the few distinctly Marxist ideas that he did accept.

6. Auden repeats the definition in *Prose II* 436, *FA* 410, *Secondary Worlds* 120, *The Enchafèd Flood* 30, and *Lectures on Shakespeare* 299.

7. To my knowledge, Auden never claimed to have read Augustine's *City of God* specifically, but his use of Augustine's vocabulary here and elsewhere suggests that he had. For example, in his essay "A Grecian Eye," a 1957 review of *The Stones of Troy* by C. A. Trypanis, he remarks that Virgil knew too much Roman political history to have treated it so idealistically, pointing out that "Virgil . . . knew about the Punic wars, Marius, Sulla, etc., and that should have been enough" (*Prose IV* 75). Those examples of Rome's dark side are familiar to anyone who knows Roman history, but they are especially emphasized in Augustine's *City of God*.

8. Williams uses the phrase not only in *The Descent of the Dove*, but also as the opening statement in a 1939 essay "Sensuality and Substance" on D. H. Lawrence in the journal *Theology*, which Auden very well may have read when it was first published. The article was reprinted in *The Image of the City* (68–75), a posthumous collection of Williams's essays that Auden reviewed in 1959.

9. Auden identifies Caliban, along with Ariel and Prospero, as one of only five mythic characters in Shakespeare's plays (*DH* 408). The other two are Falstaff and Hamlet, Hamlet being "a myth for actors only" because the role is open to endless interpretive variation, although the fairies of *A Midsummer Night's Dream* as well as some of the fools (e.g. Feste and Lear's fool) also seem to fit Auden's definition.

5. POETRY AND TRUTH

1. Mendelson notes Auden's erroneous spelling "*acte gratuite*" and regularizes it to the correct "*acte gratuit.*" See textual note to *Prose II*, xxxiv. I have followed Mendelson's correction.

2. See 13.9, though the equation of love and will permeates the whole work.

3. Matthew Mutter shows that Auden's critique of poetry-as-enchantment was rooted not only in his aesthetic concerns, but in his political sensibilities as well. Mutter explains that Yeats and others tended toward an elitism that Auden rejected, and he notes "how important the occult was to the rise of Nazism" (64).

4. See *Christianity and Literature* 59 (2010): 619–44.

5. Mendelson explains that "The 'You' who was arriving in Kirchstetten was not Kallman, who was already there, but Adrian Poole, later an academic sociologist, then a twenty-five-year-old student working toward an honors degree in jurisprudence at Oxford, where Auden had met him, and who visited Kirchstetten for about two weeks in September 1959" (*Later* 433). Mendelson also notes that "Poole enjoyed Auden's company but felt no sexual attraction to him; Auden, who sensed Poole's feelings, never made a closer approach, but enjoyed an exhilarating sexual attraction to the younger man without intruding on him by expressing it" (433).

6. Given these sentiments, it is interesting that, as Mendelson notes, Auden began writing "Dichtung und Wahrheit" only after Poole, the "You" of the unwritten poem, had left Kirchstetten, not the day before his arrival as the "poem" indicates (*Later* 433).

7. The speaker refers to the ingenuous love-poet-turned-political-poet as an "old sly boots" (*CP* 621), and while the political circumstances described in the poem are clearly modern, Auden also identifies Geoffrey Chaucer as another poet of the same type: "Politically, judging by his career, [Chaucer] must have been rather an old sly boots, to keep in favor at Court through so many upheavals, to survive Richard the Second's downfall and even get a pension from his successor Henry the Fourth" (*Prose IV* 81).

8. *Caveat lector:* Unlike most other books, the index of *A Certain World* lists Augustine and other canonized saints under "S" for "Saint."

9. The statement risks oversimplification of Plato's (and Socrates') attitudes toward poetry, but most readers will agree that Socrates' Republic will admit poets only on the conditions that they submit to the role of propagandists and agree to a policy of severe censorship, which conditions make it practically impossible for them to function as poets at all. Auden understood the rationale but thought that the Platonic suspicion of poetry rested on a false view of what poetry is supposed to do. In a 1958 essay on Werner Jaeger's *Paideia*, Auden states, "Plato's condemnation of the poets as educators would seem to indicate that the Greeks of his day reacted to *The Iliad* more or less as we do," that conventional readings of Homer tended to promote either imitation of the behavior of the gods or disbelief in the gods entirely (*Prose IV* 147). Auden points out that Plato "was wrong however, if the reaction was 'Goodness me, I never realized till Homer showed me, how ridiculous and immoral some of my notions of the gods have been: I must seek a true notion of what the gods are really like.' In so far as poetry is 'a mirror held up to Nature' the moral effect it has depends upon the conscience of the beholder; it passes no judgments, but each reader is judged by how he reacts" (147).

10. This aspect of Augustine's thought is too seldom recognized even by theologians, to say nothing of literary critics. Even Alan Jacobs claims that Augustine "has no use for [pagan poets], or at least not use for their literature" ("Paganism" 669). Jacobs goes on to argue that "to

Nietzsche's claim that for the Christian 'the truth of God . . . relegates . . . *all* art to the realm of *falsehood*,' Augustine would surely reply, 'Of course'" (119–70). But that is not quite true. While Augustine is no aesthete—he does not accept all poetry without qualification as valuable—he does, in fact, use even pagan poetry in *The City of God* and other works as evidence for his arguments and as subjects for analysis, and he commends certain statements in pagan poetry for their truthfulness. One might also note Augustine's most lyrical passages in the *Confessions* (e.g. 10.27), as well as his evident delight in the Psalms, as evidence of his appreciation of poetry.

SELECTED BIBLIOGRAPHY

Alighieri, Dante. *Paradise*. Trans. Anthony Esolen. New York: Modern Library, 2004.

———. *Purgatory*. Trans. Allen Mandelbaum. New York: Bantam, 1984.

Auden, W. H. *A Certain World: A Commonplace Book*. New York: Viking, 1970.

———. *Collected Poems*. Ed. Edward Mendelson. New York: Vintage, 1991.

———. *The Complete Works of W. H. Auden: Prose*. 4 vols. to date. Ed. Edward Mendelson. Princeton, N.J.: Princeton University Press, 1996–.

———. *The Dyer's Hand*. New York: Vintage, 1988.

———. *The Enchafèd Flood: or The Romantic Iconography of the Sea*. Charlottesville: University Press of Virginia, 1950.

———. *The English Auden: Poems, Essays and Dramatic Writings 1927–1939*. Ed. Edward Mendelson. London: Faber, 1977.

———. *Forewords and Afterwords*. New York: Vintage, 1989.

———. *Juvenilia*. Ed. Katherine Bucknell. Princeton, N.J.: Princeton University Press, 1994.

———. *Lectures on Shakespeare*. Ed. Arthur Kirsch. Princeton, N.J.: Princeton University Press, 2000.

———. *New Year Letter*. London: Faber, 1941.

———. "Pride and Prayer." *Episcopalian* (March–May 1974): 6–8.

———. *Secondary Worlds*. New York: Random House, 1968.

Augustine. *Concerning the City of God against the Pagans*. Trans. Henry Bettenson. London: Penguin, 2003.

———. *Confessions*. Trans. E. B. Pusey. London: Everyman's, 1907.

———. *Confessions*. Trans. Henry Chadwick. Oxford, U.K.: Oxford University Press, 1998.

———. *The Enchiridion on Faith, Hope and Love*. Trans. J. B. Shaw. Washington: Regnery, 1996.

———. *Homilies on the First Epistle of John*. The Works of Saint Augustine: A Translation for the 21st Century. Vol. 14. Trans. Boniface Ramsey. Ed. Daniel E. Doyle and Thomas Martin. New York: New City, 2008.

———. *Nature and Grace. Answer to the Pelagians*. part 1. The Works of Saint Augustine: A Translation for the 21st Century. Trans. Roland J. Teske. Hyde Park, N.Y.: New City, 1997. 225–70.

———. *On Christian Doctrine*. Trans. D. W. Robertson Jr. Upper Saddle River, N.J.: Prentice Hall, 1997.

Bertram, James. "W. H. Auden: A Modern Poet's Quest for the Holy Grail." *From Dante to Solzhenitsyn: Essays on Christianity and Literature*. Ed. Robert M. Yule. Wellington, NZ: Tertiary Christian Studies, 1978. 209–37.

Bozorth, Richard R. *Auden's Games of Knowledge: Poetry and the Meanings of Homosexuality.* New York: Columbia University Press, 2001.

Bridgen, John. "Auden on Christianity—A Memoir." *Auden Society Newsletter* 3.3–4 (1988): 3–4.

Bruce, Cicero. *W. H. Auden's Moral Imagination.* Lewiston, N.Y.: Edwin Mellen, 1998.

Callan, Edward. *Auden: A Carnival of Intellect.* New York: Oxford University Press, 1983.

Carpenter, Humphrey. *W. H. Auden: A Biography.* Boston: Houghton, 1981.

Cochrane, Charles Norris. *Christianity and Classical Culture: A Study of Thought and Action from Augustus to Augustine.* London: Oxford University Press, 1944.

Conniff, Brian. "Answering Herod: W. H. Auden, Paul Tillich, Ernst Toller, and the Demonic." *W. H. Auden: A Legacy.* Ed. David Garrett Izzo. West Cornwall, U.K.: Locust Hill, 2002. 297–328.

———. "Auden, Niebuhr, and the Vocation of Poetry." *Religion and Literature* 25.3 (1993): 45–65.

———. "What Really Became of Wystan? Auden, Niebuhr and *For the Time Being.*" *Christianity and Literature* 44.2 (1995): 133–44.

Curtis, Jan. "W. H. Auden's 'Vespers': A Christian Refutation of Utopian Dreams of Ultimate Fulfillment." *Renascence* 52.3 (2000): 203–17.

D'Arcy, M. C. *The Mind and Heart of Love: Lion and Unicorn, a Study in Eros and Agape.* New York: Holt, 1947.

Davenport-Hines, Richard. *Auden.* New York: Vintage, 1995.

Dulles, Avery. "Love, the Pope, and C. S. Lewis." *First Things* January 2007. 20–24.

Emig, Rainer. *W. H. Auden: Towards a Postmodern Poetics.* New York: St. Martin's, 2000.

Fuller, John. *A Reader's Guide to W. H. Auden.* New York: Farrar, 1970.

———. *W. H. Auden: A Commentary.* Princeton, N.J.: Princeton University Press, 1998.

Goldman, David P. "Hast Thou Considered My Servant Faust?" *First Things* (August/September): 2009. 31–34.

Gottlieb, Susannah Young-ah. *Regions of Sorrow: Anxiety and Messianism in Hannah Arendt and W. H. Auden.* Palo Alto: Stanford University Press, 2003

Hannah, Sarah. "Only Through Time: Structure and Temporality in Three Modern Sequence Poems." Diss. Columbia University. 2005.

Harp, Richard. "Conjuror at the Xmas Party." *Times Literary Supplement* 11 December 2009: 13+

Hecht, Anthony. *The Hidden Law: The Poetry of W. H. Auden.* Cambridge: Harvard University Press, 1994.

Hobson, Theo. "Songs Against the Devil: The Exorcistic in Auden." *Literature and Theology* 13 (1999): 17–33.

Hoggart, Richard. *W. H. Auden.* London: Longmans, 1957.

Hufstader, Jonathan. "Auden's Sacred World." *Essays in Criticism* 59.3 (2009): 234–54.

Isherwood, Christopher. *Christopher and His Kind.* New York: Farrar, 1976.

Jacobs, Alan. "Auden and the Limits of Poetry." *First Things.* August–September 2001. 26–32.

———. "Paganism and Literature." *Christianity and Literature* 56.4 (2007): 667–79.

———. *What Became of Wystan.* Fayetteville: University of Arkansas Press, 1998.

Jarrell, Randall. *Randall Jarrell on W. H. Auden.* Ed. Stephen Burt. New York: Columbia University Press, 2005.

Jeffrey, David Lyle. "Courtly Love And Christian Marriage: Chretien De Troyes, Chaucer, And Henry VIII." *Christianity And Literature* 59.3 (2010): 515–30.

———. *People of the Book: Christian Identity and Literary Culture.* Grand Rapids, Mich.: Eerdmans, 1996.

Kay, Sarah. "Courts, Clerks, and Courtly Love." *The Cambridge Companion to Medieval Romance.* Ed. Roberta L. Krueger. Cambridge, U.K.: Cambridge University Press, 2000. 81–96.

Kelley, Henry Ansgar. *Love and Marriage in the Age of Chaucer.* Ithaca, N.Y.: Cornell University Press, 1975.

Kirsch, Arthur. *Auden and Christianity.* New Haven, Conn.: Yale University Press, 2005.

———. Introduction. *The Sea and the Mirror: A Commentary on Shakespeare's* The Tempest. By W. H. Auden. Ed. Arthur Kirsch. Princeton, N.J.: Princeton University Press, 2003. xi–xlii.

Larkin, Philip. "What's Become of Wystan?" *Required Writing.* New York: Farrar, 1983. 123–28.

MacIntyre, Alasdair. *God, Philosophy, and the University.* Lanham, Md.: Rowman, 2009.

McDiarmid, Lucy. *Auden's Apologies for Poetry.* Princeton, N.J.: Princeton University Press, 1990.

Mendelson, Edward. "Auden and God." *New York Review of Books.* 6 December 2007. 70–75.

———. *Early Auden.* Cambridge, Mass.: Harvard University Press, 1983.

———. *Later Auden.* New York: Farrar, 1999.

Milne, A. A. *The Complete Tales and Poems of Winnie-the-Pooh.* New York: Dutton, 2001.

Milton, John. *Paradise Lost. The Riverside Milton.* Ed. Roy Flannagan. Boston: Houghton Mifflin, 1998. 349–710.

Murphy, Michael. "Neoclassicism, Late Modernism, and W. H. Auden's 'New Year Letter.'" *Cambridge Quarterly* 33.2 (2004): 101–18.

Mutter, Matthew. "'The Power to Enchant That Comes from Disillusion': W. H. Auden's Criticism of Magical Poetics." *Journal of Modern Literature* 33.2 (2010): 58–85.

Niebuhr, Reinhold. *The Nature and Destiny of Man: A Christian Interpretation.* Vol. 1. Louisville, Ky.: Westminster John Knox, 1996.

Osborne, Charles. "Auden as a Christian Poet." *W. H. Auden: The Far Interior.* Ed. Alan Bold. London: Vision, 1985. 23–46.

———. *W. H. Auden: The Life of a Poet.* New York: Harcourt, 1979.

Pearce, Donald. "Fortunate Fall: W. H. Auden at Michigan." *W. H. Auden: The Far Interior.* Ed. Alan Bold. London: Vision, 1985. 129–57.

Replogle, Justin. "Auden's Religious Leap." *Wisconsin Studies in Contemporary Literature* 7 (1956): 47–75.

Robertson, D. W. "The Concept of Courtly Love as an Impediment to the Understanding of Medieval Texts." *The Meaning of Courtly Love.* Ed. F. X. Newman. Albany: State University of New York Press, 1968. 1–18.

Rougemont, Denis de. *Love in the Western World.* Trans. Montgomery Belgion. New York: Harcourt, 1940.

Ruleman, William Arthur. "Auden's Vision of Human Society in Light of Augustinian Thought." Diss. University of Mississippi. 1994.

Schlesinger, Arthur. "Forgetting Reinhold Niebuhr." *New York Times* 18 Sept. 2005. Accessed 14 May 2012. www.nytimes.com/2005/09/18/books/review/18schlesinger.html?pagewanted=all.

Schmidt, Michael. *Lives of the Poets.* New York: Vintage, 1998.

Schuler, Stephen J. "'Turn her desperate longing to love': W. H. Auden, Denis de Rougemont, and Lyric Love Poetry" in *Christianity and Literature* 59 (2010): 619–44.

Smith, Stan. *W. H. Auden.* Rereading Literature series. Ed. Terry Eagleton. Oxford: Basil Blackwell, 1985.

Spears, Monroe K. "The Divine Comedy of W. H. Auden." *Sewanee Review* 90.1 (1982): 53–72.

———. *The Poetry of W. H. Auden: The Disenchanted Island.* London: Oxford University Press, 1968.

Spender, Stephen, Ed. *W. H. Auden: A Tribute.* New York: Macmillan, 1974.

Wetzsteon, Rachel. *Influential Ghosts: A Study of Auden's Sources.* New York: Routledge, 2007.

Williams, Charles. *The Descent of the Dove: A Short History of the Holy Spirit in the Church.* New York: Longmans, 1939.

———. *The Image of the City and Other Essays.* Ed. Anne Ridler. London: Oxford University Press, 1958.

Woodhouse, A. S. P. *The Poet and His Faith: Religion and Poetry in England from Spencer to Eliot and Auden.* Chicago: University of Chicago Press, 1965.

York, R. A. "Auden's Study of Time." *Orbis Litterarum* 54.3 (1999): 220–38.

INDEX

ABOUT THE AUTHOR

STEPHEN J. SCHULER holds a Ph.D. in English from Baylor University. He is an assistant professor of English at the University of Mobile in Alabama, where he teaches British literature and honors English. Schuler lives in the Mobile area with his wife, Grace, and their four children.

Library of Congress Cataloging-in-Publication Data

Schuler, Stephen J.
    The Augustinian theology of W. H. Auden / Stephen J. Schuler.
        pages cm
    Includes bibliographical references and index.
    ISBN 978-1-61117-243-0 (hardbound : alk. paper) 1. Auden, W. H. (Wystan Hugh),
1907–1973—Religion.
    2. Theology in literature. 3. Christianity and literature—England—History—
20th century. 4. Augustine, Saint, Bishop of Hippo—Influence. I. Title.
PR6001.U4Z815 2013
811'.52—DC23   2012048820